CROSSING
BOUNDARIES

CROSSING BOUNDARIES

Feminisms and the Critique of Knowledges

Edited by
Barbara Caine, E.A. Grosz,
and Marie de Lepervanche

Sydney
ALLEN & UNWIN
Wellington London Boston

First published in 1988
Allen & Unwin Australia Pty Ltd
An Unwin Hyman Company
8 Napier Street, North Sydney, NSW 2060, Australia

Allen & Unwin (New Zealand) Ltd
60 Cambridge Terrace, Wellington, New Zealand

Unwin Hyman Limited
15–17 Broadwick Street, London WIV 1FP, England

Allen & Unwin Inc.
8 Winchester Place, Winchester, Mass, 01890, USA

National Library of Australia
Cataloguing-in-publication entry:

Crossing boundaries: feminisms and the critique of
    knowledges.

    Bibliography.
    Includes index.
    ISBN 0 04 305004 2.

    1. Feminism.   2. Feminist criticism.
    3. Women's studies.   I. Grosz, E.A. (Elizabeth A.).
    II. De Lepervanche, Marie M.   III. Caine, Barbara.

305.4

Library of Congress Catalog Card Number: 88-70247

Set by Graphicraft Typesetters Ltd., Hong Kong
Printed in Singapore by Kim Hup Lee Printing Co.

Contents

Contributors

CAROLE E. ADAMS lectures in modern history at the University of Sydney. She has recently completed a book about female white-collar workers in Germany before World War I. Her research interests include women's waged work and the relationship of class and gender, particularly for white-collar workers.

JUDITH ALLEN is an historian and lecturer in the School of Humanities, Griffith University. She convenes a women's studies program, and publishes on crimes involving women in Australian history, the history of feminism, and feminist critiques of knowledges. At present she is preparing a book on the feminist career of Rose Scott (1847–1925) and co-authoring with Barbara Caine a series of essays on English and Australian first-wave feminism.

MARY BARNES is Officer-in-Charge of the Mathematics Learning Centre at the University of Sydney. She was responsible for setting up the centre, which helps students who have difficulties as a result of inadequate preparation in mathematics, and in particular those who have been disadvantaged by reason of gender. Mary's interests include projects to increase the participation of women in science and technology and ways of teaching mathematics which will make it more accessible to women. In a current research project she is investigating students' understanding of concepts in elementary calculus.

BARBARA CAINE lectures in history at the University of Sydney. She has recently published a book on Beatrice Webb and her eight sisters. She is at present working with Judith Allen on a collection of essays on first-wave English and Australian feminists and is about to begin work on a group of nineteenth-century English and American female expatriots who spent their adult years in Italy.

BETTINA CASS is Associate Professor of Social Policy in the Department of Social Work, University of Sydney. In 1986 and 1987 she was Consultant Director of the Social Security Review. Courses taught have included the development of Australian social welfare policies; studies of poverty and the development of tax/transfer and the labour market; theories of the welfare state. Her research and writing focus on Australian social security and taxation policy; women, work and welfare; family policies.

ANN CURTHOYS is an historian, and Associate Head in the School of Humanities and Social Sciences at the New South Wales Institute of Technology. She has been involved in research and writing about feminist theory, women and work, and women's history since 1970, publishing in journals such as *Refractory Girl* and *Hecate* and in books of collected essays like this one. She has also worked in other fields, including the history of racial immigration policies in Australia, Aboriginal–European relations, and the development of television.

MOIRA GATENS teaches philosophy at the Australian National University. She is at present completing a book on feminist theory and philosophy to be published in 1988 by Polity Press. She teaches courses on gender and philosophy, philosophy and literature and the history of philosophy.

E.A. GROSZ teaches philosophy in the Department of General Philosophy at the University of Sydney. She is the co-editor, with Carole Pateman, of *Feminist Challenges. Social and Political Theory*, and, with Terry Threadgold et al. of *Futur* Fall. Excursions into Post-Modernity*. Her current interests include methodologies of feminist theory and feminist philosophies of the body.

JUDITH KEENE teaches modern European history at the University of Sydney. Her research interests are in social history, particularly that of those whose existences are marginal to the mainstream: children, peasants and the urban poor. She is at present doing research on Australians who became involved in the Spanish Civil War.

MARIE DE LEPERVANCHE teaches anthropology at the University of Sydney. She is interested in forms of structural oppression, and has worked extensively on racism and ethnicity in Australia and increasingly on the location of women in society. Her most recent work is *Ethnicity, Class and Gender* which she edited with Gil Bottomley.

CAROLINE RALSTON teaches Pacific history and other courses including Women in History, Aboriginal History and South Pacific Literature at Macquarie University in Sydney. Her long-term research plan is a history of the changing patterns of gender relations in Polynesia from pre-contact times to the 1980s. In the interim she has written several articles on aspects of the larger project.

LESLEY ROGERS is in the Physiology Department at the University of New England, where she lectures in neurophysiology and animal behaviour. Her main area of research is concerned with structural and functional asymmetries in the developing brain and the effects of sex hormones on brain development and behaviour. She publishes widely in these research areas. She is a scientist who is concerned with the implications of research to society in general. Consequently she also writes on issues dealing with science and society, and especially on feminism and biology.

SUSAN SHERIDAN lectures in women's studies at the Flinders University of South Australia, and is co-founder and review editor of the journal *Australian Feminist Studies*. She is completing a book on Christina Stead's fiction, and editing two collections of papers from the 1986 Feminism and the Humanities Conference Series, which she convened. A graduate of the University of Sydney and University of Adelaide, she has published on women's studies and Australian cultural history as well as literature.

Preface

This book grew out of the Women's Studies Conference, held at the University of Sydney in 1985, to commemorate the centenary of the University's first two women graduates. At the conference there were over 60 papers, covering almost the entire range of women's scholarship in Australia. We have selected only a very small number from this initial offering, concentrating on those papers which clearly and explicitly challenged existing disciplines and fields of study from a feminist perspective, contesting their presumptions and questioning and crossing their boundaries.

The papers included here do not represent a single, unified point of view, a single line of research or even a shared political commitment. Our aim has been to illustrate something of the diversity of approaches to feminist theory and scholarship which is evident in the work of feminists working in a number of academic disciplines.

Despite the different disciplines from which many of the papers originate, they address a number of common themes. As a result of this, we have arranged them in four sections, each of which has a brief introduction, outlining the themes and issues raised and providing a general context for the papers.

The only paper which was not presented at the conference, but written specifically for this volume, is 'Feminism and Science' by Marie de Lepervanche and E.A. Grosz. This began as the introduction to the section on 'Women and Science', but soon outgrew this framework. Our belief that it was necessary to provide an entry point both for those trained in the sciences, but not familiar either with feminist critiques of science or with feminist researches in the natural sciences, and for those well acquainted with general trends in feminist theory but not with scientific literature made it imperative that this 'introduction' provide an overview of the extensive literature on women and science which is currently available. This attempt resulted in what is now the longest paper in the volume, but one for which we think that there is a great need.

This project would not have been possible without the enthusiasm and support of a number of individuals. We would like to acknowledge those who were instrumental in planning and organising the original Women's Studies Conference: Alison Turtle without whose enthusiasm and organising skills the Conference would not have occurred—and who urged us to produce this book; Susan Dorsch for her support; all those who worked on the various conference committees and who helped to select the papers for this volume, particularly Gretchen Poiner and Deborah Marr. Victoria Gollan provided us with invaluable assistance both in organising the conference and in preparing these papers for publication. Finally we would like to thank Venetia Nelson for her editorial assistance and advice, and Allen & Unwin for its continuing belief in the commercial viability of Women's Studies.

PART I
WOMEN AND THE
SCIENCES

MARIE DE LEPERVANCHE

Introduction

Although women in the humanities may have produced more critical feminist material on their own disciplines than women in the natural and biological sciences, feminist scientists have made extremely significant contributions to understanding their experiences in the traditional patriarchal disciplines of science. Many are now beginning to question many of science's assumptions and values. The political and epistemic privilege of science, its image as objective, verified truth etc. have made it exceptionally difficult for its practitioners to hold established scientific wisdom up for scrutiny.

In her contribution, Lesley Rogers undertakes this formidable task. In the conventional dichotomies governing biology (nature/nurture, male/female), she locates a misplaced emphasis on absolute sex differences rather than on biological similarities or even a range or continuum of differences. She discusses the presumed correspondences between sex differences and the differentiations of brain function, claiming that although brain differentiation does occur, it cannot be directly correlated with sex differences. The interconnections between the genetic potential of these organisms and the various environmental stimuli they encounter is much more complex than models of genetic determinism imply.

Feminists working in the sciences are beginning to recognise the extent to which their milieu is male-dominated; it thus makes sense that many would call for female 'recruits' to join them in the ranks of science. As Barnes points out in her essay, it is imperative not only that women move into science itself but also into decision-making positions so that their interests are reflected in future choice in curricula and teaching programs. She stresses that change will not occur if women simply follow established male models.

The essay by Grosz and de Lepervanche draws on the work of a number of scientifically trained feminists to present an overview of feminist interventions into science and case studies to illustrate concretely some possibilities of change. They argue that the subordinate position of women in science is not only a matter of unequal numbers of males and females doing science. The social construction of scientific knowledges must be directly addressed as must its political investments. This involves reexamining the collusion of scientific methods and ideals with masculinity, and with its effects on the subordination of concepts of femininity.

The sciences are founded on a series of oppositions (between fact and theory, pure and applied science, etc.) and on notions of truth, objectivity and nature. Each discipline within the sciences develops its own world-view, protocols of experimentation, technology and terminology. These founding presumptions remain unexamined, and are given an apparently unquestioned status that serves to perpetuate the male dominance and patriarchal character of science. In short, masculine ideals of control and mastery permeate the sciences. Feminists must be mindful of these ideals. There are alternative ways of producing knowledges about the natural world, ways that female scientists may help to create.

E.A. GROSZ AND MARIE DE
LEPERVANCHE

1 Feminism and science

Science today maintains an extremely high social profile. It is not
only regarded as the purest and most ideal form of knowledge, it
also acts as a paradigm for *disinterested, objective* and *proven*
knowledge, incontestably providing our most secure sources of
truths about the world. This may explain why feminists have had
a good deal of difficulty and often reluctance in demonstrating the
complicity of the natural sciences in the oppression of women. If,
as science claims, it is true, observer-neutral, unbiased, repeatable
and thus 'objective', it is difficult to see how it could contribute
to or participate in women's oppression. Many feminists working
within the sciences can accept that the various social apparatuses,
institutions and practices *surrounding* science—the funding and
administration of scientific projects, the hiring of staff, practical
applications of science, the development of technologies, etc.—are
bound up with social values and power relations; but some consider
it more difficult to criticise science itself. 'Pure science' is usually
considered immune to these sociological/political 'issues'. It is hardly surprising, then, that the topic 'women and science' has generally
focused on issues like 'Great Women Scientists', the Marie Curies
of science, that is, on those *individuals* within science who have
made 'Great Discoveries' and who also happen to be women.
While this kind of analysis is important in raising consciousness
about the difficulties women face in undertaking careers in the
natural sciences, it only addresses the most superficial level of the
problem. In this paper, we examine some deeper, *structural investments* and *patriarchal commitments* in science, including their implicit
presumptions, their preferred, validated methods (methodological
claims) and the criteria by which sciences are evaluated (epistemic
claims).

We use two very brief 'case histories' of women scientists to draw out some of these deeper patriarchal commitments. This involves discussing a range of feminist responses to and critiques of science and its methods.

There are a number of qualifications, cautionary notes and distinctions that need to be made (or ignored) in order to clarify and survey an otherwise exceedingly complex terrain and highly controversial series of issues. First, we must regard a number of distinctions and oppositions circulating within the sciences with great suspicion. Among the more problematic oppositions used to defend science against any external criticism, including those used by feminists, are the following: the distinctions between scientific 'facts' and theories (see, for example, Kuhn, 1970; Chalmers, 1976); between pure and applied sciences (see Chalmers, 1976); and between science on the one hand and its abuses on the other (raised in its most potent form in the debates about the atom bomb and, most contradictorily, in Einstein's simultaneously complicit position in his research and his highly critical personal protests against its use). Although problematic in their own terms and increasingly criticised within the sciences, these oppositions have nevertheless functioned as devices for placing science above any mode of political or non-scientific involvement, let alone criticism.

Second, we must be wary of a familiar defensive tactic used to undermine any serious questioning of science: the strategy of distinguishing between different sciences, accepting criticism of the less secure versions while presuming that the more secure forms are immune to these criticisms. For example, it can be more readily accepted that social, political and economic factors operate within, say, medicine and the biological or life sciences than that they do in the 'purer' sciences, such as physics, chemistry or astronomy. Third, we need to affirm some distinctions that are often blurred or ignored in the sciences, separating considerations about *who does science* from the science they practise. In other words, we must not elide two different issues: one, the question of the sexual identity of *the scientist*, raising as it does the matter of *sexual discrimination* within the training, selection, evaluation and funding of scien*tists*; the other, the question of how science qua science operates. Here we need to consider science more in terms of its assumptions, methods, procedures, criteria of evaluation, self-images and the awareness and justification of its practices, that is, the *patriarchal form* of scientific knowledges must also be examined. Both are clearly issues relevant to feminist analyses, but each leads to different objects of investigation and different remedial projects and counterstrategies.

Although it is beyond the scope of this essay, a comprehensive

6

study of women and science requires a detailed analysis of *scientists*: who does science, what sciences they choose (and why they choose them), the statistics marking various rates of student entry into appropriate educational institutions, their success rates, the types of employment available to them and the funding they receive. The sex of scientists is also relevant but perhaps less important than the methods they use and the association of these methods with the attributes of masculinity or femininity. In other words, it seems to matter little whether it is men or women or both who practise science; it is a question of how, why, and with what presumptions and effects their scientific findings, 'factual evidence' or new discoveries are made. The question is not simply who does science but how it is done.

We divide discussion into three parts: in the first we discuss the sexual discrimination operative in the sciences, which disadvantages women and provides often unrecognised privileges for men. Here we concentrate mainly on the biological or life sciences, although our position could be generalised to apply to the other natural sciences. In the second section we examine the internal functioning of the sciences, the presumptions upon which they rely and the methods they use. Here we adopt a more general approach in considering some of the assumptions and methods shared as a kind of common denominator in all of the natural sciences. In the concluding section we examine the possibility of reconceptualising science so that it may become compatible with feminist insights.

WOMEN AND SCIENCE

In examining the ways science has participated in a culturally sanctioned discrimination against women, we discuss the discriminatory barriers preventing women from equal access to the sciences which account for the relatively limited numbers of women working within science. Second, we examine the ways in which many of the sciences actively or 'passively' participate in women's oppression and social subordination, through the rationalisation and justification of pre-existing sexist practices (e.g. in sociobiology) or by devising new forms of mastery and control over women's bodies (e.g. the medical interventions into women's fertility). Third, we discuss the differential evaluations of the scientific work done by women, using as an illustration the rather extreme but well-documented case of Rosalind Franklin.

Restrictions on women as subjects of science

Since the inception of western sciences, women have been excluded from full participation (Alic, 1986). This has sometimes occurred through legislation prohibiting women's access to qualifications or the experience necessary for entry into scientific communities. At other times, it has meant that women are not actively prevented from entering the sciences, but they are strongly discouraged in so far as their femininity has been opposed to the skills and accomplishments allegedly necessary for the scientist. Women have therefore had to choose between being regarded as scientists or as feminine. At present, although women are not forcibly prevented from becoming scientists, they still make up a relatively small percentage of practitioners.

In Australia today, as in the past, science is a male-dominated discipline, even if women have enrolled as students in increasing numbers in certain courses, especially those related to biology and the life sciences—medicine, pharmacy and veterinary science (Temple, 1983:153, 159). In examining figures from the Australian Bureau of Statistics for 1980 and 1985, Temple shows that the proportion of women in occupations requiring scientific or technical training, while increasing during the 1980s, is still very low (Temple, 1985:2–3). The percentages of women working in the sciences are surprisingly small. For example, female medical and dental practitioners constitute only 0.4 per cent of all working women, while the draftsperson/technical subgroup is only 1.1 per cent (Temple, 1985:3).

Temple also shows a clear discrepancy between the proportion of undergraduate students in science and medicine courses and the proportion of female staff in teaching positions in these disciplines. In 1980, the University of Sydney's faculties of Science and Medicine had 16 per cent and 19 per cent female academic staff respectively, whereas the percentage of female students enrolled for their first degrees in these faculties comprised 39 per cent and 33 per cent respectively (Temple, 1983:156). *Some* of the discrepancy between enrolments and participation in teaching is an effect of the time-lag between larger numbers of female students and their continuous training as staff. Changes in levels of women academics will require several years to become visible. These figures are not unusual, and are confirmed in studies undertaken both in Australia and elsewhere. Commenting on a study of PhD research in the USA entitled 'Who Will Do Science', Barbara Wilson notes that there is no evidence of a higher drop-out rate for women than men within quantitative study programs, despite a common assumption that women often do drop out earlier and more frequently than men. Rather, according to Wilson, 'attrition occurs primarily at those points where choices must be made about future educational investment' (1987:3). She argues that there is a close correlation between students' careers in science and their career expectations while still at school. By the 9th grade, over one-third of those who will complete a bachelor's degree in science already expect to take this career path. By the 12th grade, the pool of future scientists is established. After this, there is only a movement (mainly by women) out of the pool. Of those who have completed the necessary advanced mathematics courses only 21 per cent of women, compared with 51 per cent of men, choose a quantitative field of study in their first years at university. And 50 per cent fewer women than men advance towards a master's degree, a percentage which diminishes as advancement towards a PhD occurs (Wilson, 1987:4).

Among the contributing factors streaming women out of scientific occupations, Temple, Wilson and Mary Barnes (in this volume) recognise the involvement of the educational system in sustaining everyday beliefs about women's mathematical and scientific abilities. As Temple and Barnes note, girls tend not to pursue higher-level mathematics because, in this masculine domain, women are considered 'unnatural' or are believed to become masculinised (Barnes, this volume). Girls are led to believe, in accordance with the stereotypes about them, that science is 'a masculine area into which they should not intrude, to think that subjects like physics are "hard" and that engineering and mathematics are unfeminine'. (Temple, 1983:153). Although there is no statistical evidence that women are unable to cope with mathematics, Wilson quotes research to show that the first year at university may have a devastating effect on women's self-esteem: 'while 21 per cent of the women and 23 per cent of the men rated themselves as far above average in intelligence during their senior year in high school, by the end of freshman year only 4 per cent of the women (compared to 22 per cent of the men) still perceived themselves to be in this category' (Wilson, 1987:5).

It is significant that this effect seems to occur *only* in co-educational institutions, not in all-women's colleges!:

> ... a common complaint of female science majors is that their male faculty members are more likely to establish a sense of camaraderie with their male students, and to take their educational and career aspirations more seriously ... By our society's norms, women are still by and large expected to defer to men socially, and to avoid direct competition ... Breaking with cultural norms may be particularly stressful in environments such as science departments, in which women represent only a small minority of the population, and have few role models or even peers to turn to for support and validation of their new behaviour. (Wilson, 1987:5–6)

In short, there are a number of pressures outside the sphere of science proper—education, social expectation, implicit ideals—that make it considerably more difficult for women to enter the sciences than men. When women do gain professional qualifications this in itself is no guarantee that they will have the same employment or research opportunities as their male counterparts. Science, of course, is not unique in this respect. But it has more actively resisted attempts to redress this imbalance than the social sciences or humanities. Moreover, the sciences lag behind in recognising their own forms of discrimination against women, and in implementing remedial programs. As we discuss below, this deficiency has been generally justified by the assertion that science needs to maintain high, neutral standards, which are admittedly difficult to achieve, but are not sexually biased.

Women as objects of scientific investigation

If women acquired positions as *subjects* or producers of science only with great difficulty, they have long been the *objects* of (male) scientific speculation. It is not surprising that women today remain the objects of the sciences, especially the biological sciences. Indeed, science remains a powerful technique for the subjugation of women (and other oppressed peoples: the working class, migrants, colonised groups), and it often serves to legitimise existing power relations.

To take one striking historical example, in Darwin's schema of natural selection and the doctrine of the survival of the fittest, women are treated as a priori subordinate and inferior to men. His account of the species survival of *homo sapiens* is sexually hierarchised with women occupying a *naturally* subordinate position, which is 'shewn by man's attaining to a higher eminence, in whatever he takes up, than can women—whether requiring deep thought, reason, or imagination, or merely the use of the senses and hands' (Darwin 1922:858). Granting women the powers of intuition, 'rapid perception' and imitation, Darwin argues that these attributes confirm women's inferiority as 'some, at least, of these faculties are characteristic of the lower races, and therefore of a past and lower state of civilization' (Darwin, 1922:858; cf. Alaya, 1977). Ironically, Darwin relies on the work of a number of dubious social theorists, like Malthus, Spencer, Lubbock, Galton and McLennan for much of his material on sexual difference. These theorists frequently elevated the everyday assumptions of their day to the status of 'scientific and universal truth', or as 'naturally pre-ordained' (cf. Darwin, 1922:66, 222, 858, 870, 896; and Richards, 1983; Hubbard, Henifin and Fried, 1979, 1982; Brighton Women and Science Group, 1980;

Alaya, 1977). Granted that Darwin is a progenitor of the modern biological sciences, it remains a largely unexplored question as to how much the problematic notions of sexual difference form an essential part of the theory of evolution and the doctrine of the survival of the fittest. Clearly a large number of contemporary biologists would wish to distance themselves from his pronouncements about women while accepting his understanding of evolution; the degree of dependence of the latter on the former needs to be addressed.

Arguably the most insidious contemporary form of scientifically sanctioned misogyny, and a direct heir to Darwin's legacy, is contemporary sociobiology, whose adherents are committed to seeking out the determinants of social behaviour in the genetic code—a sophisticated version of the claim that anatomy is destiny! Initially developed at Harvard in the 1970s (cf. E.O. Wilson, 1975, 1978), sociobiology has become a powerful contemporary version of Darwinian evolutionism regarding sexual differences. It invokes conceptions of 'natural' hierarchies, competition and (biologically based) domination and subordination, and thus legitimises existing social inequalities of sex, race and class, which are naturalised and regarded as unchangeable. Social and especially sexual differences are assumed to be innate, given capacities and proclivities rather than the consequences of social, historical and political factors (cf. Rose, Kamin and Lewontin, 1984).

Within sociobiological models, men are regarded as 'naturally' aggressive, competitive and promiscuous, whereas women are taken to be 'naturally' nurturant and maternal (E.O. Wilson, 1975; Trivers, 1978). Van den Berghe even brings together the peculiarly economic notions of 'price' and 'investment' into his explanation of sex-specific characteristics. He argues that because ova 'are big, few and therefore costly [and] sperms are small, abundant and therefore cheap ... [the male] maximizes his fitness by being promiscuous and by outcompeting his rivals in access to reproductive females', while females, by contrast, are more passive but, because their 'investment' in each ovum is greater, they seek to 'maximize their fitness by being choosy about their mating partners. They seek to pick the best possible mates in terms of genetic qualities and resources they have to offer' (1981:26). Not only does he presume that by some 'natural' means women are more attuned to the evaluation of behavioural and genetic qualities in men than men are in women, he is inconsistent in his conclusions. If, as Ruth Hubbard points out, the average western woman produces around 400 ova in her lifetime to 'invest' only in an average of 2.2 offspring, and the average man, billions of sperm for the same 'investment', it seems as if her 'economic' sense is surer than his and her investment more likely to reap dividends (Hubbard, 1979:25; see also Rose, Kamin and Lewontin, 1984; Gould, 1981; and Jacob, 1982 for critiques of sociobiology developed by men).

The Darwinian and sociobiological 'sciences' not only justify existing social inequities as natural and inevitable, they are the crudest and most visible forms of scientific discrimination. Yet, they are certainly not the *only forms* nor are they the most insidious and powerful ones operating in the control of women's lives. Within the biological and medical sciences generally, women are usually considered only in terms of *universal* (i.e. male) models and norms (cf. Sayers, 1982). Judged in these terms, women's bodies can only be regarded as anomalous, imperfect and in need of explanation whereas men's bodies are taken for granted as adequate representatives of 'human' attributes. Women's womanliness or femininity requires explanation in ways that men's manliness or masculinity does not.

Feminists have long recognised the complicity of medicine in rendering women's bodies as unfit, passive, and incapable in comparison to men's (Ehrenreich and English, 1979). It is significant, for example, that a whole branch of medicine—gynaecology and obstetrics—is devoted to women's specific biologies and above all, their reproductive capacities, while the branch of medicine reserved specifically for men—urology—is not directly concerned with men's reproductive positions. With the exception of gynaecology and obstetrics, medicine is *about* men or about what is considered 'human' in its most reductionistic sense, that is, about what men and women share, without adequate recognition of what distinguishes sexually different beings. Despite the specialisations mentioned above, medical problems specific to women are still under-researched, trivialised or given a non-medical character in their categorisation as hysterical or hypochondriacal (cf. Bowling and Martin, 1985:312). That is, they are often treated as inherent 'deviations' of a *human* biology.

Feminists challenge all these imbalances between men's and women's positions as scientists or subjects on the one hand, and objects of investigation on the other—positions correlated with active and passive roles respectively. In constituting the objects of the (male) scientists' speculations, women continue to remain passive in the control and analysis of their own bodies. This has been crucially demonstrated in the In-Vitro Fertilisation program, in the various definitions of life used for or against the availability of abortion and in the creation of 'artificial wombs'. Together with the cross-species experiments in genetic engineering, these developments have

12

aroused the anger, indeed, horror of many feminists. There is a well-justified apprehension on the part of many women about these techniques for manipulating and controlling human reproduction and fertilisation largely through the control of *women's fertility* rather than men's. Many of these projects are not necessarily in the best interests of women as a whole, even if particular women have willingly participated in various fertility or other programs. In general, feminist responses to the male domination of the very sciences that regulate and supervise women's bodies and lives have thus largely focused on the socio-personal consequences of medical practices, the effects these have on women's health and control over their own bodies, reproduction and daily lives. More recently and specifically, women working within the various life sciences have begun to contest the validity or relevance of many hypotheses and presumptions within medicine, genetics and biology, and to ask if there are not other ways of proceeding, other methods and assumptions that could be used, other projects to be funded and developed.

Such a position, which is critical of scientific assumptions and methods from a perspective *within* the sciences, is well represented in this volume by Lesley Rogers who challenges a number of inferences pervasive to sociobiological, genetic and physiological research regarding sexual differences. She is concerned with the ways in which scientific research accords with stereotypical social representations of the two sexes rather than, as is commonly presumed, social images finding their 'truth' in independently established scientific statements. She argues that although we are categorised as male or female on the basis of genital characteristics (or as she accurately claims, on the presence or absence of the penis), this binary opposition does not necessarily correspond with differentiations in brain functions. As she also suggests, arguments based on genetic or biologically determined functions must be questioned. The relationship between genetic and environmental factors is far more complex than genetic determinism would let us believe, for it is not clear to what degree each of these factors functions to influence or determine the other. The human 'data' on which the sociobiologist works are already a complex result of genetic *and* environmental factors which cannot be readily extricated from each other.

In short, biological evidence which is granted a scientific status cannot simply be taken as neutral, disinterested or pure. This is not of course to suggest sinister or conspiratorial motives in the work of scientists: rather, there may be unrecognised *structural and political adherences* operating within the sciences, particularly in those which help regulate our lives, and which scientists unwittingly reproduce.

13

That is, sciences do not simply *reflect* socio-cultural norms but, more insidiously, they develop scientific norms, procedural rules and regulatory criteria which are active contributions to (and not merely passive reflections of) social relations. Knowledges of the life-processes are always in some way or other implicated in the socio-political and cultural norms of their times, but this remains largely unrecognised by biologically oriented researchers. Those who practise the more 'hard-core' sciences such as physics and mathematics may recognise these implications in the life sciences, but cannot always perceive them in their own.

A 'case study': Rosalind Franklin and DNA

Rosalind Franklin's scientific life (Sayre, 1975) provides a fascinating case study of the ways in which women's contributions to science are often denigrated, ignored or actively appropriated by men (Sayre, 1975:150–54). It illustrates some of the techniques used by (some?) scientists (occasionally with the best of intentions) to deny women recognition of their contributions to science, and to relegate them to the status of an object out of place, displaced from their 'natural' element.

Franklin developed her crystallographic work in the 1950s while contributing to research which led to the discovery of the structure of DNA. Like many of her female scientific predecessors (cf. Alic, 1986), her contributions were not acknowledged by the men—Crick, Watson and Wilkins—who eventually shared the Nobel Prize for their work on the genetic structure. In James Watson's version of the DNA story, published in *The Double Helix* (1968), he gives virtually no credit to Franklin and is at pains to denigrate her in both personal and scientific terms. He portrays 'Rosy' (a name neither Franklin nor her friends ever used) as a peculiar, idiosyncratic individual with 'personality problems' and an inability to control her emotions (Watson, 1968:18; Sayre, 1975:138)—a standard stereotype of femininity used to discredit her productive role.

Franklin was isolated from her male colleagues at the sex-segregated Kings College in London. They tended to shun her, according to Sayre, claiming she did not know or understand the implications of her experiments with DNA (Sayre, 1975:107, 124, 128ff). Franklin worked with one of three teams (in London, Cambridge and California) working on discovering the secret of DNA, the 'Rosetta Stone for unravelling the true secret of life' (Watson, 1968:14), in what some of the men openly claimed was a competitive race. The overcoded significance of this male quest was, it could be argued, conditioned on the exclusion of women, for, as

Mary Shelley illustrated so brilliantly in *Frankenstein*, the male desire for self-production, for a reproduction free from any dependence on women, has long pervaded our culture (Jacobus, 1986).

Franklin and her co-researcher, Maurice Wilkins, made painstaking measurements of molecular cell structures using X-ray diffraction techniques. Wilkins had a proprietorial attitude towards the DNA project and tried to position Franklin as his assistant; Franklin, however, saw herself as his equal, and the project as much her own as his.

Franklin's stubbornness, her refusal to comply with the position of 'assistant', 'helper' or subordinate to Wilkins, were among the reasons which led to her denigration and, eventually, to her leaving the project (Sayre, 1975:137–38). Watson regarded her as more difficult than she was worth (although, ironically, she did provide the empirical data on which Crick and Watson based their findings (cf. Jacobus, 1986:98). Even so, they quite self-consciously saw her rebelliousness as a problem and devised various means to 'get rid of her': 'Clearly, Rosy had to go or be put in her place. The former was obviously preferable because, given her belligerent moods, it would be very difficult for Maurice [Wilkins] to maintain a dominant position that would allow him to think unhindered about DNA' (Watson, 1968:17).

The men used a number of strategies to belittle her contribution and to render it invisible. For example, the network of connections between male colleagues—Wilkins, Crick, Watson and Perutz—meant that Franklin's experimental results were discussed and disseminated without her participation (Sayre, 1975:152). She was effectively silenced, excluded, and her work was represented by others as if it were theirs. She was continually personalised in Watson's account and treated merely as 'a woman', as if being a scientist and a woman were mutually exclusive. Reduced to a bundle of whims, neuroses and symptoms, Watson even speculates that she was 'the product of an unsatisfied mother who unduly stressed the desirability of professional careers that could save bright girls from marriages to dull men' (Watson, 1968:17). It is significant that Watson's psychological 'gifts' were not directed towards the psyches of the other men involved in this scientific race (for example, to Crick's obsession with the sex lives of Cambridge au pair girls (Jacobus, 1986:98).

Franklin was clearly the victim of a kind of intellectual persecution of the most malicious and self-conscious type. She was also simply a 'character' in a fantasied scenario surrounding, as Watson implies, the quest of gods for the key to womanless reproduction!

(cf. Watson, 1968:14). This representation is, as Jacobus points out (1986:99), coded in openly sexual terms: the men see themselves as predators, explorers, adventurers, tracking down, penetrating a crucial and feminine mystery. In his book, *Life Itself* (1981), Crick even refers to the RNA and DNA molecules as 'the dumb blondes of the bio-molecular world' (1981:72). If, instead of the woman, the DNA molecule is the femme fatale, the heroine, then Franklin is presented as the wicked witch or prudish mother figure, standing between man and his conquest. She obstinately refused to play the role of daddy's helper and was consequently belittled, ridiculed and excluded.

FEMININITY AND SCIENCE

If the various practices associated with scientific discovery, training and employment and the 'applied' results of science have, until now, discriminated against women, there are many who still believe that science itself, its methods, data and forms of proof are not discriminatory. What is true is true! Although many admit that the procedures *surrounding* science have political effects, they usually believe these effects are peripheral to the actual operations of science itself. In this section, we concentrate mainly on a series of criticisms feminists have posed to 'pure science', some of which they share with male epistemologists and philosophers of science.

These criticisms also make clear the limitations inherent in attempts to institute reforms in the procedures surrounding science which leave its fundamental assumptions and techniques intact. There seems to be a strong commitment to the belief that although it is possible to reform the induction into and implementation of science, science itself is or should be immune to political criticism. That is, if it is to be criticised, science can only be criticised from within science itself. Only a *more* scientific view is capable of validly criticising a less scientific position. We hope to show that an unquestioned belief in the truth, the purity, the political/social neutrality of science amounts to an acceptance of some of the most insidious and least recognised forms of male domination—the male domination over, and the restriction of, knowledge itself.

Epistemological critiques of science

Some male critics of sciences or, rather, of the self-images and self-representations of science, have forcefully challenged its apparently neutral and universal status. Perhaps the first and most significant of the twentieth-century critics is Karl Popper, for whom science is not simply the neutral gathering of observation-statements or 'facts', which are then generalised, through induction, to provide scientific laws or universal statements. As long ago as the eighteenth century, David Hume demonstrated that the use of inductive arguments—those based on generalisation or universalisation of large numbers of particular instances—could not be reasonably justified. Popper continues the Humean critical position by arguing that sciences cannot be *verified* or *confirmed* by observations. Science does not proceed by the patient adding together of confirming instances; indeed, no finite number of confirmations can ever verify a universal scientific law of even the most elementary type (e.g. scientific laws in the form of the statement 'All metals expand when heated'). These universals are problematic when we realise that in spite of millions of instances of confirmation, a universal hypothesis needs only one counter-example to be considered false. Popper argued that the criteria by which statements can be regarded as scientific are thus not based on verification, but on *falsification*. Only those propositions that make some claim that could *in principle* at least be falsified can be considered scientific.

Thus for Popper, the bolder the proposition is, the more it risks being falsified, the greater is its scientific status and the more information about the world it conveys to us:

> I can ... gladly admit that falsificationists like myself much prefer an attempt to solve an interesting problem by a bold conjecture, *even (and especially) if it soon turns out to be false*, to any recital of a sequence of irrelevant truisms. We prefer this because we believe that this is the way in which we can learn from our mistakes, and that in finding that our conjecture was false we shall have learnt much about the truth, and shall have got nearer to the truth. (Popper, 1969:231, emphasis in the original)

Although there are clearly many problems with Popper's position, he does pose serious problems for naive empiricist concepts of science as that which is simply based on 'the facts', on 'objective observation' unmediated by a theory or prior beliefs and thus untouched by political or extra-scientific concerns. In this respect, his work was further elaborated and developed, though in quite different directions and with quite different ends in mind, by the philosopher and historian of science, Thomas Kuhn.

In *The Structure of Scientific Revolutions* (1970), Kuhn argues that science should not be regarded as the gradual and cumulative march towards truth, or as a fundamentally progressive development of statements where later ones replace earlier ones. Science is a social category. It does not rely simply on brilliant individuals or great minds, but on the existence and operation of scientific communities of researchers who share common techniques, preoccupations, language, methods and training.

Kuhn defines these shared community practices and presumptions in terms of *shared paradigms*, that is, of 'universally recognized scientific achievements that for a time provide model problems and solutions to a community of practitioners' (Kuhn, 1970:viii). These paradigms are not simply shared conceptual systems or shared world-views, but shared material practices. For any particular scientific community, its paradigms are 'revealed in its textbooks, lectures, and laboratory exercises. By studying them and by practising with them, the members of the corresponding community learn their trade' (Kuhn, 1970:43). Kuhn introduces the concept of scientific paradigm in order to explain the historical changes in directions, digressions and detours that mark the history of science.

In opposition to Popper, Kuhn argues that science does not function through falsification. In fact, if the 'Great Scientists' had adhered to the principles Popper espouses, some of the most unexpected and innovative scientific discoveries could not have occurred (e.g. those of Galileo, Newton and Einstein). In his view, science undergoes a series of dramatic and often unpredictable paradigm shifts, radical upheavals in shared presumptions, which require a distinction between what he calls 'normal science' and 'scientific revolutions'.

During periods of normal science, the scientific community shares a common set of problems, terminology, techniques and criteria. The aim of normal science is 'puzzle-solving', providing answers to already existing questions, which are not devised by individual scientists but are dictated by the paradigm itself (1970:24). Because the practitioners within a scientific community tend to be intolerant of new theories and alternative paradigms, which are judged only from the perspective of the paradigm already held, they are unable to judge other paradigms independently. The established paradigm tends to insulate the scientific community from new discoveries and from 'those socially important problems that are not reducible to the puzzle form, because they cannot be stated in terms of the conceptual and instrumental tools the paradigm supplies' (Kuhn, 1970:37).

Scientific revolutions occur when anomalies, puzzles that cannot be solved, are not so much explained in alternative ways as contextualised differently so that other puzzles are posed. Out of a mass of competing paradigms (during the breakdown of normal science) one emerges to recast the questions posed, the answers sought and the criteria devised for their assessment. The new paradigm renders the old one irrelevant, taking up a new set of issues and possibly, although not necessarily, solving the old puzzles. The shift from one paradigm to another is, on Kuhn's understanding, not a rational move from an inferior to a recognisably superior position. The process is less rational and thought out than this: to accept even the initial postulates of a new paradigm entails some renunciation of the older paradigm. Kuhn likens this shift to a religious conversion: one suddenly sees the light! He not only introduces a *relativism* to notions of scientific practice, challenging the notion of science as 'the Truth', he also introduces an irrational element into the adoption, evaluation and discarding of paradigms. He challenges Popper's assumption that observations and facts are independent of paradigms and can somehow confirm or falsify them. If 'facts' are always considered only in terms of the paradigms through which one works, then they are not independent of theory, nor are they able to provide theory with a justification through observation.

Although Kuhn's relativism generates enormous problems of its own, its opposite, empiricism, is also untenable. Both Popper and Kuhn seriously shake the foundations of everyday beliefs about scientific justification. They problematise naive adherences to a notion of science as pure truth—a pure, unmediated observational truth. These difficulties also prove to be crucial ingredients in the critiques developed by feminists. Nevertheless, in spite of their radical departures from realist and empiricist conceptions of science, neither Popper nor Kuhn raises the question of the sexual specificity of paradigms, and the social factors related to the hierarchical differences between the sexes.

Gendered science?

Granted, then, that the self-image of science as pure, motivated only by the search for truth, as non-political and objective has serious flaws, we must ask to what extent this forces us to modify our conventional conceptions of science and to accept a conception linking it more directly to social, political, sexual and economic factors. More particularly, to what extent can science (implicitly or explicitly) be regarded as gendered? That is, to what extent does it privilege masculinity and its attributes over femininity? To what extent is it implicated in prevailing patriarchal power relations? In posing these questions we do not focus on the relations between science and concrete, real *women*; instead we consider the relations between science and the elevation or denigration of masculinity and femininity. The 'masculinisation' of science here implies that the perspectives, frameworks and positions it represents concur with and privilege the masculine knower, but do not grant equal access to the knower whose position is not masculine.

19

There are varying degrees of recognition of this masculinisation in feminist literature on science. Both Temple and Wilson are aware of the extent to which the masculine/feminine opposition permeates social life and thus the lives of the men and women who become scientists. However, they locate women's subordination only at the level of particular choices made by, and obstacles in the way of, individuals. Temple refers, for example, to the association of reason and law with masculinity and imagination and creativity with femininity as being instrumental in the exclusion of women from science (1983:172). But neither Temple nor Wilson accepts the full implications of considering *science itself*, in its internal functioning, as masculine. If they accept the male domination of the sciences, each holds back from accepting the masculinity of the sciences themselves. Our argument is that this masculinity implies that feminist critiques of science should concentrate not only on getting more women into science as professionals (although this, of course, is important) but on transforming the way science is done, and what is considered part of scientific endeavour.

Jan Harding comes halfway to acknowledging science as gendered. Her research distinguishes between two kinds of thinkers whom she calls 'convergent' and 'divergent' thinkers, the former proceeding systematically towards a single answer, the latter ranging over various possibilities. Boys who choose science tend to be convergent thinkers, and boys who choose the humanities tend to be divergent thinkers. Significantly, she notes, these results do not apply for girls. Girls choosing science tend to be divergent thinkers (Harding, 1986:5). Harding, suggests that the girls' choice of science correlates with 'the perception that science has social implications' and thus, she says, girls 'seemed to be choosing something rather different from what the boys were choosing' (Harding, 1986:6). Although she does not explore further the sexualisation of science, she raises the possibility of different perspectives among the male and female practitioners of science. She argues that girls tolerate ambiguities more easily and perceive science as a way of 'helping other people' more frequently than boys who, by contrast, tend to regard science more as a form of mastery. In short, Harding explains that, empirically speaking, women tend to do science with different aims from men, yet the models that the sciences themselves actively affirm accord largely with the masculine rather than the feminine responses (Harding, 1986).

Evelyn Fox Keller moves a step closer to a recognition of the specificities and limits of the sciences as they are practised today, and towards the possibility of developing equally (if not more) viable alternatives. She sees the sciences as imbued with ideologies associated with the values of objectivity, neutrality and masculine dominance (1985:76). Like other feminists, she attributes the widespread functioning of binary oppositions with some role in these ideologies. For example, she argues that the opposition between Mind (the knower) and Nature (the knowable) is sexually coded to correlate with the oppositions between masculine and feminine respectively (Fox Keller, 1985:79).

Fox Keller first locates the explicit sexualisation of the ineradicable metaphors, terminology, and linguistic associations that function within science:

> When we dub the objective sciences 'hard' as opposed to softer (that is, more subjective) branches of knowledge, we implicitly invoke a sexual metaphor, in which the 'hard' is of course masculine and 'soft' feminine. Quite generally, facts are 'hard', feelings 'soft'. 'Feminization' has become synonymous with sentimentalization. A woman thinking scientifically or objectively is thinking 'like a man'; conversely, a man pursuing a non-rational, non-scientific argument is arguing 'like a woman'. (1985:77; and cf. Le Doeuff, 1980)

She recognises however that locating the problem at the level of the language and metaphors of science is not to position it in a trivial or easily transformable form. On the contrary, the 'use of language and metaphor can become hardened into a kind of reality' (1985:78). If mastery over nature, opening up nature's secrets, the conquest of the atom, the quest for the DNA structure are all metaphoric and rhetorical forms necessary for conceptions of science, they reveal their sexual resonances. And given their tenacity and centrality in how science is actually conceived and practised, the transformation of these uses requires a change in the way science functions.

Fox Keller locates a second-order problem in the differential socialisation practices in the rearing of children. Here, she relies on object-relations theory and the work of Nancy Chodorow (1978) on mothering to associate femininity with a tendency towards merging with the mother and the environment, neither of which is sharply differentiated from the subject; and masculinity with the striving towards independence, autonomy and separateness from the mother and from objects. These attributes are attached generally to female and male subjects in our culture, and therefore to female and male scientists working within it: 'Along with autonomy the very act of separating subject from object—objectivity itself—comes to be associated with masculinity' (Fox Keller, 1982:595). In spite of problems in Chodorow's position, Fox Keller clearly recognises the implications of attributing masculinity to the bases of objectivity. This ideal of objectivity, so strongly desired within the sciences, reveals its own (political) limits: it problematises the universality and necessity of conventional scientific positions by demonstrating the complicity of knowledges in patriarchy. As Fox Keller recognises, 'in characterising scientific and objective thought as masculine, the very activity by which the knower can acquire knowledge is also genderized' (1985:79).

'Case study' 2: Barbara McClintock

Fox Keller's biography of the Nobel prize-winning geneticist Barbara McClintock provides a significant contrast with Sayre's account of Rosalind Franklin. McClintock discovered genetic transposition, that is, the way in which genetic elements 'move, in an apparently coordinated way, from one chromosomal site to another' (Fox Keller, 1985:159). Where Franklin has been re-presented as a victim (to some extent through her own complicity) of the discrimination against women within the sciences, McClintock, by contrast, provides a positive example of the ways in which alternative scientific frameworks and perspectives, those more appropriate for women, may be developed. Like Franklin, she was largely isolated from the mainstream of the scientific community, denied access to a proper job and suffered the general humiliations and denigration women usually undergo in entering male-dominated domains. One prominent geneticist, for example, referred to her as 'just an old bag who'd been hanging around ... for years' (Fox Keller, 1983:141). Yet McClintock revealed that there was more than one way to solve problems, and that the existing paradigms within her field required reconceptualisation.

Fox Keller uses Kuhn's conception of paradigm shifts to explain how McClintock's transgressions were able to gain recognition and eventual acceptance. She reads McClintock's career as 'a story about the languages of science—about ... the process by which worlds of common scientific discourse become established, effectively bounded, and yet at the same time remain sufficiently permeable to allow a given piece of work to pass from incomprehensibility in one era to acceptance (if not full comprehensibility) in another' (Fox Keller, 1985:161).

Describing her own work, McClintock did not divorce herself from the organisms she studied, nor did she adopt a pose of objective disinterested neutrality. She maintained that nature was infinitely complex. Plants, for example, 'can do almost anything you can think of' (Fox Keller, 1983:200). Instead of conceiving of the scientist as an outside observer, she believed the scientist should 'hear what the material has to say to you' (1983:198). Rather than seek the expected with a penetrating intelligence, she invokes here a

literary or interpretive skill. It is significant that, where many of the
social sciences aspire to natural scientific status and forms of proof,
McClintock's breakthrough involved seeing science more on the
model of the humanities. She believed that one had to develop a
'feeling for the organism' (1983:198), to respect and interact with its
specificity, to see/listen to what it has to say: 'The important thing is
to develop the capacity to see one kernel [of maize] that is different,
and make that understandable ... If [something] doesn't fit, there's
a reason, and you find out what it is' (Fox Keller, 1985:163).

Her method involved what she saw as an openness to the 'object'
she interrogated, one that modelled itself on communication.
McClintock anticipates many of the insights developed by feminists
working in the humanities and social sciences about the problems of
binary polarisations and oppositions (see, for example, Irigaray,
1985a; Lloyd, 1984; Jay, 1981). According to Fox Keller, she re-
gards a *non-oppositional* relation of *difference* (the A/B model, not
the A/-A model) as crucial to understanding how the sciences could
work. Where polarisation and division sever the connections and
impose distance, McClintock's recognition of difference 'provides a
starting point for relatedness'. As Fox Keller continues:

> ... difference constitutes a principle for ordering the world radically
> unlike the principle of division of dichotomization (subject–object,
> mind–matter, feeling–reason, disorder–law). Whereas these opposi-
> tions are directed toward a cosmic unity typically excluding or devour-
> ing one of the pair, toward a unified, all-encompassing law, respect for
> difference remains content with multiplicity as an end in itself. (Fox
> Keller, 1985:163)

Fox Keller emphasises that McClintock's unconventional approach to her work, her attempt to rethink her data and entertain
quite different conceptions from her colleagues, nevertheless provided testable, repeatable results. While, in other words conforming
to some of the major criteria adopted by the sciences, she questioned the methods of procedure, the fundamental techniques and
axioms of her chosen field. In seeking an answer to the question
'how do genes work?', McClintock did not limit herself to the
genetic structure or mechanisms, as others did, but examined how
genes function in relation to the organism's cells and to the organism as a whole, thereby blurring the traditional border dividing
genetics from developmental biology. In her work, she placed the
gene in an eco-systemic order where it was defined by its general
position within the whole (not unlike contemporary views of language itself!).

In discovering that genetic sequences are not fixed, given that
genetic transpositions have occurred, McClintock's work problema-

tised the prevailing understanding of the DNA as 'the central actor in the cell, the executive governor of cellular organisation, itself remaining impervious to influence from the subordinate agents to which it dictates' (Fox Keller, 1985:169. Cf. Sayre, 1975:198)—a clearly anthropocentric and androcentric metaphor (reflecting the hierarchised system of social stratification in our culture). Instead of presuming that nature functions as a modern corporation, she regarded it as an environmental system in which signals external to the cell account for reorganisation of the DNA molecule. DNA could thus be regarded not simply as a genetic *transmitter* of biological information, but also as a receiver, and thus as a communicational circuit.

Although recognised today by most geneticists, McClintock's position is still not altogether accepted. Her methods and approach differ considerably from accepted scientific norms. It is ironic that, although she was explicitly committed to a gender-free notion of science, her work was itself quite different from that of her male colleagues: 'the relevance of McClintock's gender . . . is to be found not in its role in her personal socialization but precisely in the role of gender in the construction of science' (Fox Keller, 1985:174). McClintock *did* effect a radical subversion of many key terms and presumptions within her own field, demonstrating that there is always more than one way of approaching any problem: she insisted on 'a different meaning of mind, of nature, and of the relation between them' (Fox Keller, 1985:175), an insistence that helped transform her discipline.

FEMINIST SCIENCE?

The most radical, far-ranging feminist analyses of the alleged sexual neutrality of science no longer maintain, as McClintock does, that science could, if reformed, become gender-neutral. Instead they wholeheartedly affirm the sexual specificity of science and its representation of masculine positions and perspectives. These feminists attempt to develop different models of knowledge which can also be openly affirmed as sexually specific, but this time representing women's positions and interests. This approach implies both the development of critical analyses, pointing out the limits and unwarranted assumptions of prevailing models of science and the masculinity belying its apparent sexual neutrality; and of experimenting with and devising new or different procedures and paradigms.

Although she only schematically outlines it in her works, Luce Irigaray (1984; 1985) offers one of the more perceptive and challenging conceptions of science. Irigaray's position is related to her conception of the production of knowledges: all knowledges are produced from certain positions that have somewhere left their trace in what they produce. Within the sciences, she argues, the 'common force of production' (1985:74) has always been man. But if man, men, produce science, where is it possible to locate this force of production in the product (science, knowledge) thus produced? Irigaray suggests that man effaces his masculinity and particularity to proclaim instead the global relevance and *perspectivelessness* of his construct. Thus the claims that science makes about its own truthful, objective, neutral and global position are in fact attempts to resist recognising its masculinity.

While Irigaray does not attempt to formulate a specifically feminine or feminist science—after all, this is a project for women in science to achieve—she does help to pinpoint a number of the commitments operative within science that reflect or reinforce the social and patriarchal privilege of masculinity. She implies that these commitments are congruent with the attributes and values accorded to men within our culture. In other words, the ideals men attribute to themselves are projected onto the forms adopted by knowledges, so that the latter are forms of masculine self-reflection—not unlike man's representation of God as a reflection of his own form.

She includes the following among the features of scientific activity which are problematic: 1) the presumption of a singular reality which is distinct from and observable by the knowing subject; 2) the imposition of models and grids, structures and paradigms which, far from being instrumentally useful tools, are ideologically motivated self-images, projected onto reality as if they emanate from the real; 3) a privileging of the visible and its equation with the sensible—in other words, an 'ocularocentrism' (vision-centredness) that denigrates the information provided by the senses other than sight; 4) the presumption that the use and intervention of technological equipment is neutral and can be accounted for in the extraction of scientific laws and rules—in other words, the imposition of a mediating set of instruments between the knower and reality, whose influence on the data is considered neutral; 5) the construction of conceptual models or ideals that are isomorphic or congruent with the knower's position as subject; 6) the presumption that proof, repeatability are criteria of objectivity when this assumes the identity or sameness of two experimenters; and 7) the equation of the ability to manipulate and control with progress and knowledge (Irigaray, 1985:78–79).

This list of presuppositions operative within science justifies a series of methodological procedures which separate scientific and potentially scientific hypotheses from non-scientific ones. There are certain minimal conditions that must be met if a proposition is to be included within a scientific category. First, there is the substitution of symbols for proper nouns: this ensures that science remains hermetically sealed and opaque to all outsiders who are not familiar with its terminology. Only those 'things' which can be represented in symbolic terms can be scientifically formulated. Second, Irigaray cites the condition under which terms must be quantifiable rather than qualifiable. Indeed, the numerical condition seems to be a major prerequisite of science, necessary for the rigour and precision of its terms and discoveries. Third, she describes the condition of formalised language, which 'serves to define the rules of the game so that the participants will play the same game and will be able to rule over a particular move in the case of disagreement' (Irigaray, 1985:80).

According to Irigaray, masculine science requires rigour, precision, accuracy, repeatability, a neutral, clear language, a clear-cut set of procedures for assessing propositions, a manipulable, controllable set of experimental techniques, not in order to make science absolutely truthful or objective, but to provide man, the knower, with a set of guarantees about the stability and certainty of his position.

> The scientist now strives to stand before the world; naming it, legislating it, reducing it to axioms. While he manipulates nature, using it, exploiting it, he is forgetting that he, too, is *within* nature—that he is still part of the physical world and not just placed before phenomena whose physical nature he occasionally misreads. He progresses in accordance with an objective method which would provide a shelter from any instability, any 'change' of mood [*humeur*], any sentiments and affective fluctuations, any intuition not programmed in the name of science, any admixture of his desire, especially those differentiated by sex, in his discoveries ... He is living in fear of and sterilizing anything tending toward disequilibrium, however necessary these disequilibriums may be for happening upon a new horizon of discovery. (Irigaray, 1985:83)

Irigaray's point here is that until the masculinity inherent in science is recognised as such, until, that is, the *partiality* of existing scientific theories, laws and techniques are seen as one among many possible ways of proceeding, science will remain the privileged domain of the masculine. Men in general seem to have too much invested in their positions as authoritative knowers to be able to recognise this: it is thus largely up to women to challenge the norms and ideals within which they were trained in order to seek other ways of knowing, other techniques of proof, and perhaps another status for science. Irigaray does not present a feminist science. What she does show is that those techniques of knowing that we call science are not singular, truthful and incontestable positions. In doing this, she makes clear the exclusions, disqualifications, silences that the sciences effect over competing paradigms, and the intellectual coercion and domination that established paradigms hold over others. She therefore clears a space which must be reexplored, a terrain of intellectual positions that must be reinvestigated for their effectivity and explanatory power. She shows that if science as we know it up to now has reflected male interests, this problem is not dissolved by purging it of *all* interests. Rather, it is necessary to acknowledge the specificity of any particular interest in order that other interests may also be explored and even provide the bases for the production of knowledges.

Women have only recently begun to enter the sciences in large enough numbers to provide support for each other and to provide challenges to the sciences that cannot simply be dismissed as 'female neurosis' or individual idiosyncrasy. Only when they are firmly entrenched can women actively produce methods and discoveries that depart from male norms to produce different kinds of knowledges, and only then will the male domination of science be overcome.

The feminists we have surveyed in this paper have in their different ways participated in the dawning recognition that it is not necessary to accept masculine norms as the only ones possible. Different kinds of science, different relations of knowing can also be devised and, indeed, *must* be if women are to have some effect on the power over life and death that science today exerts.

MARY BARNES

2   Mathematics: a barrier for women?

> As decidedly as that two and two make four, what a monstrosity is a woman who is a professor of mathematics, and how unnecessary, injurious and out of place she is.

These were the words of the Swedish writer August Strindberg on the occasion of the appointment of Sonya Kovalevskaya in 1884 as professor of mathematics at the University of Stockholm (quoted in Mozans, 1974:163). In declaring mathematics an inappropriate activity for women, Strindberg was expressing the common belief that most women are not capable of such abstract study, and that those who do succeed in it are in some way unnatural. This belief has in the past motivated parents to try to prevent their daughters from studying mathematics, as in Kovalevskaya's own experience. As a young woman, she found that universities in Russia were not open to her, and her father refused to permit her to travel abroad to study. She managed, however, to achieve a neat solution to this problem. A young man of radical views was found, who supported the higher education of women, and a 'fictitious' marriage was planned. By pretending to elope, she forced her parents into permitting the marriage and the young couple later set off for Heidelberg, where Kovalevskaya was able to pursue her mathematical studies (Koblitz, 1983:55–87).

More recently, Emmy Noether, who more than any other female mathematician has influenced the shape of mathematics as we know it today, was for many years unable to gain a teaching position at Gottingen because of her sex (Dick, 1981:32). And even after her death, we find in the middle of a memorial address by Hermann Weyl, who intended to praise her and her work, remarks which can only be regarded as insulting: 'She was heavy of build and loud of voice, and it was often not easy for one to get the floor in competition with her.' Weyl, it appears, did not approve of assertive women. He continued: 'No-one could contend that the Graces had stood by her cradle; but if we in Gottingen often chaffingly referred to her as "der Noether" (with the masculine article), it was also done with a respectful recognition of her power as a creative thinker who seemed to have broken through the barrier of sex' (Weyl, 1935:219). In other words: we were not just being rude about her appearance, we were really paying her a compliment by implying that she could think like a man!

WOMEN'S PARTICIPATION IN MATHEMATICS

The idea that mathematics is a field in which women are 'out of place' and in which no normal woman can be expected to achieve, is still prevalent today both within the mathematical community and in society at large, although it is seldom stated as explicitly as in the examples above. This belief that mathematics is a male domain forms part of the complex network of factors which helps explain women's lower participation in mathematics and mathematics-dependent occupations.

To see the extent of this lower participation, let us consider the selection of courses by girls and boys at school. A review of enrolment patterns in mathematics courses throughout Australia (Dekkers et al., 1983) shows that more girls than boys choose 'terminal' mathematics courses, that is, courses not designed as a preparation for any future studies involving mathematics. Approximately equal numbers of girls and boys enrol in courses designed to provide sufficient competence for tertiary studies with minimal mathematical content, while those courses designed to lead to tertiary studies which have mathematics as an integral component attract between two and three times as many boys as girls.

As an illustration of this, Fig. 1 shows the percentage of females in the total candidature in each of the four mathematics courses offered in the New South Wales Higher School Certificate. By way of explanation, Mathematics in Society is a terminal course, 2 unit Mathematics provides minimal competence for further study, 3 unit Mathematics is the normal preparation for tertiary mathematics, and 4 unit Mathematics is a specialist course.

Although there has been over the last few years a gradual trend towards an increase in the proportion of girls at all levels, they are still seriously underrepresented in the more specialised courses. In New South Wales in 1984, only 35 per cent of the total 3 and 4 unit candidature were girls. Looked at in a different way, only

Figure 1 **Participation in mathematics examinations—New South Wales Higher School Certificate**

Source: Board of Senior School Studies and Dekkers et al. (1983)

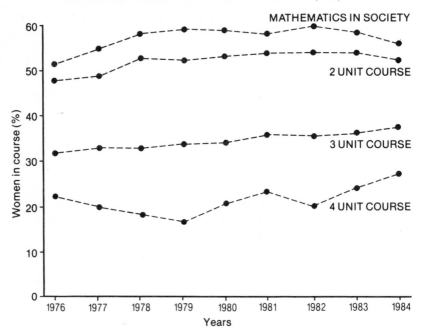

16 per cent of female Higher School Certificate candidates took 3 or 4 unit Mathematics compared with 30 per cent of males.

Data from other States are very similar, the main difference being that in some States, for example Victoria, a much higher proportion of students in the final year of school study no mathematics at all. 'More than 25 per cent of boys satisfied tertiary entry requirements with higher Mathematics, Physics and Chemistry but only about 6 per cent of girls did so. About 45 per cent of boys did so with at least general mathematics, compared with less than 20 per cent of girls' (McGregor, 1985).

As students move on to the tertiary level, the percentage of women in mathematics courses steadily decreases. Fig. 2 shows the percentage of honours degrees in mathematics awarded to women by all Australian universities in recent years. Although there has been an increase from an average of around 10 per cent in the early 1960s, the present figure is still only just over 20 per cent (Petocz, 1985a).

30

**Figure 2   Percentage of honours degrees in mathematics awarded to women
(All Australian universities)**
Source: Petocz (1985)

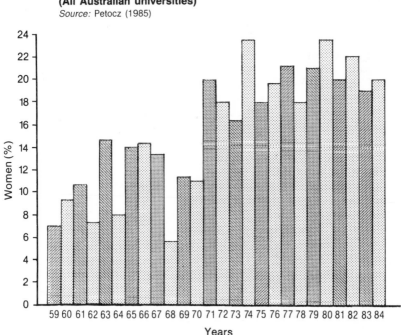

At the postgraduate level, women gained 18 per cent of research masters degrees and 14 per cent of PhDs in mathematics awarded in 1979–83 (Petocz, 1985b). This should be compared with the average over all disciplines: in 1982 women gained 28 per cent of masters degrees and 22 per cent of PhDs (ABS University Statistics, 1982).

Results of this kind are not confined to Australia. A similar pattern appears in virtually all developed western countries: as soon as mathematics becomes optional, girls choose to drop out of it in greater numbers than boys; as soon as there is a free choice in the level of mathematics studied, girls choose lower levels more than boys do. Keeves, reporting on the first international mathematics study, carried out in 1964, found mathematics 'predominantly a male activity' at the end of secondary schooling in ten countries (Keeves, 1973:49). Recent reports indicate that, although there have been some changes, mathematics at this level remains male-dominated in most countries (Atkin, 1984; Hiddleston, 1984; Kuendiger, 1982; Wily, 1984).

ACHIEVEMENT IN MATHEMATICS

Boys' superiority in mathematics used to be taken as a 'well established' fact, (Maccoby and Jacklin, 1974:352), but the picture nowadays is less clear. The conclusions reached by recent studies depend on the age of the students, the specific groups sampled, the mathematics tasks to be performed and the way in which the performance is measured (Leder, 1984). Nevertheless some general patterns emerge. There are few differences between the sexes in overall performance on mathematics tests up to about age thirteen. After that, differences in favour of males begin to appear, but when the number of hours spent learning mathematics is taken into account, these disappear entirely or are greatly reduced (Moss, 1982:59; Leder, 1984).

A rather altered picture appears when we look at the performance of boys and girls on different types of mathematics problem. Data from the School Certificate Reference Test, which is taken by all Year 10 students in New South Wales schools, reveal no overall sex difference. Yet when responses to individual items are analysed, it is found that boys perform better on questions of a practical nature, especially those involving measurement, percentages or ratio, that is, questions requiring spatial visualisation or interpretation of graphs or diagrams and problems requiring multiple steps for their solution, while girls do better on algebraic and arithmetical questions usually involving application of a memorised rule (Thomas, 1981). Pattison and Grieve (1984) found that girls achieved better than boys on certain types of abstract logical or algebraic problems, while boys, again, excelled on measurement, proportion and spatial problems. Very similar results have been obtained in New Zealand (Wily, 1984), Canada (Hanna, 1984) and England (APU, 1982:72 and 143–45), while some other Australian studies provide partial confirmation (Moss, 1982:19–21; Kudilczak et al., 1979).

At the highest levels of achievement in Australia, gender differences are more pronounced. Boys greatly outnumber girls among prizewinners in mathematics competitions, for example, and on tests designed to select talented students for special programs (Leder, 1984:5). This, too, parallels results from overseas (Benbow and Stanley, 1980).

THE MATHEMATICS BARRIER

Before discussing the reasons for these observations, let us first ask how seriously we should regard them. Should we simply accept that women have other interests and other aptitudes, and leave men to play their own games, along with a few somewhat 'unnatural' women?

On the contrary: we must take action to bring about change for a number of reasons. The first is the effect of lower participation in mathematics on employment opportunities for women. Mathematics, often described as a 'critical filter' in the job market, is one of the factors which contribute to the gender segmentation of the workforce. The occupations (and tertiary courses) in which women are clustered are mainly those which need little or no mathematics. On the other hand, those occupations and tertiary courses which are most male-dominated are those which require mathematical skills: engineering, surveying, computing, business and financial studies (including economics, accountancy and actuarial work), and to a lesser extent nowadays, pure science (see e.g. Poiner, 1983). In general, job opportunities are better in the male-dominated areas mentioned, while employment in many traditional women's jobs is decreasing as a result of technological change and economic pressures. The same pattern is seen in those jobs which require training in Technical and Further Education (TAFE) colleges. Trade courses, except for hairdressing, are overwhelmingly male-dominated (Women's Bureau, 1983:36), as are most technician-level courses. Many of these require a competency in mathematics at an appropriate level. As the pressure on TAFE for places in courses with good vocational prospects increases, some sections are instituting their own selection procedures, which can include mathematics-based selection tests or use of Higher School Certificate results in mathematics (Craney, 1985:8).

Further, looking to the future, young people planning careers today need to bear in mind the possible impact of technological change and the need to be flexible and able to adapt to new requirements. Mathematics is being used increasingly not only in the physical sciences but in the biological and social sciences, economics and business, and the introduction of computers to almost every area of human endeavour means there is an increased need for analytical thinking and problem-solving capabilities, which the study of mathematics can help to develop. Thus a lack of mathematical skills constitutes a barrier for many women, leading to reduced employment opportunities and the restriction of their life options.

There is a second reason why more women should study mathematics (and science) and prepare themselves to enter scientific and technological occupations. I believe it is important for the future of our society to have more women in positions where they can influence decision-making. This means not only more women in leading positions in politics, business and the public service, but also more women among the 'experts' who advise the decision-makers —such as economists, engineers, scientists, town planners and architects—all male-dominated professions. These people can limit the options for the decision-makers by telling them what, in their opinion, is possible and what is not. They can also influence the decisions reached by the way in which they present their advice. It is also important to have women with technological or scientific expertise who can speak out when scientific issues which affect our society are being debated: examples include the arms race; pollution and control of the environment; conservation issues of all kinds; mining, especially uranium mining; and priorities for expenditure on medical and scientific research. Too often women's contributions to such debates are dismissed because 'they don't understand the issues'. We need women whose scientific expertise is beyond question and who can speak out on behalf of other women.

But there is a caution here: little will be gained by encouraging more women to qualify in mathematics and science if, in the process of being socialised into the scientific community, they adopt the values and ideologies of the men who dominate that world. There is a real danger of this, especially in the most male-dominated disciplines where the pressures on a young woman to conform can be very strong. The education of a mathematician or scientist, female or male, is frequently very narrow, allowing little opportunity for consideration of philosophical issues or the impact of scientific research and new technology on the broader society. Although we do need more women in the world of science, they need also to be politically aware, ready to speak out on issues which affect women, to search for a feminist perspective in their work and its applications and, wherever possible, to try to remove the barriers which prevent other women from entering these disciplines. Given the hierarchical structure of most scientific organisations, and the isolation which many women in science experience, they need the support of other women if they are to achieve these objectives.

THE SEARCH FOR AN EXPLANATION

Whenever the issue of the lower participation and achievement of women in mathematics is discussed, the suggestion is inevitably brought forward that males have 'superior ability' in mathematics (see e.g. Benbow & Stanley, 1980; 1982). The implication (sometimes explicitly stated) is that this is a result of biological differences in cognitive function. However boring it is to return repeatedly to this question, it is nevertheless important because the belief in a biological cause is frequently an excuse for lack of action to change the educational environment or provide support and encouragement for young women undertaking studies in mathematics-based disciplines. Girls' lower levels of interest and achievement are regarded as 'natural', and efforts to bring about change are seen as misguided.

These assertions, however, are based on a number of misunderstandings. The first concerns the magnitude of observed sex differences on mathematical tests. In most cases the differences between the mean scores of boys and girls is very small in comparison with the standard deviations. If the number tested is large, these results may be highly significant statistically, but their educational significance is doubtful, and they do not adequately explain the much lower numbers of women in advanced-level mathematics courses and mathematics-based occupations. The second has to do with the measurement of ability in mathematics (or anything else). Although ability is a concept most people believe they understand, tests which purport to measure it are in fact tests of performance, and presume that every individual tested is equally interested in attempting the test, and has had the same opportunity to learn and practise whatever is being tested. Since boys and girls are treated differently almost from the moment of birth, resulting in different motivations to learn mathematics and different learning experiences, this presumption is quite unwarranted. Tests of ability are better regarded as measuring the interaction of innate intellectual potential with the environmental influences which have shaped the individual's development. The fallacies in biological determinist theories in general have been discussed in detail by Rogers (1985), who points out that frequently insufficient attention is paid to the effect of environmental influences on brain development and function.

There is indeed a growing body of research indicating that environmental factors are the main source of sex differences in mathematics (see e.g. Barnes, Plaister and Thomas, 1984:24–25). An even greater number of investigations has sought to discover which factors are of greatest importance and just how they affect mathematics learning and decisions about course-taking. These have been reviewed in detail elsewhere (e.g. Barnes, 1983; Chipman and Wilson, 1985), so only a brief outline will be presented here.

A large number of variables have predictive value for the selection of mathematics courses. The most powerful of these is previous achievement in mathematics, but this appears to contribute little to the explanation of gender differences. Those predictor variables in which significant gender differences have been found include educational and career aspirations, the perceived usefulness of mathematics, confidence in one's mathematical ability, and the expectations, encouragement and support of parents, teachers and, to a lesser extent, classmates. Social class position has been found to be a more significant predictor for girls than for boys. Enjoyment of mathematics is also a predictor of course selection, but a less important one than might be expected, and there are no observed gender differences (Chipman and Wilson, 1985).

These variables are not, of course, independent of one another. For example, past achievement influences aspirations towards mathematics-based careers, and career aspirations clearly affect the perceived usefulness of mathematics to the individual. Past achievement might also be expected to influence confidence in one's mathematical ability, but here an important gender difference emerges. For the same level of achievement, girls generally have less confidence in their mathematical ability and lower expectations of future success than boys do. Closely related to this are the explanations which children give for their successes and failures in mathematics. It has been found that girls are more likely than boys to explain their success as due to effort or luck, while boys are more likely to attribute success to ability. Girls, on the other hand, are more likely to explain their failures as due to lack of ability. These attribution patterns are dysfunctional for girls' achievement in mathematics: if a girl believes that she has failed because of lack of ability, she has little motivation to persevere with the task, whereas if a boy believes that he has succeeded because he does have ability, his expectations of future success will be increased, and he is less likely to give up when he runs into difficulties (Leder, 1981). These conclusions do not really solve our problem, but merely push it one step further back. We now have to ask the questions: why do girls have less confidence, and why do they make these dysfunctional attributions?

To help make sense of the large number of variables, and the connections between them, I would like to present a theoretical model developed by Kuendiger (1984), who is using it in the analysis of data from the Second International Mathematics study (Fig. 3).

Kuendiger suggests that the variables can be grouped under two headings: the general beliefs held in a community and the personal learning experiences of the individual. General beliefs may concern the place of women in the society, their need for education and careers, and which occupations are considered suitable for them. There may also be beliefs about the nature of mathematics, how important or useful it is, how difficult it is. Together, these determine the extent to which mathematics is perceived as a male domain and beliefs about how appropriate it is as a subject for women to

Figure 3

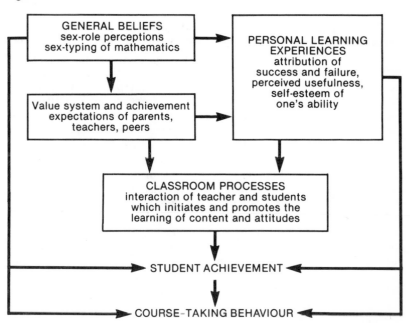

study. Personal learning experiences include enjoyment, or other-wise, of the subject matter, success or failure, confidence and motivation to succeed. These all come together in the classroom itself, where interaction with others allows their attitudes and expectations to influence the learning process.

Most of the research reported above was carried out in the United States, although much of it has also been replicated in Australia (Leder, 1984). One interesting line of research pursued in Australia, which has not been given so much attention overseas, concerns gender differences in preferred styles of learning. Owens (1981) has found that girls prefer a cooperative mode of learning, while boys have greater preference for a competitive mode. Female teachers and teachers of humanities are more inclined to teach in a coopera-tive style, while male teachers, and especially teachers of mathema-tics and science have much greater preference for a competitive style. Thus there seems to be a mismatch between the learning preferences of girls and the preferred styles of mathematics teachers. Owens speculates that, when selecting courses, 'girls, dis-inclined to favour competitiveness in learning, and faced with male teachers and subject matter that seems oriented towards competitiveness, opt out and transfer their enthusiasm to other subjects' (1981:149).

The main thrust of all the research reported above has been to explain differential selection of mathematics courses. Observations of gender differences in the patterns of achievement on various types of mathematics tasks have been much less thoroughly investigated. It has been suggested that boys' better performance on applications of mathematics such as measurement and ratio arises from experiences outside the mathematics classroom, either in other school courses such as physics or manual arts (Wily, 1984), or through hobbies such as model-building in which more boys than girls take part (Hanna, 1984). It has also been suggested that girls' socialisation makes them more compliant, more willing to do what is expected of them, solve problems in the way they have been shown, memorise formulae and practise what they have been taught, that is, to become 'submissive achievers'. If this is the case, it would explain why girls do better on computational tasks, which would be facilitated by the approach described above, but less well on problem-solving, which requires more independent thinking. These speculations, if borne out by research, would help to explain both the achievement differences, and the smaller proportion of girls in higher-level courses, since those skills in which girls are weaker become more important as the level of mathematics increases. It is clear, however, that much more research needs to be done here.

WHAT WOMEN SAY

As we have seen, beliefs, attitudes, confidence and anxiety play an important role in determining the amount of mathematics women study. I have gained further insight on these from informal interviews with several groups of women in which we talked about their views of mathematics and of themselves as learners of mathematics. They were in no sense a representative sample: some came to a workshop because they were concerned about their children's mathematical difficulties, while others were mature-age students who had returned to study or were thinking about doing so; some had done no mathematics since leaving school and others were enrolled in university mathematics courses. Nevertheless common themes emerged in our discussions which I believe are important, and which are similar to responses reported by researchers in England and the United States.

First, those not studying mathematics had a very restricted view of its content and methods. They saw it as dealing mainly with number, with getting right answers and memorising rules. It was supposed to be rational and logical, but many said that it never made sense to them and they felt that they could not relate to it. Most of these women did not expect to be able to understand mathematics. A very frequent comment was 'I just don't have a mathematical mind'. They saw the world as divided into two sorts of people—rational, logical ones who could do mathematics, and those who could not. If I suggested that mathematics could be creative and imaginative, or that intuition had an important place in it, they expressed incomprehension or disbelief. Buerk (1985) obtained similar responses from the women in her study. One of these expressed her ideas more succinctly than any of those I have spoken to, and in a delightfully imaginative way:

> On the eighth day, God created mathematics. He took stainless steel, and he rolled it out thin, and he made it into a fence, forty cubits high, and infinite cubits long. And on this fence, in fair capitals, he did print rules, theorems, axioms and pointed reminders. 'Invert and multiply.' 'The square of the hypotenuse is three decibels louder than one hand clapping.' 'Always do what's in parentheses first.' And when he was finished, he said 'On one side of this fence will reside those who are good at math. And on the other will remain those who are bad at math, and woe unto them, for they shall weep and gnash their teeth.'
>
> Math does make me think of a stainless steel wall—hard, cold, smooth, offering no handhold, all it does is glint back at me. Edge up to it, put your nose against it, it doesn't take your shape, it doesn't have any smell, all it does is make your nose cold. I like the shine of it—it does look smart, in an icy way. But I resent its cold impenetrability, its supercilious glare. (Buerk, 1985:59)

Another group were less negative about mathematics. Often they had enjoyed it in their early school years, but had become lost at some later stage. There was an almost wistful quality about the way in which they reiterated: 'I wish I had the opportunity to go back and learn it again; I'd like to try again sometime and see if I can make sense of it'. Even women with high achievements in other fields expressed to me feelings of inadequacy about mathematics and seemed to feel a need to apologise for their lack of mathematical ability. It is almost as though there is some guilt associated in the minds of many with the fact that they lack competence in mathematics. This may perhaps derive from experiences in the mathematics classroom. Many talked about fears associated with mathematics at school and recounted incidents, sometimes quite horrific, in which they had been subjected to scorn or public shame. This recalled the observations of Buxton (1981) who identified three factors which triggered panic about mathematics in his adult subjects: pressure to give an answer quickly, fear of being 'shown up' in front of others, and the threat inherent in being judged by an authority figure, usually the mathematics teacher. Associated with this he noted some semantic confusion about 'right' and 'wrong' with their strong moral implications which sometimes led people to a feeling that they were less worthy because they had failed in mathematics.

Those mature women who have returned to the study of mathematics often described how they were 'filtered out' of mathematics at a fairly early stage, and were told that it was not necessary for girls. One uttered a cry from the heart: 'Why did no-one ever tell me that mathematics was important?' As they gradually began to master the concepts which had seemed so confusing, and experience success, these women expressed delight and a tremendous sense of achievement. Their growing confidence in themselves as learners of mathematics was exciting to watch, and as one student wrote, 'this confidence spreads to all other subjects'. But in spite of this they are very vulnerable. Some have experienced repeated put-downs by male students, tutors and lecturers in mathematics or related courses, which sap their new-found confidence. They have also reported feeling alienated from women friends who are studying humanities courses: their friends simply cannot relate to the fact that these women are doing mathematics and enjoying it.

Finally, what about those women who chose to specialise in mathematics to honours or postgraduate level? Mura (1984) interviewed a group of Canadian mathematics students about their attitudes towards the subject and their reasons for choosing to study it. Both males and females were interviewed and quite a few gender-related differences were revealed. For instance, many more women than men said they were attracted to mathematics because of its logical rigour. Mura suggests that this attitude affords a cultural interpretation: women might seek in mathematical logic the fairness that is often denied to them elsewhere in society. Men, on the other hand, repeatedly mentioned the appeal of challenge. Mura believes that this is in agreement with men's cultural conditioning to link their personal value to their external achievements. Mathematics, with its endless problems to be solved, offers men endless opportunities to reassure themselves of their value.

BREAKING DOWN THE BARRIERS

Much of the foregoing suggests a conflict between women's attitudes and preferences and the mathematical environment. As Mura says, 'Women's present minority status in mathematics is not a reason for regarding their attitudes as deviant and men's as normal ... Both women and the mathematical environment are candidates for change' (1984:2).

Most intervention programs, here and overseas, have concentrated on the women. The programs have attempted to change women's perceptions of the usefulness of mathematics by changing career aspirations, or they have attempted to build confidence and decrease anxiety. Although these initiatives may bring about useful changes, doubt has been cast recently on their effectiveness (Lantz, 1985). I believe they may even at times be counterproductive. By concentrating on changing women, they promote the idea that women are deficient. In the United States, the wide publicity given to 'mathematics anxiety' has resulted in it becoming 'a respectable and prestigious neurosis'! (Lantz, 1985:341) If too much publicity is given to intervention programs of this kind, the general public could become more firmly convinced that women really are inferior at mathematics.

Further, we must be careful of the values which are being promoted in programs which emphasise career choice. Although we should encourage girls to aim high, I think we should be careful about promoting competitiveness or a purely utilitarian attitude. For both boys and girls, enjoyment of mathematics has been found to decrease as they move through high school (Chipman and Wilson, 1985:299). Stressing the importance of mathematics as a credential, without doing anything to increase intrinsic interest, could result in more girls studying mathematics but, like many boys, regarding it as a 'necessary evil'.

A better approach is to try to change the mathematical environment so that women can relate to it better. This can mean decreasing stereotyping in textbooks and including more applications that will be relevant and interesting to women and girls. It can also mean monitoring classroom interaction and trying to ensure that girls are not harassed and that they get a fair share of the teacher's attention. But more than this is needed. As we have seen, the authoritarian and competitive atmosphere in the traditional mathematics classroom is one of the principal factors which destroy women's interest in mathematics and sap their confidence. The teacher dominates and is the source of authority. Students believe that there is only one right way to do a problem and that getting the right answer quickly is all-important. 'Gender-inclusive' mathematics should stress cooperation and communication, with a teacher who is prepared to listen and accept students' ideas rather than being in too much of a hurry to explain his or her own. To help students to make sense of mathematics for themselves, there needs to be plenty of opportunities for discussion and, where appropriate, practical work with structured materials. By learning to express mathematical ideas in words, rather than only as symbols on paper, students may learn to avoid the meaningless manipulation of symbols. We need to present mathematics as a human creation, involving imagination and intuition, by undertaking investigative and problem-solving activities and by studying its history. A.H. Read expressed it very well:

> One of the most common sources of difficulty to the student of mathematics is that a piece of work is very rarely presented to him [sic] in the form in which it was worked out by its originator. It has been condensed, polished up and rearranged in logical order, the idea which gave it birth concealed like the works of a clock behind the clockface. So does the mathematician appear as a super-mind because we cannot follow the trend of his thought. (Read, 1951)

This reminds me of that hard, shiny steel wall. This is how mathematics is usually presented, not only in research papers but in textbooks at all levels, and in lectures and classroom teaching. The joy ⅰ discovery is removed from mathematics, as is the exploration, imagination, intuition and the sudden flash of insight. Our students plod routinely through exercises which are to be done by a method they have been taught. We think we are making it easier for them, but in removing the problem-solving from much of mathematics, we have removed the 'pay-off' that makes it exciting.

It may be argued that the suggestions I have made here would benefit all students and not only women: I would agree. Mathematics educators regularly put forward similar ideas. The fact remains, however, that the traditional mathematics classroom still exists. It is competitive and elitist. Certain groups of males who are confident, assertive and ambitious appear to thrive in it, and women and others are placed at a disadvantage. By changing the way we teach mathematics we can remove some of the barriers, and help a wider group of people to succeed in mathematics and enjoy their study.

LESLEY J. ROGERS

3 Biology, the popular
weapon: sex differences in
cognitive function

From the 1970s on there has been renewed interest in biological
determinist theories for explaining human behaviour and the structure of human societies. These theories have been applied to race,
class and sex in that natural selection is postulated to have selected
for genetic differences between blacks and whites, men and women
and different social classes (Rose and Rose, 1976; Lewontin et al.,
1984).

By purporting to explain the structural divisions within society as
'natural', these theories have been used to reconfirm the status quo,
and to argue that to work towards equality between the sexes, races
or classes is to go against biology. They have been incorporated into
the ideology of the New Right and as such they have been used as
powerful political weapons not only by small extremist groups, such
as the National Front in England, but also by the media in general.
Not coincidentally, the increased interest in biological determinism
of sex differences in behaviour occurred when the feminist movement was making major gains.

Biological determinist theories for sex differences in behaviour
are of course not new (Salzman, 1977; Sayers, 1982). Biologism
dates back to the last century (Rose, 1976), but over recent years
the theories have been revamped into somewhat different forms. In
the case of sex differences in behaviour, it is no longer claimed that
women lack the area of the brain concerned with intellect but,
rather, female brains are more asymmetrically organised than male
brains, or they are less so, according to which theory you follow!

Two related paradigms of thinking underscore all biologism, viz.,
reductionism and division into dichotomous categories. Reductionism is that thinking which attempts to explain the properties of
complex wholes in terms of the units which comprise the whole

(Rose, 1984). For example, it is argued that the behaviour of a society can be explained on the basis of the individuals within it and, in turn, that the behaviour of the latter can be explained in terms of the genetic constitution of each individual. In other words, a causal chain is said to begin at the level of the genetic units and run through the society as a whole. Thus, genes have been postulated for aggression, territoriality, intelligence, altruism, homosexuality and a number of other complex human behaviours (see Caplan, 1978). In the case of sex differences in behaviour, genes are said to play a causal role in determining male/female differences by being expressed through the sex hormones (testosterone, oestrogen and progesterone), which act on the brain (see Bleier, 1984). Thus complex human behaviour is reduced to explanations of subcellular mechanisms.

A partner to reductionism is thinking in terms of dichotomies: black versus white, male versus female, maleness versus femaleness, male sex hormone versus female sex hormone (Birke, 1982). A dichotomy is a polarisation with discontinuity which ignores overlaps. Differences are seen to be more interesting than similarities and there is a tendency to see these differences as absolute. As a consequence of this thinking, the psychological literature has placed undue emphasis on sex differences in behaviour at the expense of similarities.

The behaviour differences between the sexes are not absolute or as common as both scientific and non-scientific reporting has given us to believe, and even the biological differences between males and females are not absolute (Rogers, 1981; Kaplan and Rogers, 1986). Males secrete the so-called 'female' sex hormone, oestrogen, and females secrete the 'male' sex hormone, testosterone. Indeed, some females have higher plasma levels of testosterone than do some males. In the brain, where sex hormones are meant to act to cause sex differences in behaviour, the distinction between the sexes becomes even less distinct. There are no known sex differences in the binding of oestrogen in the hypothalamic area of the brain, let alone binding at higher levels of brain organisation; and testosterone must be converted to oestrogen intracellularly before it can act on neurones (Clark and Peck, 1979).

People are divided into male and female on the basis of genital sex (actually, on the presence or absence of a penis). This is a biological reality, although not without some degree of overlap. During foetal development, undifferentiated tissue differentiates into either a female or male genital structure according to the circulating levels of sex hormones. It is often assumed that the brain differentiates into the same male/female dichotomy as the genitalia.

44

Thus, an anatomical division into the male and female genital sex is extrapolated to the brain and to a functional division between femaleness and maleness. But differentiation of the brain, the most complex organ of the body, is not the same as for the genitalia, although many assume that it is. In male rats, female nerve circuits are not lost. The male animal can be induced by appropriate stimulation on hormonal administration to perform female sexual behaviour and other patterns of behaviour more characteristic of females (Sodersten, 1984). The development choice of the brain is not a discrete one of either male or female, even in rats. It is therefore incorrect simply to extrapolate the differentiation processes of the genitals to the brain (Beach, 1971). (Such extrapolation formed the basis of the thesis put forward in the BBC film *The Fight to be Male*, shown on Australian television and now used in many physiology and psychology courses in Australia; see also the popular, sensationalised paperback by Durden-Smith and Simone, 1983.)

In experiments using rats exposed to androgen (male sex hormone) during the first five days after birth it was found that androgen-exposed animals displayed in later life sexual behaviour typical of the male (i.e. mounting behaviour) irrespective of whether their genetic sex was male or female. Castrated males and females, not exposed to androgen in early life, were found to develop sexual behaviour typical of the female (i.e. the lordosis posture). It was these findings, made in the 1960s, which suggested that the presence of androgen in neonatal life directs the brain to develop in a typical male-type direction, and that in its absence a typical female-type brain develops. Androgen appeared actively to operate a switch mechanism channelling brain differentiation towards maleness; hence the 'fight' to be male! Despite the fact that there is no evidence for long-lasting effects of early androgen exposure in primates, researchers influential in the field of sexology (e.g. Money and Ehrhardt, 1972; Dorner, 1979) have extrapolated to humans the data obtained using rats (see Rogers, 1981). Money and Dorner go so far as to suggest that male homosexuality is caused by insufficient exposure of the genetic male to androgen in foetal life, and lesbianism is due to excess exposure to androgen of the genetic female. The work of Money and Dorner has been criticised extensively elsewhere (Birke, 1979; Ross et al., 1978; Rogers and Walsh, 1982). Here I wish to discuss new evidence making it necessary to reinterpret the original data obtained in the experiments with rats.

Celica Moore has now shown that mother rats treat their male and female offspring differently, and that this is dependent on the androgen condition of the pups. Male pups, or female pups administered testosterone, receive more licking by their mothers in the anogenital region, and pups which have received more licking show altered sexual behaviour and increased androgen secretion in adulthood (Moore and Morelli, 1979; Moore 1982). In other words, the earlier experiments, which were thought to have demonstrated that early androgen exposure of rats causes the brain to differentiate in a male-type direction due to the action of the sex hormone on the brain, must be reinterpreted. The androgen treatment in early life could be altering maternal behaviour, and thus indirectly altering the development of behaviour through external, environmental stimuli, or a learning process. Researchers have been all too ready to assume that behaviour patterns in animals are directly genetically and/or hormonally controlled. Moore's experiments illustrate an indirect route of influence on sexual differentiation involving environmental inputs, and therefore an interaction between genetic and environmental factors. As Moore states, 'evidence fails to support generally accepted views that early hormones affect behaviour through direct effects on brain differentiation ... Hormones coact and interact with other factors throughout development ... Hormone-based sources of sex differences may be located throughout the body and in the social surround' (1985:18). If male and female rats are raised differently by their mothers and thus, even in rats, we cannot ignore the role of environment in the development of sex differences in behaviour, how much more must this be so for humans!

To complicate matters further, at a cellular level, while the genitals recognise testosterone as testosterone and oestrogen as oestrogen, the brain does not. In the brain, testosterone is converted to oestrogen and another androgen. It is not known whether brain cells can distinguish between oestrogen and testosterone, or indeed whether the distinction is relevant to them, particularly as far as behaviour goes.

The more scientists conduct experiments designed to understand the mode of action of hormones on the brain, the more 'confused' becomes the distinction between the sexes. Or, is it only 'confusion' in so far as we have placed an artificial male/female dichotomy on biology, and constantly try to push biology into this polarisation which has been constructed for social purposes and is not an accurate reflection of cellular biology, especially in the brain? Since sex differences in behaviour exist, it has been inferred that brain organisation must differ between the sexes, and that this is genetically and/or hormonally determined.

Sometimes biological theories for causation of human behaviour are formulated, expounded and believed, even in the absence of supporting scientific evidence. For example, Geschwind and collea-gues (Geschwind and Behan, 1982; Geschwind and Galaburda, 1985) have proposed that testosterone retards development of the left hemisphere of the brain, and this is why there are more left-handed males and why males are better in mathematics and females better in language. This theory has been widely propagated in the Australian media, and widely accepted among scientists. Yet, in formulating this theory, Geschwind and his co-workers had no evidence suggesting that testosterone might in-fluence the development of the left or right hemispheres. It was pure speculation, which has been propagated as if it were scientific truth based on some sort of facts.

This brings me to the special case of asymmetrical brain function and sex differences in behaviour. Asymmetry or lateralisation of brain function simply means that one side of the brain functions differently from the other. One hemisphere may be said to be dominant over the other for control of a given behavioural function. Functional asymmetry may be linked to structural asymmetry but it need not be (Rogers, 1985).

Asymmetry in the human brain was first discovered as long ago as 1836 by Dax, who noted that patients suffering from speech disturb-ances had damage in the left, but not the right, cerebral hemis-phere. Soon after, Broca reported a number of cases of muscular weakness on the right side of the body coupled with inability to speak. Autopsy revealed neurological damage in the left frontal lobe of such patients. This is now known as Broca's area of the brain. In 1874 Wernicke found that damage further back in the temporal lobe on the left side could cause loss of understanding of speech while not affecting speech production. This area became known as Wernicke's area. Later studies revealed anatomical asym-metry in these regions of the human brain, the left being larger than the right (Geschwind and Levitsky, 1968; and Blakemore, 1977).

This historical introduction to asymmetry focused on asymmetry for language and handedness and led to the belief that asymmetry was confined to the human species (Levy, 1977; Herron, 1980). It is now known to be present in a number of animal species (Harnard et al., 1977).

Understanding of asymmetry in the human brain was advanced considerably by the work of Sperry, mostly in the 1960s, in which he tested 'split-brain' patients. The latter were people who had under-gone an operation known as commissurotomy, section of the corpus callosum, the large system of pathways connecting the left and right hemispheres of the brain, given as treatment for intractable epilepsy. By appropriate tasks requiring special techniques of visual presentation, in the extreme peripheral fields, he was able to demonstrate asymmetry for a number of brain functions (see Corballis, 1983; Segalowitz, 1983). For example, and putting it in a rather oversimplified fashion, the left side of the brain is concerned with language, manual performance and more analytical thinking, while the right side is used for spatial perception, music appreciation, emotional responses and handling information in a more 'gestalt', whole sense. This is oversimplified because, for example, although the left hemisphere is dominant for language, we now know that the right processes some aspects of word form. Indeed, an extra centre for language has been found in the right side of the brain of females (Bradshaw and Nettleton, 1983). These researchers claim, without supporting evidence, that this sex difference in brain asymmetry is genetically determined. No other sex difference in asymmetry, functional or structural, is known.

The human brain is asymmetrically organised, although in the intact brain the left/right dichotomy may not be as absolute, as indicated by the original experiments with split-brain patients (Kinsbourne, 1980a). More evidence for at least some degree of organisational differences in asymmetry between male and female brains may yet be discovered. Meanwhile, apart from the above example and evidence for a larger splenium area of the corpus callosum in females, there is no other clear evidence for any difference in organisation of male and female brains (Swaab and Hofman, 1984). Opposing views exist on postulated differences in the degree of asymmetry in females versus males, and proponents of each view seem to take little cognisance of the other.

One of the earliest theories suggested that, because females are more emotional than males, they are right-hemisphere-dominant (see Starr, 1979). This theory ignores the fact that females are known to have superior language ability and inferior spatial ability, which indicates left hemispheric dominance. Yet, it is obviously not acceptable for females to have left hemispheric dominance as analytical ability is a property of the left hemisphere (Bleier, 1984)!

Another, somewhat more sophisticated theory, argues that female brains are less lateralised (show a lesser degree of asymmetry) than male brains. This has been referred to as the Levy-Sperry hypothesis (see Starr, 1979; Levy, 1977). Some evidence for this theory has been provided by experiments conducted by McGlone: however, McGlone herself has concluded that the overlap in the data between men and women is so great that basic patterns of male and female asymmetry seem to be more similar than different (see Corballis, 1983:96–99). Nevertheless, researchers such as Sperry and Levy adhere to the idea that female brains are less lateralised than male brains, and suggest that this is why males are better at performing visuospatial tasks. This is so, they reason by a circular route, because good visuospatial ability requires more hemispheric specialisation. According to this theory, then, females are less lateralised than males and they are therefore equivalent to left-handed males. Thus, females and left-handed males have more interhemispheric crosstalk. In left-handers language is said to be mediated by both sides of the brain (at least, according to these workers, although evidence for this is contradictory). Therefore, in females and left-handed males some language processing occurs in the right hemisphere and this interferes with the spatial abilities of the right hemisphere. As mentioned earlier, there is evidence for an extra language-processing centre in the right hemisphere of females (Bradshaw and Nettleton, 1983), but this has not been investigated in left-handed males. Moreover, the claims of the theory are hardly consistent with the evidence that there is a higher than average representation of left-handers amongst architects (Geschwind and Galaburda, 1985).

A contrary theory has been proposed by Gray and Buffery (Buffery, 1981). This claims that females are more lateralised than males, and the reason why females are inferior on visuospatial tasks is because this ability requires use of both hemispheres. As for the previous theory, the latter is obviously an ad hoc deduction.

Kinsbourne raises the important consideration that any sex differences in brain organisation are likely to be given exaggerated attention: 'Under pressure from the gathering momentum of feminism, and perhaps in backlash to it, many investigators seem determined to discover that men and women "really" are different. It seems that if sex differences (e.g. in lateralisation) do not exist, then they have to be invented' (1980b:124). This is essential to remember in any discussion of sex differences, but the issue being addressed in this paper is 'What may be the cause of sex differences in brain organisation?', irrespective of how significant these differences may be.

The brain is able to learn and in so doing its biochemistry and cellular structure are changed. Thus environmental influences alter its storage and capacity to process information, and thus can affect the course of brain development (Rogers, 1985). This is often forgotten in discussions of brain structure and function. The brain is seen as a controller determining behaviour, and often insufficient attention is paid to feedback of behaviour and other environmental influences on brain development and function. Although it is possible that sex hormones can influence brain development, it is equally possible that environmental factors can do the same. Thus, the different cultural environments in which women and men are raised could become manifest in sex differences in brain organisation. No one has looked at asymmetry in the brains of males and females raised in ways which diverge from conventional gender-typing. There are subjects which could be tested thus, but researchers have so far shown no interest in approaching the problem from this direction of inquiry. It appears that the automatic assumption that sex differences in asymmetry are biologically caused shields researchers from any need to consider further scientific investigation of the issue. Many outspoken statements are made, data are over-interpreted, theories are followed or formulated on a rather arbitrary basis, but no well-conducted research inquiry proceeds. Belief systems, personal biases shaped by social and political needs have more to do with discussion of sex differences in asymmetry than does any genuine desire for understanding.

Such biases have also carried over into research on brain asymmetry in animal species. There are ever-increasing reports documenting the presence of asymmetry in animal species (Harnard et al., 1977), but few investigators have been interested in studying the development of this.

When I discovered asymmetry of brain function in chickens (Rogers and Anson, 1978), many people immediately assumed that it was genetically programmed. The asymmetry was seen in a static sense and was assumed to have a unitary cause. However, subsequent experiments have shown that the chicken embryo's experience of light before hatching influences the development of asymmetry (Rogers, 1982). In the egg, the chick embryo is oriented so that its left eye is occluded by its body, while the right eye remains uncovered and able to receive light entering through the shell. It is this asymmetrical input of light which influences the asymmetry of brain development. Chickens hatched from eggs incubated in darkness do not show the normal development of asymmetry. The orientation of the chicken in the egg must have genetic determinants, but these interact with environmental stimulation to influence the development of asymmetry. Added to this, we have found that testosterone can reverse the direction of asymmetry in the chicken brain (Rogers and Zappia, 1985). Thus, in the chicken, asymmetrical organisation of the brain depends on the complex interaction of genetic, environmental and hormonal factors. No unitary, reductionistic, causal explanation for asymmetry will suffice. There are sex differences in behaviour in chickens; these must result from a complex interaction of many factors. Our studies have provided the first evidence that testosterone can indeed influence the development of asymmetry of brain function. But in no way does this provide evidence in support of Geschwind's proposition that testosterone is *the* biological cause for sex differences in human asymmetry. The effect of testosterone does not occur in the absence of environmental influences and it cannot be considered in separation from these.

Similar studies by Denenberg (1981) have shown that the development of asymmetry in rats can be influenced by handling the animals in infancy.

Despite this evidence for the inseparable interaction of genes and environment in influencing asymmetry, the majority of animal researchers still adhere to unitary genetic determinist theories for asymmetry in animals. Theories of biological determinism of animal behaviour may simply represent narrow-minded thinking, but application of similar thinking to human behaviour is socially and politically dangerous. Some feminists have accepted the biological causation theories for asymmetry of brain function and therefore argue for reform instead of revolution (e.g. Lambert, 1978). Some use them to explain male domination, or to reverse the argument, in favour of female superiority. But these are theories and not fact. If, even in chickens and rats, unitary causes do not apply, how much more so must this be the case in humans? It is obviously premature and oversimplified to argue backwards from the behavioural sex differences to biological causes.

PART II
WOMEN AND THE
HUMANITIES

E.A. GROSZ

Introduction

Humanity, Humanities: ... learning or literature concerned with human culture; a term including the various branches of *polite scholarship*, as grammar, rhetoric, poetry, and especially the study of ancient Latin and Greek classics (*OED*)

The humanities and social sciences form the institutional backdrop against which feminist theory has tended to develop. It has also increasingly become the object of feminist critiques. Given women's historical exclusion from the 'hard-core' natural sciences, and given the orientation of the *humanities* to apparently *human* concerns, it is not surprising that women have gravitated towards those knowledges considered 'softer' than the 'hard-core' natural sciences. But given the clear masculine orientation of the humanities and social sciences, feminists may have been disappointed by the apparent absence and exclusion of women and femininity from most discourses constituting the so-called 'sciences of Man'. Not content with merely noting these exclusions, feminists today pose the question of what can be done to enable us to participate in knowledges and knowledge production *as women*.

This may mean locating those regions where women are either missing or misrepresented in traditional masculine knowledges. Of course, this is no easy task: to locate *an absence*, a *misconception*, implies that one has either independent information or knowledge through which the absence can be discerned and prevailing models can be compared; or that one can 'master' knowledges well enough to be able to infer or deduce from their internal features what remains unspoken or unrecognised but nonetheless necessary for knowledges to function as such.

If locating or pinpointing problems in the ways women are treated in knowledges is the first step in transforming women's convention positions, it is not enough. Listing those places where women are conceptually oppressed, inadequately theorised or absent, constitutes a lament of tragic proportions, a catalogue of wrongs done to women in the name of Truth or knowledge. As such, it only adds to women's oppression by the sheer weight of a demonstrably pervasive misogyny. If this lament is not accompanied by positive alternatives or by productive, transforming critiques, this list confirms rather than questions women's subordinated intellectual status. The ways women are treated in social knowledges should provide a lever by which the burden of an oppressive political/sexual weight can be lifted from women's backs.

Feminists have devised a number of strategies over the last decade and more to ensure that this lever challenges and subverts prevailing patriarchal methods, terms and frameworks. These strategies range from the invocation of a higher, more encompassing truth (patriarchal knowledges are false because they are *partial* knowledges, which, when 'corrected', are capable of generalisation or universal applicability) to the tactics of parody, excess and outrageousness—from the 'serious' to the 'audacious'.

'Serious'-minded feminist critiques adapt and modify the norms and criteria governing knowledges—often using *ad hom(me)inem* arguments—assessing them by their *own* criteria to see how well they measure up. This may mean, as Susan Sheridan explains in her chapter, the creation of a counterknowledge or paradigm to 'balance' out the maleness of prevailing knowledges (in Sheridan's case, literary theory) by developing a women-centred 'gynocritical' perspective, that is, a feminine mirror-reflection or correlation of masculinist knowledges. This type of critique invokes an 'alternative truth', and a 'counter-objective' which affirms both a truth and the evaluative processes of judgment operating in patriarchal knowledges. It is almost as if there is an underlying belief here that if gynocriticism and patriarchalism could be combined, between them they could provide *the whole truth*.

In more 'audacious' critiques, feminists seek the weaknesses, blind spots, or unspoken investments of patriarchal knowledges in order to magnify and render explicit what remains intolerable for 'malestream' knowledges. Moira Gatens' chapter illustrates this powerful technique of speaking the unsayable. As she argues, if the history of philosophy has dichotomised being into the oppositions between mind and body, and male and female, it has invested an enormous intellectual energy to negate and subordinate the secondary terms of binary pairs, body and female. Their secondary status is the condition for dominant terms, namely, reason, mind, culture, public. Gatens' strategy is audacious in so far as she develops precisely the kind of philosophy that could accommodate corporeality and femininity, that is, a philosophy that could articulate what cannot be spoken in philosophical paradigms derived from Cartesian dualism. In the face of this pervasive dualism, it is indeed audacious and threatening to call for a non-dualist (in this case, Spinozist) philosophy, for this reveals what is at stake in dominant (i.e. dualist) models.

The tactic of re-naming appears in striking form in Caroline Ralston's chapter. Once it is recognised how interests and values proliferate through the ways in which terms and discourses are defined and presented, feminists can engage in the re-formulation of these terms and in devising new ones in order to announce an entirely different point of view. To describe the sexual activities of Tahitian women, for example, as 'promiscuous' and as forms of 'prostitution' not only imposes western morality and values, as Ralston points out, but also entails the surreptitious imputation of a singular male perspective as the only possible one (and thus not really a perspective at all). To conceive of femininity and women as profane, polluting or impure, is to refuse the evidence proffered by other cultures for ours to decipher. It is a refusal to accept another perspective, an otherness different from our own identities and culture, an other with whom we can exchange (knowledges) and thus grow.

My chapter is a methodological reflection on the unsettling and subversive place of feminism within knowledges. Although it may take a number of forms, feminist theory tends to unsettle and problematise the entire history of western knowledges, a history that effaces its own masculine interests and orientations. Feminist theory is, by contrast, anomalous in so far as it *openly* states that knowledge is necessarily limited, representing only some possibilities. It recognises and affirms its own perspectival, partial and invested position in the production of knowledges. Unlike patriarchal knowledges it is able to accept a place that is acknowledged as limited, politically implicated, and representative of some, but not all interests.

Taken together, these papers show that those knowledges of *human* social, personal and linguistic relations, while they may be *about* men *and* women, represent the perspectives and interests of only one sex. If we recall the definition with which I opened this introduction, the term humanity or humanities refers to three things: it refers to 'culture and civilisation', that which separates the human from animal existence on the one hand and the divine on the other. It also refers to a self-consciously *classical* or *Græco-Roman* model of knowledge, that provided by the 'classical texts' of Plato and Aristotle. Finally, it refers to a *polite scholarship* involved in the study of languages: the human, the knowable and the definable. Yet, like the strategically ambiguous use of the term 'Man', 'the humanities' can now also be seen as equivocal, as motivated and localised. It does not simply refer to a subjectivity, a culture or language in neutral, sexually indifferent terms. Instead it is *motivated* knowledge, one that cannot accept the interests it serves. It is incapable, in short, of accepting its masculinity and the privileges and values it proffers to those elements associated with or furthering men's interests.

The following papers all attempt to reveal the masculinity of the various frameworks within the humanities from which they derive. At the same time, they develop the beginnings or outlines of different kinds of knowledges, different critical and evaluative practices, and different speaking and reading positions, ones more amenable to the representation and characterisation of women, and thus, ultimately, of both sexes.

4 Towards a feminist
philosophy of the body

Feminists have made women's bodies a focal point around which
many campaigns have been fought. The right to the autonomy of
the female body has been argued in relation to abortion, contraception and birthing methods. The right to knowledge about the female
body, the right to the health of the female body and the insistence
on the autonomous pleasure of the female body have all been
stressed by feminists in various contexts. Attempts to claim
or assert these 'rights' have often involved direct defiance of both
church and state. The meaning of the early women's liberation
slogan, 'The personal is political', took on an added, and unwel-
come, dimension when acts that women saw as *personal* choices
were forbidden or penalised by the state. This raises the question
of the relation between woman's body and the state. In spite
of this social and political concentration on the female body, I
would still argue that feminists have offered little by way of a
coherent theory of the body. In particular, there has been little
critical work done on the *conceptual* dimension of the relations
between women's bodies and the state: between the body of woman
and the body politic. In the absence of such theory, it is culturally
dominant conceptions of the body that, unconsciously, many feminists work with.

What I propose to do in this paper is, first, critically examine
some of the features of these dominant conceptions. Second, I will
argue that traditional philosophical conceptions of corporeality
are counterproductive to the aim of constructing an autonomous
conception of women's bodies along with the possibility of women's
active participation in the politico-ethical realm. Finally, I will
suggest that the onto-ethical writings of Spinoza can provide a

rich resource in working towards a feminist theorisation of corporeality.

Whatever else we say about conceptions of the body, it is clear that *how* we conceptualise the body forms and limits the meaning of the body in culture in various ways. The historical and philosophical associations between women and corporeality are multiple and complex (see Spelman, 1982). Significantly, cultural attitudes to both women and corporeality are often negative and function conceptually as the underside to culturally valued terms, such as reason, civilisation and progress. Many philosophers have tended to treat the soul or mind as, in essence, sexually neutral. Apparent differences between minds are generally seen to be due to the influence of the passions of the body. This element of sensuous and passionate corporeality allows philosophers to maintain the essential neutrality of the mind while allowing for individual and sexual differences. The most superior minds suffer least from the intrusions of the body. Women are most often understood to be less able to control the passions of the body and this failure is often located in the a priori disorder or anarchy of the female body itself. Some feminists have argued that this dualist notion of the body involves an implicit alignment between women and irrationality. The ideal conception of the rational is, in other words, articulated in direct opposition to qualities typical of the feminine (Lloyd, 1984; Le Doeuff, 1980).

This notion of the female body as intrinsically anarchic or disordered has repercussions for women's suitability to political participation. Some feminists—especially the egalitarians of the eighteenth and nineteenth centuries—argued that women are not essentially irrational but are *trained* to be so (e.g. Wollstonecraft, Taylor, J.S. Mill). Given proper training, they argued, women would be capable of rational political participation. This does not seem, in our present time, the most productive way of approaching the relation between woman and her access to the political realm. As Lloyd has shown in another context, it is not so much that women are explicitly conceptualised as irrational but rather that rationality itself is defined against the 'womanly'. In this context it may be profitable to explore the idea that it is not so much that women are biologically unsuited to political participation, as political participation has been structured and defined in such a way that it excludes women's bodies. If this is so then fighting to have women included in the present body politic will be counterproductive unless it is accompanied by some analysis of the exclusions of women's corporeality that still define that body politic and a working framework from which to think and live other ways of being, of being political and of being ethical.

MOTHERLESS BIRTHS: THE MIRACLE OF MASCULINE
AUTO-REPRODUCTION

The seventeenth century was witness to at least two births of interest to us here. First, the birth of the human *subject*: who is both the subject *of* governance—of an internal relation of domination, where mind or reason should dominate the body and passion—and one subject *to* governance. Second, the birth of the modern body politic which is represented as a product of reason, designed to govern, manage and administer the needs and desires of its subjects. A twin birth? Clearly, each being presupposes the other. This embryonic contiguity, between the modern body politic and the modern subject, suggests that in order to understand modern conceptions of the human subject, including its corporeality, one needs to understand its reflexive relation to the modern body politic.

Modern political theory typically conceives of political life as a state created by a contract, entered into by rational decision, and designed to ensure the protection and safety of the body and its needs. As it is a contract entered into by men only, one must surmise that it is a contract designed to secure the needs of male bodies and desires. This contract is also thought to create an *artificial* body: Hobbes' leviathan, for example, is an 'artificial man'. What a feminist theorist must consider is woman's relation to this 'artificial man'. Here, I will simply signal the importance of traditional conceptions of the female body and the way these conceptions function in political discourses to justify women's historical (and present) social role.

Woman in fact never makes the transition from the mythical 'state of nature' to the body politic. She *becomes* nature. She is necessary to the functioning of cultural life, she is the very ground which makes cultural life possible, yet she is not part of it. This division between nature and culture, the division between the reproduction of mere biological life as against the production and regulation of social life, is a division reflected in the distinction between the private and the public spheres, the family and the state. These divisions are conceptually and historically sexualised, with woman remaining mere nature, mere body, reproducing in the private familial sphere. These associations are viewed as having their ground in woman's ontology. The distinction between the sexes is taken to be a fundamental feature of nature that could only be represented in culture in this dichotomous way. The notion that culture constructs nature or that cultural practices construct bodies as dichotomously sexed is theoretically *inadmissible* in the modern account.

In the modern view the body is understood as part of 'raw'

nature, which is progressively integrated or surpassed by the development of culture. Here I will merely signpost the resonances of this view in feminist theory. Both Firestone and de Beauvoir, for example, have a clear nature/culture, body/social split, where both nature and the body are conceived as outside culture and outside history. Yet the effects or the power of both nature and the body are able to be progressively eroded in history by the advances of culture. The sex/gender distinction, so crucial to early 1970s feminist theory, also displays this acceptance of the division between bodies on one hand and culture on the other (see Gatens, 1983). Sex is understood to be a fact of bodies, gender a socialised addition to sex. It is important to note the extent to which these early feminist critiques share the modern conception of the body as a non-cultural, ahistorical phenomenon. All history and culture can do, on this model, is intervene as a mechanic intervenes into the functioning of an already constituted machine.

The anti-humanist stance marks a definitive break with this tradition. This stance seriously questions the idea that the body has a priori needs, desires or functions which determine the form of culture and politics. Foucault, for example, thoroughly rejects the idea that the body has a fixed character which sets the limits to possible socio-political structures in which that body could 'live'. He inverts the modern problematic and suggests the exploration of how socio-political structures construct particular kinds of bodies with particular kinds of needs and desires. One could argue, for example, that the sexed body is not a product of nature but rather is constituted as dichotomously sexed by elaborate and pervasive practices that act on and through the body (see Foucault, 1978; 1980). Rather than viewing the forms and functions of bodies as determinant in the organisation of culture, we can view them as products of the way that culture organises, regulates and remakes itself. This approach allows us to shift the conceptual ground from the question 'How is the body taken up in culture?' to the more profitable question 'How does culture construct the body so that it is understood as a biological given?'

The most conspicuous contribution of feminists to the anti-humanist critique involves exposing the masculine bias of the supposed 'neutral' humanist subject. Recent feminist research has shown how paying attention to the specificity of female embodiment disrupts and belies the supposed liberal principles of equal treatment and the right to bodily integrity. However, this critique has paid insufficient attention to the congruence between the (implicitly masculine) subject of these rights and principles on the one hand and representations of the body politic on the other. Many theorists seem to assume that this relation of congruence merely reflects an historical fact about the privilege accorded to masculine experience in the construction of both political life and representations of political life. I think it necessary to go beyond this 'man-as-author' understanding of political life. In particular, I think it is necessary to consider the isomorphism between philosophical representations of the 'neutral' human body and the body politic.

The work of Luce Irigaray is an excellent example of recent feminist criticism which seeks to reveal the masculine bias of western culture. She has argued that an examination of philosophy reveals a certain isomorphism or mirroring of form, between philosophy and the male body, a mirroring which implicitly privileges the masculine form in western constructions of logic, language and metaphysics (Irigaray, 1977). Her main target is metaphysics, which she seeks to undermine by an internal disruption which creates a space to re-present femininity (Irigaray, 1985a). Using aspects of her approach, we can present a challenge to the masculine nature of representations of the human body, the body politic and the links between these two. This may open a space where different political and ethical relations can begin to be thought, a 'space' that will be opened by questioning what is repressed in current representations of politico-ethical life.

In this context Freud offers an interesting observation on the mother–son relation, which is for him the primal 'hinge-relation' between the pre-social and the social. It is this relation, after all, that for Freud lies at the heart of the riddle of culture; it is the riddle the Theban Sphinx poses to Oedipus. Freud writes: 'All his [the son's] instincts, those of tenderness, gratitude, lustfulness, defiance and independence, find satisfaction in the single wish *to be his own father*' (1978:173). This primal wish, to take the place of the father, is expressed in political terms by the fantasy of the generation of a man-made social body: a body that is motherless and so immortal. Our cultural unconscious is littered with examples that suggest that those *not* born of woman have awesome powers. Macbeth, who smiles with scorn at '. . . swords brandish'd by man that's of woman born', can only be slain by the unbirthed Macduff. The motherless Athena can fearlessly confront the Furies, rebuking them for their vengeful pursuit of the matricide, Orestes. Asserting her authority by sending them (literally) underground she establishes the priority of (male) citizenship over blood ties and thus institutes the classic patriarchal state, which even bears her name: Athens. Unmothered, such beings are autonomous, immortal and quintessentially masculine. The motherless body politic, product of the fecundity of man's reason, is also a body untouched by death.

This fantasy of masculine auto-reproduction is not uncommon in western political theory. It appears in Greek, medieval and modern writings and it is a fantasy that feminists need to address.

Discourses on the body and discourses on the body politic each borrow terms from the other. This mutual cross-referencing appears in their shared vocabularies, for example, 'constitution', 'regime' and 'diet'. A philosophically common metaphor for the appropriate relation between the mind and the body is to posit it as a *political* relation, where one (the mind) should dominate, subjugate or govern the other (the body) (see Spelman, 1983). These conceptual interconnections are historically unstable. They take their present form, in whatever definitive sense can be given them, largely in response to a series of dichotomies that came to exist around the seventeenth century.

Descartes, Hobbes, (and later, La Mettrie) are names commonly associated with the mechanisation of the body. This involved positing a faculty of reason able to dominate a body-machine. Seventeenth-century discourses are obsessed with the question of the legitimate exercise of power in at least two contexts: first, how to enforce the legitimate power of reason over the unruly body (see, for example, Descartes' *The Passions of the Soul*); second, how to establish (or discredit) the legitimacy of the power of the King (the head) over the social (body). These debates concerning the legitimacy of social and political authority had considerable effects not only on conceptions of the appropriate governing relation between minds and bodies, kings and subjects, but also on the relations between men and women.

Pateman (1984) has argued against understanding the patriarchal body politic as the 'rule of the father'. She argues that the sons (cf. Locke) may well have defeated the fathers (cf. Filmer and Hobbes) but what they introduced was not a democracy but a fraternity. It is also crucial to stress, in this context, that the triumph of the sons required a strict separation between natural and conventional authority. Although the authority of father over son was questioned, the authority of man over woman was not. In order for men to 'legitimately' dominate women it was necessary to exclude women from the political sphere, i.e. from the 'artificial body'. This involved reducing women to roles that have meaning only in relation to men: wife/mother/daughter. It is worth mentioning that considerable physical coercion was employed in late-seventeenth- and eighteenth-century politics to ensure that women were confined to the private/familial sphere. Any attempt by women to take advantage of the considerable social unrest was often severely quashed. The justification for the often harsh measures used to keep women out of the body politic were commonly put in terms of protecting the health of the social body from invasion, corruption or infection (see Abray, 1975).

One of the many petitions put before the revolutionary government in Paris between 1792 and 1794 demanded that women be given 'a voice' in the newly formed body politic. The terms in which this petition was rejected confirms many of the points I have made here:

> If we take into account the fact that the political education of men is still at its very beginnings, that all the principles are not yet developed, and that we still stammer over the word 'liberty', then how much less enlightened are women, whose moral education has been practically non-existent. Their presence in the *sociétés populaires*, then, would give an active part in government to persons exposed to error and seduction even more than are men. And, let us add that women by their constitution, are open to an exaltation which could be ominous in public life. The interests of the state would soon be sacrificed to all the kinds of disruption and disorder that hysteria can produce. (Abray, 1975:56)

If women are admitted to the social body and given a 'voice', the feminine disease of hysteria may be transposed to the social body which would result in *political* hysteria. We can see in the above passage, the shift that Foucault notes from concern over the well-being of the king's body to concern for the health and asepsis of the social body (see 1977; 1978). Amar, the speaker quoted above, was representing the newly formed 'Committee for General Security', a committee whose task it was to police the health and safety of the nascent social body. That part of this task involved the quarantine of women is instructive. As Cixous (1980; 1981), Lyotard (1978), and others have commented, in so far as woman is socially 'initiated', she is initiated by decapitation, either metaphorically (mutism) or literally (recall the guillotining of Mme Roland and Olympe de Gouges). She has nothing to forfeit but her 'voice', her head, her reason. Her relation to the body politic will be limited to the corporeal and to her use as a natural resource. She will continue to function as the repressed term 'body', thus allowing the fantasy of the masculine body politic to 'live'.

Recent feminist writing has responded to the self-representation of philosophers by pointing out that the body politic that men give birth to assumes both the appropriation and the disavowal of woman's ability to reproduce life (Pateman, 1984; Irigaray, 1985a, 1985b). This response allows us to read the modern political writers in a new light. Clearly, many of the writers of this period have in common the fantasy of political man's autonomy from both women and the corporeal, specifically, autonomy from the maternal body. It is tempting to argue that the modern body politic has yet to be *embodied*. Any attempt to begin conceptualising the embodiment of the body politic runs up against immediate problems: the 'neutrality' of the modern subject; women's exclusion from the rational and hence from the political and the ethical also. This situation, then, requires a radical rethinking of the connections between reason, the body and politico-ethical relations. What is required is a theoretical space that is not dominated by the isomorphism between male bodies and political bodies. Part of what I attempted to show in this section is that feminist reflections on modern accounts of embodiment and politics reveal that the philosophers' 'slip' is showing, or perhaps more appropriately, his mother's petticoats.

The lever that this feminist critique provides can be a starting point for exploring other ways of being. Woman's historical exclusion from these discourses and relations can thus be seen as a strength. The construction of alternative perspectives presents us with both practical and theoretical difficulties. The conceptual difficulty of trying to construct other ways to live human corporeality using dominant categories of thought is partly because these categories are tied in complex ways to present forms of social, political and ethical life. Descartes' dualist conception of subjectivity, for example, can be viewed as an essential development in western ontology that has functioned to validate a body politic that is characterised by the notion that the mind, by an act of will, can alienate the labouring capacities of its body-machine in return for a wage. Offering a coherent account of woman's relation to wage-labour has long been problematic for political theorists. It seems fair to suggest that there are conceptual exclusions operating against developing such an account. Of course, theories of being or politics cannot be created *ex nihilo*. We are constrained by our theoretical as well as our practical histories. However, the history of philosophy has a much richer store of conceptions of the body than appears in dominant accounts. For the remainder of this chapter I propose the use of a tradition of conceptualising the body that 'begins' with Spinoza and has been largely neglected in Anglo-American philosophy. This tradition offers a multivalent ontology that may provide a basis from which to develop a multiple and *embodied* politico-ethics.

SPINOZISTIC BODIES

It may seem a little odd to return to a seventeenth-century conception of the body given the advances in biology and physiology since then. I think, however, that there are several good reasons to prefer such a remote account as Spinoza's. His theory may offer another perspective from which to assess the claims and findings of a science and a biology that have been articulated in the shadow of dualism. I also think that there is some reason to scrutinise the seventeenth century as it was a crucial transition period in our culture. If women are going to play an active part in contemporary politics then it is important to begin the task of thinking through how one participates in a context where female embodiment is denied any autonomous political or ethical representation. It is important to begin the exploration of other ontologies which would be developed hand in hand with a politico-ethical stance that accommodates *multiple*, not simply dichotomously *sexed* bodies.

It seems important, in this context, to argue that feminists who are in a position of (relative) social power do not use this power to further entrench polarities that function negatively in relation to other social groups as well. Given the history, and the discourses surrounding the history, of the modern body politic it is necessary for feminists to exert a strong counterforce to the explicit and implicit masculinity of that body. This counterforce will necessarily involve the assertion of a certain homogeneity in the specific situations of women. This seems to be a necessary initial response to a substantive historical fact about political society. But this response must be viewed as based in tactical *nous* rather than in an ontological truth about women that is closed to history. It is necessary for feminist theory to develop an open-ended ontology capable of resisting entrenchment in a romanticism which so often accompanies the 'underdog' position.

The kind of political practice that I am suggesting could be developed from Spinozist metaphysics would require the reconsideration of several dominant feminist principles. The polarisation between men and women is a part of our socio-political histories which cannot be ignored. But to accept this dualism uncritically is merely to perpetuate relations whose construction is not fully understood. The kind of political practice envisaged here is one where difference could not be decided a priori but rather recognised in the unfolding of shared (or conflicting) aims and objectives of groups of bodies. To seek to create a politico-ethical organisation where all, in their own manner, seek to maximise the possibilities of their activity must take into account different beings and their desires, and their understandings of their being and their desires. It is an unavoidable (and welcome) consequence of constructing an *embodied* ethics that ethics would no longer pretend to be universal.

Spinozist philosophy is capable of suggesting an account of the body and its relation to social life, politics and ethics that does not depend on the dualisms that dominate traditional modern philosophy. Yet neither is it a philosophy which neutralises difference. Rather it allows a conceptualisation of difference which is neither dichotomised nor polarised. Spinoza's writings offer the possibility of resolving some of the current difficulties in the much-debated relation between feminist theory and dominant theory (see Gatens, 1986). This 'resolution' is not so much concerned with 'answers' to these difficulties as with providing a framework in which it is possible to pose problems in quite 'different' theoretical terms.

The division between the (bodily, natural, feminine) private sphere and the (rational, cultural, masculine) public sphere is a division that has proved particularly resilient to feminist intervention. To address the tension between the political and the familial sphere is to address the tension between the conceptions 'men' and 'women', and so ultimately to address the tension *within* the present politico-ethical structuring of the 'universal' human subject. The Spinozist conceptions of reason, power, activity and conatus (the tendency of all things to persist in their own being) offer a provisional terminology in which to begin working towards dissolving these tensions. By abandoning the dualist ontology of mind versus body, nature versus culture, we can circumvent the either/or impasse of contemporary feminist theory between affirming an essential mental equality, which the progress of civilisation can be entrusted to expose, or affirming an essential bodily difference. The Spinozist view does not lend itself to an understanding of sexual difference in terms of a consciousness/body or sex/gender distinction. For Spinoza the body is not part of passive nature ruled over by an active mind but rather the body is the ground of human action. The mind is constituted by the affirmation of the actual existence of the body, and reason is active and embodied precisely because it is the affirmation of a *particular* bodily existence. Activity itself cannot be related especially to body, mind, nature or culture, but rather to understanding the possibilities of one's participation in one's situation as opposed to the passive 'living' of one's social, political or even brute existence. This active understanding does not, and could not, amount to the mental domination of a body-machine, since thought is dependent for its activity on the character of the body and the manner in which, and the context in which, it recreates itself.

The Spinozist account of the body is of a productive and creative body which cannot be definitively 'known' since it is not identical with itself across time. The body does not have a 'truth' or a 'true' nature since it is a process and its meaning and capacities will vary according to its context. We do not know the limits of this body or the powers that it is capable of attaining. These limits and capacities can only be revealed by the ongoing interactions of the body and its environment.

Traditional political theory takes the body, its passions, its form and function as virtually given. This form is then understood to be taken up in culture in the way that it is because of this a priori or biological nature. Entertaining a non-mechanical view of nature and a non-dichotomised view of nature and culture would involve acknowledging the cultural and historical specificity of bodies. The particular form, structure, character and capabilities of a body confined to the domestic sphere and to the role of wife/mother may then be seen as an historically specific body whose capacities are reduced by its sphere of activity and the conditions under which it recreates itself. This perspective makes essentialist accounts of the female form and its capacities problematic. It allows one to question the traditional alignments between the female body and the private sphere and the male body and the public sphere without disavowing the *historical* facts that support these alignments. One could rather note the ways in which the respective activities of these distinct spheres construct and recreate particular kinds of bodies to perform particular kinds of tasks.

For feminists working in philosophy—or any academic discipline— the most pressing difficulty in relation to affirming the presence of woman is the theoretical exclusions implicit in the discourses we have to deal with. Creating other modes of conceptualising human culture that do not involve the passivity or invisibility of women is obviously of the greatest importance. A philosophy of the body that addresses the connections between representations of sexed bodies on one hand and representations of the politico-ethical on the other is an essential component of any alternative view. Recent work on the body by French feminists (see Marks and Courtivron, 1980; Eisenstein and Jardine, 1980; Irigaray, 1977; 1985a; 1985b) which stress *morphology* over biology, cultural constructions of embodiment over the 'natural' body, break with traditional boundaries between desire and instinct, between consciousness and bodies. Morphological descriptions of the body construct the body as an active, desiring body since the form of the body *is* its being, its form *is* its desiring. I take this conception of morphology to be a useful bridging device—a device that is necessary to get beyond the dilemmas of dualism. Many feminists are working on the creation of an alternative topos from which to reject or work through these dominant dualisms of the mind and the body, nature and culture, biology and psychology, and sex and gender. What I have tried to show in this chapter is that the theorisation or clarification of this topos could benefit from the Spinozist framework. I have suggested that his work offers exciting possibilities in terms of conceptualising the body as productive and dynamic: a conception which defies traditional divisions between knowing and being, between ontology and epistemology, and between politics and ethics.

No doubt there are other non-dualist conceptions of subjectivity that should be explored. I am not presenting Spinoza as a unique exception in the history of philosophy. Some aspects of the work of Nietzsche, or more recently the work of Foucault and Deleuze, may also prove useful to feminists. My personal preference for the remote figure of Spinoza stems from a worry that more contemporary figures may entrap feminism in the transferential position, to which it is so very vulnerable (see Le Doeuff, 1977). Establishing an autonomous relation to one's discipline, and to its history, is a step towards at least *theoretical* independence.

CAROLINE RALSTON

5   Polyandry, 'pollution',
'prostitution': the problems
of eurocentrism and
androcentrism in Polynesian
studies

Since the 1950s, publications and research in Pacific history have
concentrated almost exclusively on the impact of western products,
peoples, ideologies and economic practices on the island world.
Serious and successful attempts have been made to present islanders
as rational active agents in the processes of contact and subsequent
change, but usually they have been perceived as homogeneous
populations. Differential responses, initiatives or adaptations from
the various groups within island societies, or between male and
female, have rarely been recognised let alone studied (Ralston,
1985). In Polynesia the islanders most likely to come in contact with
foreigners were male chiefs, and too frequently histories of contact
have been written as if the experiences of these chiefs were typical
of all. Like so many other areas of academic discourse, Polynesian
history has been gender-blind, referring specifically to women only
when their presence and 'scandalous' behaviour (for example
flocking on board foreign vessels seeking sexual liaisons) exposed
them to misinformed and judgmental comment and stereotyping.
    As a product of this school of Pacific history, I find that little of
my conventional training prepares me for the research work I am
now engaged in: the study of gender relations in Polynesia and
their transformations since contact with the west. I am particularly
concerned to elucidate Polynesian concepts of the nature of female
and male, the positions, power and daily activities of women in
pre-contact societies, and then, how these have changed since
contact with the wider world. Changes in concepts of masculinity
and in Polynesian men's power, positions and status have
necessarily directly affected Polynesian women's lives and therefore
also demand attention.

In many ways I am faced with starting a totally new academic endeavour. My interest in the Pacific and Polynesia in particular remains unchanged, but to investigate the lives of women and gender relations demands expertise in a number of disciplines and methodologies new to me, particularly women's studies and women's history but also cultural anthropology, archaeology and linguistics. No simple absorption of the latter fields, however, will suffice. Given the intellectual milieu in which these traditional disciplines were created and developed, and by whom, their principles and procedures must also be critically examined. The body of knowledge women's studies scholars isolate and analyse has always been considered peripheral to mainstream, masculinist disciplines whose models and theories ignore, distort or fundamentally misinterpret the experience of women. For these reasons any research in the area of women's history or gender relations must work on and between the margins of traditional disciplines and therefore is inherently transdisciplinary in nature (Sheridan, 1985). To try to become an expert in and critic of so many fields is intimidating to say the least (Burton, 1985).

I see my long-term project as an essay into both women's history and gender relations. Neither term has a single, clearly developed or undisputed definition. 'Women's history' has been used with reference to a number of historical works of diverse ideological perspectives and methodological approaches. Biographies of great women and histories detailing women's activities during the Reformation, the American Civil War or other 'significant' historical periods, fall within this rubric, as well as the more avowedly feminist histories which reject the conventional criteria of historical significance and periodisation and take as the central problematic the experiences of women. Working from this latter perspective, I will focus upon the changing lives, opportunities and outlook of Polynesian women, both ordinary and chiefly. But these women cannot be studied in isolation. The nature and changing patterns of relations between them and Polynesian men is central to any understanding of their lives, and hence the need to study gender relations—an academic debate taken up more frequently by social scientists than by women's or feminist historians.

In the social sciences concepts of gender have been central for several decades in psychological and sociological studies of sexual difference, sex roles, childhood development and the family, and in anthropological studies of kinship. Only more recently has attention been given to gender relations or more precisely the social relations between the genders. Connell (1985:261) has argued cogently that gender relations cannot be tightly defined but must rather be understood as a complex network of arguments and issues, which includes the social subordination of women, and the cultural practices that sustain it; the politics of sexual choice: heterosexual, bisexual or homosexual; the sexual division of labour; the formation of personality, so far as it is organised in terms of femininity and masculinity; and the role of the body in social relations, especially the politics of reproduction. (This list owes much to Connell, but I have adapted his criteria so that they are less specifically related to late-twentieth-century western conditions.) Research focused upon this network of issues, combined with the approaches and skills of feminist history, seems to me to be essential in any study of Polynesian women over the past two centuries.

But a decision to concentrate on women and gender relations in Polynesia, given the extent and diversity of that area, still leaves the problem of where to start: with an individual island group—Hawaii or the Tokelaus? with a particular cultural practice—birth rituals or hula dancing? or with an attempt to look at Polynesia as a whole? Whatever the choice, certain basic problems concerning the nature of the extant evidence and the academic discourses in which it has already been incorporated must be faced. The evidence available about pre-contact and early post-contact Polynesian societies is riddled with eurocentric and androcentric preconceptions and misconceptions, and the theories and models used by nineteenth- and twentieth-century historians and anthropologists to analyse these data suffer similarly. Much of this literature is the product of the imperial enterprise. Like so many non-western peoples, the Polynesians have been seen as exotic and have been subject to racist and sexist caricatures and misrepresentations (Said, 1978). A further closely related problem is the nature of the language available to attempt to expose and counter these biases. Just some of the concepts frequently used in Polynesian contexts will illustrate this difficulty. Words such as 'prostitution', 'promiscuity', 'debauchery' and 'effeminacy' all carry with them negative, Christian judgments about sexuality, especially women's sexuality.

In this chapter I want to explore a few examples of these theoretical and linguistic problems in an attempt to expose and subsequently discard a mass of intellectual debris and obfuscation. Such an examiniation of the established disciplinary procedures and the language in which any discourse must be couched seems an essential piece of groundwork before any specific analysis of women and gender relations can proceed, in Polynesia or elsewhere. Certainly the inadequacies of established disciplinary methods and exposition are not unique to the study of Polynesia. They plague feminist analyses of any society.

THEORIES AND MODELS

The standard twentieth-century definitions of 'polyandry' as the marriage practice allowing a woman to have more than one husband at the same time, and of 'polygyny' as the marriage practice allowing a man to have more than one wife at the same time (Hunter & Whitten, 1976:310) are uncontroversial. In common usage, however, 'polygyny' appears infrequently, and 'polygamy', by definition the marriage practice of either sex having more than one spouse at the same time (Hunter and Whitten, 1976:310), is normally used to describe a man with multiple wives. What was originally a non-sex-specific term, 'polygamy', has acquired a specifically masculine definition—by no means a unique occurrence in English usage.

While the twentieth-century definition of 'polyandry' is unproblematic, the moment analysts attempt to describe and explain polyandrous societies, deep-seated beliefs about 'normal' or 'natural' sexual practices are revealed. The founding fathers of social anthropology, in particular Henry Lewis Morgan and Herbert Spencer, saw clear evolutionary usefulness in polygyny, a definite advance they believed on generalised sexual promiscuity and group marriage. Polyandry, however, was to Morgan 'an excrescence of polygamy [polygyny], and its repulsive converse', which could only occur in times of a scarcity of either 'unappropriated females' or the means of subsistence, or both (Morgan, 1871:477). Spencer considered polyandry unnatural and conducive of serious evils, particularly authority conflicts and poor social cohesion: an unlikely marriage practice to flourish in any struggle of the fittest for survival (Spencer, 1904:654–51). Such quasi-evolutionary pseudo-science has long since had its rebuttal, but only more recently have feminist scholars revealed the sexism in the conventional nineteenth-century descriptions of polyandry and polygyny, viz. 'in polyandry several men agree to share one woman; polygamy [polygyny] results when one man possesses a number of women. The reverse description would have been inconceivable: in polyandry one woman possesses a number of men; polygamy [polygyny] results when a number of women agree to share one man' (Fee, 1974:102, fn.12).

The practice of polyandry in pre-contact Marquesan society has confronted (one is tempted to say, affronted) several twentieth-century male analysts who have felt compelled to explain such an 'unnatural' marriage practice. Rather than present a detailed exposition of the nature and functioning of late-eighteenth-century Marquesan society based on traditional mythological and oral evidence, and the material from the early foreign visitors, anthropologists such as Linton (1939), Kardiner (1939) and Otterbein (1963) proceeded from the 'fact' of polyandry, conceived as an aberrant sexual and social practice, and selected or fabricated evidence to explain it. All start from a basic but totally unsubstantiated premise that in pre-contact Marquesan society men greatly outnumbered women (Handy, 1923:100; Linton, 1939:155; Kardiner, 1939:200; Otterbein, 1963:155). No other explanation seems to have been considered possible or palatable. The sex ratio imbalance they claim or suggest was the result of female infanticide. But neither the practice of infanticide, selective or otherwise, nor the sex ratio imbalance can be established in the oral or written record (Thomas, 1983; Suggs, 1966:129–30; Suggs, 1971:170). A sizeable academic literature on a mythical Marquesan culture has been created, which has to be read, only to be discarded as unsubstantiated and an amazing monument to certain western males' preconceptions and anxieties about polyandry. The beachcomber Robarts (Dening, 1974:270) in the Marquesas in the early 1800s was at least more candid about the disquiet polyandry can evoke: 'In this liberty [one woman having several husbands] these people differ from any other class of people that I ever met with. One man may have several women, but for one woman to have several men I think is a pill hard to digest.'

More recently Pacific anthropologist-historians Dening (1980) and Thomas (1983; 1984; 1987) have returned to the primary evidence available on the Marquesas, and Thomas (1983) has presented the practice of elite women having one or more secondary husbands, called *pekio*, as an integral part of the domestic economy. A *pekio*'s duties as a household servant were more important than his sexual rights and activities. It is significant that apparently all *pekio* came from the slave or landless sector of Marquesan society, and that the word itself is translated as 'the servant who copulates' (Thomas, 1983). The American Mary Ann Alexander (Alexander, 1934:168), wife of a Protestant missionary in the Marquesas in the early 1830s, emphasised the *pekio*'s servant role:

> The women are also abused by their husbands, often beaten cruelly, yet they will plead for having five or six husbands. They say, who will prepare their food? the first husband is a chief and he must not work and it is not proper for the second and therefore they must have five or six.

The cultural presuppositions underlying this statement are too complex to explore fully here, but briefly it is important to realise that the cooking and eating of food were highly significant, *tapu* activities, and, as in almost all traditional Polynesian societies, women did not cook. In such circumstances domestic help from a class of landless males became an important cultural phenomenon. Evidence about *pekio* husbands, their numbers, duties and privileges, remains scant and ambiguous, but until the 1970s male anthropologists' attempts to elucidate Marquesan polyandry have only muddied the waters.

Polyandry is by no means the only anthropological category that has been defined and/or used in decidedly eurocentric and androcentric ways. Many anthropological and historical studies of past and present-day Polynesian societies have remarked upon the impermanence of husband–wife bonds and the instability of marriage (Levy, 1973:198–99; Marshall, 1983:12), phenomena which have frequently been seen as psychopathological and in need of explanation and reform. The subtext of such analyses is a deep-seated, often unacknowledged belief that stable nuclear families are the ideal social unit. These specialists ignore the central importance in Polynesian societies of the bonds between brother and sister (Ortner, 1981:368–70; Marshall, 1983:7–12; Schoeffel, 1978:72–75; Shore, 1976:283–86; Bott, 1981:17; Rogers, 1977). For a woman her position among her natal kin as daughter, sister and aunt remain throughout her life more influential and central than her position as wife and mother among her affines (Schoeffel, 1977; Schoeffel, 1978:76–77; Ortner, 1981:368, 395; Gailey, 1980:299–300, 317–18). Similarly the long-established and frequent practice in nearly all Polynesian societies of adoption, both formal and informal (Carroll, 1970; Brady, 1976), has been considered as unnatural and abnormal by many western analysts whose belief in the primacy of genetic bonds goes unquestioned (Lowie, 1930:459–60). An historian trying to investigate the nature of gender relations or the lives of women in any past society needs to be aware of the inherent preconceptions not only in the primary material but also in the secondary analyses, the models and theories that have been brought to bear on the basic data.

THE USE OF LANGUAGE

Like man-made theories, man-made language carries with it inherent connotations and judgmental positions that should not be ignored. The nature of Polynesian sexuality, particularly Polynesian women's sexuality, has fascinated western male visitors since the time of contact. But the concepts used by participant observers and later analysts to describe this behaviour—particularly terms such as 'prostitution' and 'promiscuity'—ignore the women's own experience and their perceptions of it, and condemn it from a particular cultural and religious perspective. For example, in traditional Hawaiian culture heterosexual relations were vaunted (Sahlins,

1985:9; Charlot, 1983:83; Ralston, 1983). Chastity and virginity, except for certain dynastic marital alliances, were unimportant (Ralston, 1983). On the arrival of Cook with his officers and crew, the ordinary Hawaiian women demanded to have sexual intercourse with the men, seeking no material reward, as the surgeon's mate Samwell (Beaglehole, 1967: vol.3, part 2, 1083, 1085) made abundantly clear:

> The Young Women who were in general exceeding beautiful, used all their arts to entice our people into their Houses, and finding they were not to be allured by their blandishments they endeavoured to force them & were so importunate that they absolutely would take no denial.
>
> [We] found all the Women of these Islands but little influenced by interested motives in their intercourse with us, as they would almost use violence to force you into their Embrace regardless whether we gave them any thing or not.

The women's actions were influenced by their belief that the foreigners had close links to supernatural powers and that offspring sired by them would give the women access to supernatural benefits (Sahlins, 1981:38–41; Ralston, 1983). Later, after the repeated arrival of foreign vessels, illusions of supernatural access faded, but the Hawaiian women still made themselves readily available to foreign sailors in return for a range of highly desired goods of western manufacture (Ralston, 1983). Even at that stage, to define these sexual activities as 'prostitution', imposes Christian judgments on casual sexual encounters, which evoked no such stigma in traditional Hawaiian culture. A puritanical brand of Christianity was introduced into Hawaii in 1820 and was widely, if superficially, accepted by the mid-1820s, but until at least the 1850s it seems more appropriate and culturally neutral to describe the women's sexual liaisons as 'an exchange of sexual services', not prostitution.

In any society, including twentieth-century western, Christian, capitalist society, use of the term 'prostitution' is seen as offensive by many. As long as the men who buy sexual services are called 'clients', it is unacceptable to call the women who sell 'prostitutes'. I am not denying the real problems inherent in the sale of sexual services, particularly in western societies (Pateman 1982; 1983), but at least the language used to analyse the phenomenon should be as non-judgmental and non-sexist as possible. Similarly, the use of terms such as 'prostitution', 'promiscuity' and 'debauchery' to describe the behaviour of Polynesian women distorts and prejudges analysis, revealing much about the religious, moral stance of the commentator, but little or nothing about the people who supposedly are the focus of study.

One other example of loaded language, which has obscured rather than elucidated Polynesian analysis, should be briefly discussed. In several Polynesian societies certain young boys were deliberately brought up to dress, act and live like women, and male transvestism and homosexuality were openly practised (Oliver, 1974:369–74, 1111–12; Gunson, 1964:58; Levy, 1973:130–33; Malo, 1951:74, 256; Kamakau, 1961:234, 238). To describe the male participants in such activities as 'effeminate' or to describe the practice of treating them like women as 'emasculating' is to impose western notions of gender and 'proper' or 'natural' sex roles on people who clearly do not conceive of the nature and roles of male and female in the same way. The acceptance and prevalence of *mahu* (male transvestites), especially in Eastern Polynesia, suggest that femaleness in traditional society was not associated with negative characteristics.

Dale Spender in *Man Made Language* (1980) has clearly revealed the sexist nature of the English language, particularly the vocabulary available and used to describe women's sexuality and the nature of heterosexual intercourse, but feminist scholars must develop her analysis much further. A persistent sensitivity to the connotations of the English language is essential for any one trying to unravel the conceptions of sexuality and gender in non-western societies.

FEMALE POLLUTION?

Finally I want to consider the presumption of notions of female pollution in Polynesia. Early foreign visitors to the area witnessed the following phenomena: that women rarely participated in any major public religious ceremonies; and that in all Polynesian societies except Tonga they did not eat with men, and everywhere certain foods, associated with the gods, were denied them (Hanson, 1982:335–43). Faced with this evidence and other instances of similar kinds, most foreigners concluded that women were considered by their own societies as dangerous, disruptive and polluting, inimical influences in any religious or social context (Hanson, 1982:335–36). Early western visitors and later specialists have suggested that a timeless, inflexible dichotomy mediated all Polynesian behaviour: Polynesian man was sacred: Polynesian woman profane (Handy, 1927:38–48, 54; Howe, 1984:66). This interpretation is clearly of a piece with eurocentric, androcentric and Christian concepts of womanhood, which are centrally concerned with female sexuality and biological functions (Marcus, 1984:211–12; McLaughlin, 1974:229–30; Henning, 1974:272–73).

Evidence is slowly becoming available to refute this interpretation, but it is disparate and not always focused on the question of female pollution (Hanson, 1982; Hanson and Hanson, 1983; Driessen, 1984; Sahlins, 1985:7; Thomas, 1983; 1984; 1987). Part of the reinterpretation depends on the translation of the Polynesian words *tapu* and *noa* (or *meie*). To render *tapu* as sacred (in relation to persons, objects or activities closely associated with the gods) in this context is not disputed, but *noa*, which has usually been translated as profane, should be rendered as clear, or unrestricted (Driessen, 1984; Thomas, 1983). To define certain women as *noa* therefore meant they were unconstrained by sacred regulation rather than that they were impure, or categorically opposed to male sacredness. There were contexts in which some women, usually those of chiefly rank, were *tapu*, while non-chiefly men were *tapu* in some circumstances but not in others. There was in fact nothing inflexible or absolute about these states.

Rather than being repellant to the gods, women's reproductive functions were closely associated with the supernatural (Hanson, 1982:347–57). Among the Maori the word *atua*, god, also meant menses (Hanson and Hanson, 1983:93) and in both Samoa and New Zealand certain stillbirths and menstrual clots were believed to become a special kind of spirit or god (Schoeffel, 1978:78; Hanson, 1982:350). Parturition was immensely *tapu* (Hanson, 1982:350–51). The vagina was seen as a portal between the world of the gods and the world of humans (Hanson, 1982:350). Reexamination of Polynesian concepts of male and female has only just begun, but already the data reveal that Polynesian women were potent forces, whose close links with the gods had to be carefully restrained. To interpret women's potency as pollution or their very being as profane is to misunderstand their power and significance completely.

As the misconceptions and biases in many of the theories, models and language used to analyse Polynesian society are identified and removed, a picture of Polynesian women and patterns of gender relations in pre-contact times begins to emerge. Men and women filled sacred chiefly roles enjoying both status and authority (Herda, 1987; Schoeffel, 1987; Gunson, 1987). Ambilineal, cognatic descent rules, the importance of high chiefly women to politically ambitious but genealogically less elevated male chiefs, and the sacred superiority of the father's sister in Western Polynesian societies (Schoeffel, 1978:70–75; Shore, 1976:283–88; Bott, 1981:17; Rogers, 1977:160–62) all contributed to the political significance of Polynesian women. Only since contact with the west have notions of strict patrilineal descent and male primogeniture appeared. When male Polynesian chiefs recognised the emphasis Europeans put on these patterns of inheritance, they manipulated their genealogies to conform to the highly restrictive western notions of legitimate political descent (Gunson, 1987). In pre-contact times, the importance of kinship throughout Polynesian societies placed particular emphasis on women's roles as daughters, sisters and aunts, while as wives and mothers they were less influential. There were clear beliefs in women as potent agents, closely affiliated with supernatural powers. In general women were not conceived of as weak, dependent, passive or in need of protection.

I do not wish to argue that Polynesian women of any rank enjoyed equal status, power or opportunity with Polynesian men of similar rank, but the nature of their positions and status must not be mistakenly identified with misconceived notions of pollution or profanity. From a carefully reconstructed pre-contact base which articulates Polynesian concepts of female and male and the behaviour appropriate to each, it should be possible to explore and understand the nature of the impact of western contact on concepts and patterns of gender relations and women's lives. The persistent misinterpretations of traditional Polynesian social practices perpetrated by western missionary, trader and colonial official must be distinguished from the notions of gender relations and male/female roles they sought to impose as 'natural', most productive in an economic sense, or Christian. Only when all these different strands have been isolated and identified will it be possible to write a history of women and gender relations in Polynesia over the last two centuries.

SUSAN SHERIDAN

6 Feminist readings: the case of Christina Stead

With the development of feminist literary criticism over the past decade or so, most women writers recognised as 'major' now have a feminist as well as a mainstream reputation. Christina Stead is an interesting case in point, because the two reputations have emerged almost simultaneously and there is evidence of a struggle going on over the possession of her name. Male critics, in these early stages of Stead criticism, frequently challenge the legitimacy of feminist readings. They object to what they see as feminists 'enlisting her work in support of partisan causes' (Geering, 1978:469; Reid, 1979:112–13) and misreading her texts by an overemphasis on certain features such as her portraits of egotistical males (Clancy, 1981:42) or the 'reductive labelling' of her female characters as feminist heroines (Pybus, 1982:42).

Such objections are easily recognisable as appeals to some basic assumptions of mainstream liberal humanist criticism: that literature has nothing to do with 'partisan causes' but rises above politics and history to explore the universal 'human condition', and that distinctions of gender or other cultural differences made in relation to this 'human condition' are inevitably 'reductive', inevitably made at the expense of the literary text's self-regulating complexity. Feminist criticism challenges both these assumptions by maintaining that such claims to universality are false and that all readings—those of mainstream male critics included—are appropriations of the text and are made from a gender-marked place within a particular cultural context (Furman, 1980:52). Feminist criticism of all descriptions insists that the position from which one reads is not neutral, and certainly not neuter. Jonathan Culler describes feminism's 'hypothesis of the woman reader' and its effect as follows: 'What it does above all is to reverse the usual situation in which the perspective of a male critic is assumed to be sexually neutral, while a feminist reading is seen as a case of special pleading and an attempt to force the text into a predetermined mold' (Culler, 1983:55).

Yet such objections to feminist criticism of Stead's work can be supported by the novelist's own statements rejecting feminism as a political movement, and in this respect they are not so easily dismissed. It is a stock gesture of such 'malestream' critics to quote Stead's own denials that her fiction had any particular concern with the situation of women or with feminism. In interview after interview she reiterated the opinion that Women's Liberation was not a genuinely political movement against oppression but middle-class fanaticism, 'pure freakery' (Whitehead, 1974:246). Feminist critics are in a less advantageous position to deal with this kind of appeal to the author's authority because, generally speaking, they have developed a critical practice which does indeed refer questions of meaning back to the text's author, a practice which reads the woman writer's texts as expressions of herself, of her female conflicts and visions. This feminist criticism implicitly defines itself as the search for feminist meanings in the texts of women, and in that respect it shares the critical presupposition of its mainstream detractors that meanings reside in texts (put there, as it were, by authors), and that the task of criticism is to decipher those meanings.

This, the dominant mode of feminist criticism so far, has been called 'gynocritics' (Showalter, 1979:25 et passim). It involves the identification of feminist themes in the texts of women writers through attending to their accounts of female experience (usually assumed to be that of the writer herself). In the process, gynocritics has tended to set up a canon of ideologically sound feminist works by a pantheon of exemplary feminist writers. The fact that Stead has refused the mantle of 'feminist writer', and the difficulty of describing her later novels as 'feminist' in any clear sense, are two practical reasons for questioning the critical assumptions and practices of gynocritics. There is also the theoretical reason touched on earlier, the extent to which gynocritics shares these assumptions and practices with the mainstream criticism against which it sets itself politically (Moi, 1985:62–63). On the other hand, feminist criticism of male-authored literary works (what Showalter calls 'feminist critique'), because it cannot expect to find authentic female experience represented in them, is less interested in authorial intentions, more likely to 'trust the tale, not the teller' and to attend to the text's inscriptions of ideology rather than reading it as if its language were transparent. The gap between such a 'hermeneutics of suspicion' and the celebratory revisions of women's writing characteristic of gynocritics is remarkable. It is also a disturbing gap, if one is disinclined, as I am, to believe that only men's texts are saturated in ideology while women's writing offers the woman reader direct access to female experience. Showalter's distinction between gynocritics and feminist critique certainly describes a major divide in feminist literary criticism, but the divide itself must be questioned, not least for its reliance on authorial signatures of gender.

Feminist criticism of all descriptions insists that the gender of the reader matters. The way in which it is held to matter, however, and what it means to 'read as a woman', needs further investigation. As Mary Jacobus puts it:

> More recently American criticism has become concerned with the reader as the place where meanings are generated ... and therefore more concerned with the question of the woman reader ... The woman reader isn't simply produced by having had female experience, she's produced in some sense by the text, whether it's the text she's reading or a text that reads her. (Jacobus, 1986:51–52)

The appeal to the woman reader can be seen as a dual one: on the one hand, to the woman as social subject, whose female identity is thus 'given', and on the other hand to the woman reader as she is constantly inscribed in discursive constructions of femininity. The ground for interpretation is not so much female experience itself but whatever discourses on female experience are available, discourses which may be shaped by different feminist concerns at different times and in different cultural contexts. Such discourses constitute a feminist reader or reading position which sets itself in productive relation to the text. As Culler puts it, in slightly different terms:

> The appeal to the experience of the reader provides leverage for displacing or undoing the system of concepts or procedures of male criticism, but 'experience' always has this divided, duplicitous character: it has always already occurred and yet is still to be produced—an indispensable point of reference, yet never simply there. (Culler, 1983:63)

Interaction between these two aspects of the reading process, as I hope to show in the following discussion, can produce a high degree of instability. Gynocritical readings of women's novels depend on the model of a woman reader's identification with the female protagonist(s), but this model only works successfully when the protagonist can herself be seen as a feminist or proto-feminist, as victim or heroine of the struggle with patriarchal power. In much of Stead's work, however, the sexual politics of the female protagonist are unclear, or even anti-feminist, and the woman reader is left without firm ground to stand on, in an unstable relation to both protagonist and narrator. But if the reader is in an unstable place or field which the narrative strategies of the text attempt to organise, reading is also a process or practice, a work of producing meaning; to read is to 'produce the text, play it, open it out, make it go' (Barthes, 1979:80). Operating on a notion of reader-power of this kind, feminist criticism is in a better position to fulfil its potential for 'undoing the system of male criticism' and to develop its own proce- dures of reading which would apply equally to male- and female- authored texts, appropriating both for feminist purposes.

I want now to look at some gynocritical appropriations of Stead's best-known novel, *The Man Who Loved Children*, and to estimate their strengths and limitations. Even within the dominant liberal- humanist critical discourse, a certain feminist reading position is possible and has proved productive, as exemplified by Dorothy Green's essay 'Storm in a Teacup' (1974). Her sharp analysis of the patriarchal nature of family dynamics implicitly answers the sen- timentalities about 'the family' propounded by Randall Jarrell in his influential introductory essay to the novel. While her reading consti- tuted a powerful counter-diagnosis of major thematic issues, how- ever, it perpetuated at the same time the notion that the daughter in this family, Louisa, must escape from it because she is potentially an artist, a destiny which cannot, in this reading, be connected with her cultural fate as a woman. Green's approach could be described as one which brings to bear a woman's point of view, but within the boundaries of liberal humanist ideology. To schematise: it locates women's (and children's) oppression within the family but assumes that beyond this private sphere of life a woman (a woman artist, for instance) can enter the public sphere on the same terms as a man. It is a position similar to that of Simone de Beauvoir in *The Second Sex* (1972), with its central opposition between the immanence of women's condition within the domestic world, and the potential transcendence in the world of work and politics available to the 'independent woman'. In this oppositional scheme there is only one model of subjectivity, that of a 'universal' individualism, covertly identified with masculinity.

Out of the Women's Liberation movement which took up and extended de Beauvoir's analysis of women's oppression, radical feminism has emerged as the dominant tendency, at least in North America. In literary studies, as in other areas of knowledge, radical feminism has challenged the universalist claims of liberal humanism. It has gone on to maintain that women have not in fact been absent from cultural production but have been, in Dorothy Smith's phrase, 'eclipsed' from 'men's culture' (Smith, 1978). The study of this eclipsed female culture—gynocritics—has been a major theme of radical feminism. But in the process of recovering women's writing, gynocritics, practically speaking, inverts the categories of 'men's culture' and applies them to women, without interrogating the categories themselves. For instance, gynocritics has produced feminist versions of the dominant literary-critical categories of 'tradition and the individual talent' and of literature as expressive form. Influential books by Patricia Spacks (1976), Ellen Moers (1977), Elaine Showalter (1977) and Sandra Gilbert and Susan Gubar (1979), have set in place the major themes of gynocritics: a matrilineal history of women's writing, enabling myths of female creativity and community, and an analysis of women's texts as expressive of the female experience, in particular the specificities of feminine psychology.

Joan Lidoff's study of Christina Stead takes up these latter themes. Her analysis of *The Man Who Loved Children* is entitled 'Domestic Gothic: the Imagery of Anger' (1979), and it inevitably focuses attention on Henny, the mother, as victim; she is seen as a representative figure of the 'constricted subculture' of women denied legitimate outlets for aggression and fantasy. Louisa, the daughter, is seen as the agent of the female anger expressed in that Gothic sensibility, a sensibility which is also, Lidoff argues, shared by Stead's narrative voice. But a major problem with the theory of expressive form she is operating with is that in eliding the two characters into a single figure representing 'female experience', she manages to avoid examining the violent—indeed fatal—conflict between them. And in identifying this composite figure ultimately with the unifying narrative sensibility, everything is referred back to the 'authority' of Stead herself.

This kind of feminist criticism repeats the gestures of mainstream liberal humanist criticism in two ways. First, meaning is referred back to the author, whose creativity is seen as its single origin and whose text transmits this meaning to the waiting reader who, because she too is a woman, recognises it as authentic. Second, to operate on this theory of meaning is to divert attention from the critic's own activity as reader—in this instance, from her own choice of the feminist questions she brings to bear on the text. In a repetition of the universalising gesture of the dominant critical discourse, 'female experience' is generalised out of what in fact is a cluster of particular radical feminist themes, namely a female subculture (defined by domesticity and marked by the suppression of anger and fantasy) and a feminine psychology conceptualised in behaviourist terms, and which generalises about 'female experience' without recognising differences of class, race and sexuality.

My own analysis of *The Man Who Loved Children* is in part caught up in the same universalising tendency (Sheridan, 1985). In talking about the 'patriarchal family drama' in terms of incest (or what Elizabeth Ward (1984) has more accurately designated 'father–daughter rape') and in giving this theme a psychoanalytic reading derived from Juliet Mitchell's earlier hypothesis of a 'feminine Oedipus complex' (Mitchell, 1975), this essay buys into the continuing debate in feminist theory about whether Freudian psychoanalysis can claim to explain the universal entry into human culture of gendered subjects. It is, though, a debate about the applicability of a theoretical construct to explain the oppression of women, rather than a claim about the capacity of literature to represent female experience, and in this respect it appropriates Stead's text as a contribution to feminist theory.

It is undeniable that the best-known of Stead's novels, the auto-biographically based *The Man Who Loved Children* and *For Love Alone*, stand up remarkably well to gynocritical readings. Their concern with the transition from childhood to adult femininity, and with the dynamics of heterosexual relations, can be read as a powerfully critical representation of female experience. The linguistic excesses that mark Stead's style can be explained, as Joan Lidoff explains them, as a Gothic mode compatible with a 'feminine aesthetic', the theory of which is another major concern of gynocritics. The structural anomalies characteristic of Stead's narratives can in each case be subordinated to a utopian reading of the final outcome for the heroine: that is, Louisa's escape from her father's house in *The Man Who Loved Children*, and Teresa's emergence out of the 'womb of time' and into the 'citied plain' of human history and her own freedom, in *For Love Alone* (p.494). Yet problems begin to show when, for instance, it is recognised that *For Love Alone* has a doubled ending, in that the final scene is one of repetition, not of resolution and closure: Teresa sees her former lover-tormenter in the street and reflects 'bitterly': 'It's dreadful to think that it will go on being repeated for ever, he—and me! What's there to stop it?' (p.502).[1]

The limitations of this approach become clearly evident, however, when one looks to Stead's later novels, in particular *Letty Fox*, *Cotters' England* and *Miss Herbert* (*The Suburban Wife* and *I'm Dying Laughing*). In each case the female protagonist is neither a victim nor a heroine but a survivor, both self-deceiving and exploitative of others. None of them can be read as moral models; nor can they be read as myths of female creativity—except by ironic inversion. Their literary antecedents do not come from the female 'great tradition' celebrated by gynocritics but, more likely, from female protagonists constructed by male writers—Moll Flanders, Emma Bovary, various evil and grotesque women in Dickens. Indeed their precedents are not necessarily literary: Eleanor Herbert, as I shall argue later, is the 'ordinary woman' constructed by popular cultural forms in the 1930s and 1940s; Letty Fox, it has been suggested,[2] is a secondary figure out of 1940s Hollywood detective films, the wise-cracking, hard-boiled receptionist; Nellie Cotter is perhaps derived from folk tales, pagan residues in English popular culture. With Letty and Eleanor, the question of their representativeness as women is foregrounded—and pre-empted by the characters them-selves: Letty announces herself a 'typical New York girl' and Eleanor insists that she is 'just an ordinary woman', a pillar of the conservative middle class.

I want to take *Miss Herbert* as an extreme manifestation of the dilemmas posed for feminist readers by the assumptions of gynocri-tics. If we attempt to read this text, as Elanie Showalter recom-mended we set about reading all women's texts, in order to learn 'what women have felt and experienced' (1979:27), we are con-fronted with some unpleasant things about this determinedly 'ordin-ary' woman, things which appear to confirm many misogynist accusations of women's 'innate' conservatism. It is difficult to know how to weigh the text's construction of its protagonist, for she appears sometimes as the heroine of a realist novel, given light and shade by narrative irony, while at other times she becomes the object of satire; but the distinction between these two positions is often so slight as to be indistinguishable. Eleanor's ordinariness is of course the point, and in relation to this, Stead's writing acts as a reminder that what language gives us access to is not unmediated experience but ideology. When language appears most transparent and 'natural', it is probably closest to the dominant ideology, in-scribed in the register we expect to find. In fiction we are usually made aware of the constitutive work of language when it draws attention to its own literariness. But in *Miss Herbert* the language is remarkable for its extreme ordinariness: it is the clichés which draw attention to its ideological character. The following passage explicit-ly comments on the process of editing her reactions in conformity with the ideological norms of femininity which marks Eleanor's whole text:

> As she worked she became wrapped in herself, spoke automatically to the children, and, to her confusion, indignant phrases repeated them-selves in her mind while she recalled scenes which had left her sore— even though she had always been considerate, sensible, humane and 'exercised her saving sense of humour'. Fiery, a complaint: 'Leni comes to help Henry; no one comes to help me.' A scene. In the original: 'Henry, what you call self-reliance and self-control, I call plain self. If you would discuss our differences of opinion, you might find yourself in the wrong, so you retire into this self-sufficiency, to humiliate me. I

won't be humiliated.' This mental record ran quickly through, and she edited as it ran, till it then took on its enduring form: 'Henry dear, let us just sit down awhile and thrash this thing out. A little frank speaking and soul-searching will do this family a world of good. You and I have had love and a deep sense of togetherness, and now we have our futures and the future of our children; we have everything. It's perfect, what we have. So just let's pull the mote each from his own eye, and see this thing clearly.' Henry then ideally replied, 'I admit I am too self-sufficient; and I grant that there is a grain of selfishness in self-sufficiency. You have a better form of it, self-reliance. A mother is closer to the human race.' 'Oh, but you, too, Henry, have the human touch—' but this rainbow interchange was coarsely interrupted by fierce words hurtling across her mind: 'He gets the best end of the stick and leaves me all the dirty work. He's a brute, the cold little climbing devil.' (p.111)

We are not even offered the luxury of seeing her as a victim of those popular culture institutions which circulate such ideological norms (talk shows, advice columns, magazine feature articles on 'communication skills in marriage' [Coward, 1984]). For Eleanor writes them herself—she is actively implicated in the cultural construction of femininity, circa 1936. During a dinner party, for instance, she almost weeps because her husband queries her management of pre-dinner drinks:

> Over and over again she had read that 'before dinner just one cocktail or one glass of sherry, according to your guests' fancy and pleasure, is correct; nothing more is needed to give them that pleasant anticipatory glow.' She had written it herself. 'More leads to raised voices and flushed faces.' Now, mortified, in her mind accusing the immoderate habits of Continentals, she went away ('slipped away' she thought to herself) and put on the dinner; Henry should not have the second bottle of sherry. (p.107)

The reference to 'Continentals' here—her husband is German—is one of the many indices of Eleanor's unreflective, populist racism. She is portrayed as a dyed-in-the-wool Tory, and indeed the novel can be read, as Angela Carter has suggested, as an allegory of 'the home life of Britannia from the twenties until almost the present day' (Carter, 1982).

I would suggest, though, that the distance offered to the reader by an allegorical text is not consistently maintained here, and that while we recognise the incessant inscription of contemporary ideologies of gender, race and class, we are also positioned vis-à-vis Eleanor in such a way as to invite a certain degree of identification with her plight and her determination. Rather like reading popular romance as a feminist, it is impossible to deny the heroine's relation to ourselves as social subjects, women, caught up in the same processes even as we read critically. The notion of 'reading woman'—introduced by Mary Jacobus into the debate about 'reading as a woman' to which I referred earlier—could be useful in untangling the issues here. As I understand the notion, it can encompass several distinct concerns with the discursive construction of femininity and with gendered reading/writing: 'reading woman' can connect 'woman' as the object constructed by the text (say, Eleanor Herbert), the writer's project of critically reading cultural constructions of femininity (as Stead does repeatedly), and the woman reader's complicity in this process (through identification) as well as her critical capacity to position the text among others and to read it against the grain.

The acid test for 'reading woman' in *Miss Herbert* is the point at which the consistent ordinariness of the language shifts violently into another key, one that seems to represent passion, desire, all that has been signally absent from the story of this woman's life:

> Her heart had begun a great circular thrumming, so it felt. Round and round it gadded, making larger swoops, and her head turned, making larger swoops, as if she were floating, with her large body, round the great dome. Her heart began pounding out hard and real thoughts, like pieces of metal, too; and she heard them, forceful, unanswerable: This is love and he knows it; it would be too strong for me, my life would be carried away into a whirlpool, round and round and down, in the center, lost and gone; I wouldn't want to get out of it, I would lose myself; I'd be swept away; I don't want that. I couldn't live, then all would mean nothing. I can't live like that; what of the past and future? There'd be no meaning to the world or time, but this hour and the future hours with him would break into everything, flooding everything, everything would be washed away: I couldn't stand it, I'm not strong enough, I'm too old to go in for it—
> Meantime the people had settled, the music had begun and Eleanor, who was somewhat musical, began to be ordered by and drawn into the music. What a terrible, powerful beat the music had, threatening and promising sullenly, something tremendous, nothing good. In it was a life Eleanor had never known, and which frightened her, but now, for the first time, attracted her—a great potency, passion, which she had been always unconscious of; some great thing approached her and for the first time spoke to her, as if a new world came somewhere near her world and she felt its attraction and feared to be pulled away off the earth, out of life. (p.304)

What is at stake here is the *mode* of representation of passion. Is this a love scene from one of Eleanor's magazine stories? Is it the eruption of a utopian desire? There is no narrative resolution which would allow us to decide one way or the other. All that happens, in one sense, is that the discourse changes key, and this change is set up in the paragraph preceding the above quotation by two different modulations. First, the occasion is a visit to the opera, a perform- ance of Verdi's *La Forza del Destino*, in which Eleanor's namesake, Leonora, in following the dictates of passion, is herself destroyed and brings about the deaths of her father and brother. Yet Eleanor's resistance to such fated passion is suggested in her mistake over the name: '(for some reason Eleanor always called it *La Sforza del Destino*)' (302). Certainly, *sforza*, exertion and effortfulness, is the keynote of *her* destiny.

The second lead into the passage quoted draws on another cultu- ral form altogether, a sub-Lawrentian or Mills and Boon discourse on sexual attraction. Eleanor has just met her daughter's fiancé, at which moment he 'looked straight into Eleanor's eyes with the glance of a man who understands a woman wants him and who gives himself and means to take all, a dark look that existed long before language. Eleanor looked away, to hide it from the others' (p.303). Reading woman becomes a particularly shifty business at this point, as the female protagonist's point of view takes up a projected masculine one.

In this unnerving context of Verdi superimposed on Mills and Boon, together with such shifts in the protagonist's point of view, it is perhaps inevitable that the following paragraph of rare narratorial comment, on her response to the music, should gain a certain authoritative weight. But it does not, I think, come down on the side of Verdi or of Mills and Boon. Nor is it the last word, by any means. Eleanor is given that, as she promises on the final page to sit down and write the story of her life. If the narrative we have been reading is written from the final position of knowledge of the pro- tagonist, as it is in classical realism, then it would seem that her encounter with passion and death at the opera has made no impact at all on Eleanor Herbert (the suburban wife).

This practice of identifying the discourses at work in the text constructing sexual difference is but one of the reading practices made available to feminist criticism when it takes on 'reading' in the strong, post-Barthesian sense, as work to produce meaning. The feminism of feminist criticism, in this mode, is a function of reading, rather than something which resides in the text or in the writer's intentions. The readings made possible by available feminist dis- courses can intervene in particular debates in the interpretation of texts or in cultural studies generally. Feminist readings, as presented here, have the potential to bridge the gap between 'gynocritics' and 'feminist critique', drawing on gynocritics for its insistence on the culturally specific conditions of women's literary production.

Though it need not confine itself to texts which address or construct female subjects, feminist criticism, 'reading woman', will have a particular interest in such texts, especially in their transformations of sexual and textual norms (Miller, 1986:270–78). The case of Christina Stead, and in particular her difficult later novels, is one which both requires and rewards such reading.

NOTES

1 To ignore this is comparable to those readings of Doris Lessing's *The Golden Notebook* which celebrate the integrated heroine of the golden notebook narrative and ignore the irreconcilable ending of the 'frame' narrative, 'Free Women', where Molly remarries and Anna joins the Labour Party and becomes a social worker!
2 Meaghan Morris, in conversation, September 1985

7 The in(ter)vention of feminist knowledges

> If we continue to speak this sameness, if we speak to each other as men
> have spoken for centuries, as they have taught us to speak, we will fail
> each other. Again ... words will pass through our bodies, above our
> heads, disappear, make us disappear. (Irigaray, 1980:69)

In this paper, I discuss some of the political stakes invested in
feminist analyses of the methods, assumptions and data of traditional academic disciplines, particularly the social sciences and
humanities. In challenging the structure and prevailing models
of knowledges, feminist theory is now intellectually mature enough
to effect radical ruptures and displacements in socially dominant
knowledges, making them more amenable to the interests and perspectives of women, and not as feminists in the past have done,
limiting feminism to struggles around women's equal inclusion. Only
in the late 1980s have feminists acquired a perspective from which to
assess traditional knowledges from the point of view of their capacity to accommodate women's particularity.

From the 1960s feminist theory focused on the misogyny and
hostility explicitly directed at women and femininity from various
discourses and epistemic frameworks. In the 1970s, feminists were
more concerned with integrating feminist and radical (*patriarchal*)
theories, incorporating feminism into, say, marxist, liberal, or
psychoanalytic frameworks, gaining a justification from these other
positions. And even when these frameworks are recognised as problematic they are not thereby seen as irredeemably flawed but are
assumed to be capable of 'correction' or minor modification.

Only after experiencing both exclusion from and co-option by
patriarchal discourses and knowledges are feminists able to affirm
their own points of view and thus to gain the necessary distance to

form independent judgments about the very systems within which many were trained. By beginning to know and grapple with patriarchal discourses, its 'other' or 'opposite', we may understand the highly variable interactions and encounters between feminist theory and academic mainstreams.

In surveying the kinds of relations feminist scholars have adopted in their various encounters with mainstream knowledges, three levels or types of intellectual misogyny can be distinguished for the purposes of analysis. These will be described as *sexist, patriarchal* and *phallocentric*. Significantly, these three levels of women's oppression in western knowledges give rise to three kinds of critique (not always clearly separable in feminist texts) developed by feminists over the last three decades. Feminist critical responses will be described as liberal feminist, structuralist feminist, and autonomy-oriented feminist, respectively. While these classifications are arbitrary—in so far as what is now a vast field of feminist theory could be divided according to different criteria—this distinction may enable us to assess the current state of feminist knowledges in their relations to the traditional academic discourses out of which they developed. I do not wish to imply that feminist knowledges are *only* critical or merely reactive to male knowledges. Critiques always imply the establishment of a (provisional) position. Critique is not clearly distinct from construct. In defining feminist theoretical writings according to a classificatory system based on relations to masculine knowledges, I do not wish to denigrate the insights and issues feminists have created independent of male knowledges. Instead I will focus on the kinds of threat and revaluation feminist theory implies for prevailing knowledges.

Before proceeding further, it may be helpful to briefly explain how the terms *sexist, patriarchal*, and *phallocentric* will be used. This may also provide a brief overview of the range and scope of misogyny pervasive in but usually unrecognised by its practitioners. It represents some of the assumptions and claims feminist theory contests in its examinations of knowledges.

First, then, *sexism* within knowledges consists in a series of specifically determinable *acts of discrimination* privileging men and depriving women. By 'acts' here I mean propositions, arguments, assertions, methodologies—discernible textual references to women or femininity. Sexism is a *manifest* phenomenon, easily illustrated, for it ranges from the open expression of hostility or suspicion about women, to ignoring and excluding women altogether from being considered worthy or relevant objects of investigation. Sexism is the *unwarranted* differential treatment of the two sexes. Because misogyny can be located at an empirical, observable level, it could probably be eradicated without seriously challenging a second, more insidious and structured level of oppression.

Second, *patriarchal* knowledges comprise a more systematic form of women's oppression and containment that women experience as the objects of sexist knowledge. Even if sexism could be 'eliminated' and even if the two sexes behaved in identical ways, their behaviours would still not have the same social meaning and value. Above and beyond particular acts of sexist discrimination, patriarchy constitutes underlying structure regulating, organising and positioning men and women in places of different value and with differential access to self-determination. Patriarchal oppression provides a context, structure, support and legitimation for the various sexist acts of discrimination. In turn, it exists relatively independently of sexist acts. As an underlying structure of evaluation, it can be analysed most directly in the examination of the unspoken assumptions lying behind the postulate of apparently sexually neutral terms, Reason, Knowledge, Truth etc.

Third, prevailing models and ideals of theory also participate in *phallocentrism*, which is a discursive or representational form of women's oppression. Phallocentrism conflates the two (autonomous) sexes into a singular 'universal' model which, however, is congruent only with the masculine. Whenever the two sexes are represented in a single, so-called 'human' model, the female or feminine is always represented in male or masculine terms. Phallocentrism is the abstracting, universalising and generalising of masculine attributes so that women's or femininity's concrete specificity and potential for autonomous definition are covered over. It is thus more difficult to locate than sexist or patriarchal commitments, for it renders female autonomy and self-representations impossible and conceals alternatives. It operates as a condition of possibility for statements, methods, axioms and judgments and cannot be so readily illustrated by concrete examples as sexist or patriarchal models. It is a theoretical bedrock of shared assumptions that is so pervasive that it is no longer recognised.

In *sexist* knowledges, women are usually excluded altogether or reduced to the positions of wife, sexual object, carnal being, corporeality, sexuality; or to the functions of maternity, reproduction, fecundity, nature. In its typical forms *patriarchal* theory is not distinguished, as sexism is, by its views on 'woman' as the object of theory, but by its unspoken or repressed, unrepresented, 'feminine' foundations. The feminine may function as metaphor or image, necessary for the theory's foundations, but is incapable of being accepted by it (see also M. Le Doeuff (1980)); while in *phallocentrism*, women are construed on the model of the masculine, whether

in terms of sameness/identity, opposition/distinction, or comple-
mentarity. Women and the feminine function as silent supports for
all modes of male theory.

The three distinct yet historically related feminist responses to the
recognition of the misogyny of prevailing knowledges must also be
briefly described.

In reaction to the sexism of knowledges, there is what could be
called a liberal feminist response. It is usually based on attempts to
eliminate the barriers preventing women from equal inclusion within
theories where they are treated unequally compared to men. Its aim
is the elimination of sexist barriers preventing women from entry
into knowledges (e.g. Kate Millett's attempts to include women
where previously they had been excluded). It develops already
existing patriarchal theories so that they now deal with issues
and objects that have previously been excluded (e.g. Juliet Mitchell's engagement with and reconciliation of feminism and
psychoanalysis or marxism), theories which may exist in a conflictual
relation with feminism. Liberals are committed to the basic
frameworks of male knowledges. Including women as men's equals,
however, is not possible where there is no *theoretical space* for
women's inclusion. Women's specificity and autonomy must be
ignored to seek their commonness or sameness with men. In short,
liberal feminism leaves the patriarchal and phallocentric foundations
of theory uncriticised, orienting itself largely to the elimination of
'discrimination'. Perhaps most significantly in the context of this
paper, liberal feminism is content to continue to treat women as the
objects of theoretical speculation; 'objects' capable of being analysed better by the new discipline, 'Women's Studies', which coun-
terbalances male-biased theories and theoretical norms, creating a
genuinely sexually neutral knowledge. Women's positions cannot be
reversed, nor converted from the position of passive objects of male
knowledges to that of active subjects of knowledge, creating new
methodological criteria and new perspectives to analyse anything
women may choose to speculate on.

In recognising the patriarchal structures informing prevailing
theories, some have responded by initiating what could be regarded
as a 'conservative' feminist backlash against the liberal attempts to
reconcile feminism with traditional forms of knowledge. Conservative feminists, however, affirm the right of judgment of traditional
knowledges over feminist concerns. 'Women's issues' can be readily
incorporated into most mainstream traditions, but they must be
carefully positioned under the hierarchical dominance of mainstream criteria if they are to leave the broader framework unquestioned. Within the discipline of philosophy, for example, feminists

such as Carol MacMillan (1982) and Janet Radcliffe Richards (1982) have come to act as female guardians of male knowledges. Conservatives bring the potential upheavals feminists create back under the control of masculine norms. Such women dutifully serve their masters, using the work of their masters to chastise wayward women for going beyond the acceptable limits of their various disciplines. Male and female conservatives thus react, not only to the positions of liberals or egalitarian feminists but particularly to the more provocative, threatening questions posed by what I will call 'feminisms of autonomy'.

Whether intentionally or not, liberal and conservative feminists bolster and place beyond question the domination of masculine intellectual paradigms. Feminists of autonomy, on the other hand, undertake the challenge to the foundational reliance of knowledges on phallocentric norms, methods and paradigms. In questioning the 'contents' *and* unspoken assumptions, the preferred methods and ideals of phallocentric knowledges, these feminists are committed to the development of new or different forms of knowledge and intellectual inquiry. Within this category, feminists have analysed how concepts, values and methods have been insidiously or associatively related to masculinity, and their excluded, negative counterparts, or 'others', are connected to a devalorised femininity. Within philosophy, for example, the presumedly eternal, timeless values of the discipline—Truth, Reason, Logic, Meaning, Being—have been shown by feminists (such as Lloyd (1984), Irigaray (1985a; 1985b)) to be based on implicit but disavowed relations to their 'others'— poetry, madness, passions, body, non-sense, non-existence. These 'others' are defined as feminine by opposition to the privileged concepts, and their coding in masculine terms is the silent but necessary support of masculine speculation. Many included in this category (such as Irigaray, Cixous, Adrienne Rich, Mary O'Brien) make explicit the inherent masculinity of universal models. This, for many, is only the first step in the development of entirely new forms of theory based on women's experiences and perceptions rather than men's.

The transition from a feminism oriented to equality and opposed to sexism to one based on the specification of differences opposing theoretical phallocentrism, that is, the movement from a sixties to an eighties political consciousness, witnesses the development of new concepts and different goals by women, in their various interrogations of the knowledges in which they were trained. This transition consists in moving from a feminism which takes women as its objects of analysis, using patriarchal theories and frameworks to discuss this hitherto excluded object, to a feminism which takes theory as its object of investigation, using the perspective of women's experiences. This involves a major reversal, transforming women from the position of object to that of subject of knowledge. Feminists who tackled the pervasive phallocentrism of theory risk the recuperative forces of liberal and conservative feminists as well as more openly hostile patriarchal social and theoretical attacks coming from men. Rather than spell out the disagreements and differences between feminist positions here, I prefer to elaborate what within prevailing knowledges autonomy-feminists have problematised, and the positive alternatives some are now beginning to develop.

If phallocentrism relies on universal models to represent both sexes in terms that are appropriate only to one—the male—then feminists need to show *how* these models are invested in unspoken yet privileging assumptions about masculinity. They need to demonstrate that the values, qualities and characteristics are differentially attributed to masculinity and femininity in apparently neutral terms like 'Reason' or 'Truth', terms whose privilege derives from the repression and exclusion of alternatives, rather than from the inherent explanatory power or a priori relevance they claim. An open avowal of the *masculinity of knowledges* is necessary for feminists to clear a space within the 'universal' and to reclaim women's places in it. Ironically, phallocentrism is a *disavowal* or denial of the specificities of the *male sex*, the male body or masculine subjectivity rather than, as is commonly assumed, the imposition of clearly masculine values onto women. In attributing a masculine status to knowledges which present themselves as universal, objective, truthful and neutral, as free of all sexual determination, feminists may for the first time be able to claim a space within theory for women *as women*.

Phallocentric paradigms require clearer specification than I have yet presented. They need further elaboration in order to develop a detailed analysis of feminist challenges to them. Among their most general, interdisciplinary, adherences and commitments are some of the following:

1. The commitment to a perspectiveless, static truth, a truth that evades its own conditions of production, including the *cost by which a statement is considered true*—the invalidations, exclusions, silences imposed on what is not accorded a truth-status. In seeking this monolithic, singular truth, patriarchal knowledges aspire to a knowledge beyond change and beyond the unpredictable events of history, power and desire (cf. M. Foucault, 1972).

2. The commitment to objectivist, 'neutral' concepts of know-

ledge, considered on a *scientistic* model which postulates the fundamental *interchangeability* or *substitutability* of scientific observers,
and thus on the repeatability of experimental or 'objective' (i.e.
verifiable or falsifiable) hypotheses. This position implies the independence of epistemological results from their historical 'origin' in
the labours of particular individuals. How a theory is produced is
considered irrelevant to its truth-status. The criterion of the substitutability of observers, it is believed, is a balance against any 'subjective bias' the individual may bring to his or her conjectures. At
best, in those domains where such an interchangeable observer can
be substituted for the author/knower producing knowledges—that
is, where experimentation under strictly controlled conditions is
possible—there is nevertheless an assumption of *atomistic* notions of
individual knowers, and empiricist conceptions of the procedures of
verification (or falsification) by which a substitute observer confirms
or disconfirms a particular set of results (Thomas Kuhn's critique of
empiricist accounts of scientific knowledge makes clear the naive
presumption that falsification pinpoints a single hypothesis within a
necessarily complex network of assumptions). In any case, within
the social sciences and humanities, the ideal of objectivity and
substitutability becomes meaningless, given the impossibility of repetition or independent confirmation of 'experiments'—that is, the
impossibility of establishing control experiments, and of accounting
for all the variables in any given social and individual object of
analysis —the irreducibility of history and contingent events, and
the particularity and concreteness of the results obtained. In inter-
preting a text, developing a philosophy, analysing a social arrangement, assessing another culture, the conclusions are *unique*, specific,
incapable of independent external or 'objective' judgment. At best,
the imposition of a neutral norm of knowledge, based on a (false)
aspiration to the precision, rigour and repeatability of results presumed in the natural sciences, reduces socio-individual relations to
behaviourist modes of explanation. Behaviourism may *describe* but
it cannot *explain* social and individual relations.

    3.   The commitment to a model of knowledge subordinating the
materiality of language to a merely passive role in representing the
individual's mental processes. Ignoring the productivity and activity
of discursive or representational systems, knowledges can evade
their dependence on images, metaphors, tropes. Language functions
not just to communicate ideas that are independently formulated
but essentially private; they are an ineliminable labour of discursive
production, constitutive and not merely expressive of concepts. The
refusal of language as an active force in knowledge-production is
necessary for knowledges to sustain their self-image as purely

conceptual, enabling the processes of theory-production to remain undiscussed.

4. The commitment to a separation and distance between the subjects and the objects of knowledges, that is, between the knower and the thing known. The subject of knowledge produces true, objective, immediately or directly communicable knowledge because it can separate itself from the social, political, historical and psychic networks within which the individual knower functions and produces theory. The subject is assumed to be unimplicated in and distinct from the objects of analysis. The knowing subject must disinvest all external impingements from the theory he or she produces.

5. The commitment to an intellectual system of concepts whose validity and identity relies on its opposition to other terms. For example, instead of describing reason, truth or objectivity substantively, phallocentric discourses tend to define them in terms of what they are not, by their opposites or 'others'. Reason is surreptitiously defined by claiming it is *not* corporeal, not based on passion, nor madness, nor emotions rather than described in positive or substantive terms. The binary oppositional grid establishes a privileged model of theoretical inquiry where the identity of a privileged term is guaranteed only by the elaboration and expulsion of its opposite or other.

These are only some of the relevant features of male theory that have been challenged by feminists interested in developing alternatives. Instead of abandoning patriarchal theories altogether, (which in any case is today impossible), feminists in the 1980s attempt to negotiate with their historical pervasiveness and dominance in order to devise alternative modes of theorising in which women's interests and not men's are represented. They question the prevailing commitment to the *One*: one truth, one method, one knowledge, one mode of reason, one form of subject. Only by wresting the concept of the one from its exclusive identification with the norms of masculinity can feminists claim the right to speak, think and act *otherwise*. To be different.

I will now turn to the positive production of theories, methods and knowledges more appropriate to and expressive of women's interests than theoretical paradigms operating up to the present. Perhaps the most convenient way of indicating these developments is to point to their correlation with the problems within misogynist theory just outlined: autonomous feminist theories attempt to supersede patriarchal traditions precisely on these major points of disagreement. While well informed about the history of patriarchal knowledges, it supersedes them in presenting different kinds of knowledge. Once again in summary form, I will indicate some of the major lines of development in contemporary feminist researches and methods.

1. Instead of an adherence to truth, objectivity, neutrality and reason, considered in singular or exclusive terms, feminist theory openly admits to its own position as context- and observer-dependent—that is, as historically, politically and sexually *motivated*. This is not however, to suggest that feminists have embarked on false, subjective, irrational or biased projects either, or to sharply differentiate it from patriarchal knowledges. On the contrary, by the affirmation of its own *perspectivism*, the fact that theories elaborate particular points of view, specific aims and values, it accepts its own historicity. Feminist theory can acknowledge its own interests openly as those of women; patriarchal theory, by contrast, is unable to admit its masculine interests without risking its status and rationale.

2. Feminist theory is neither subjective nor objective, neither relativist nor absolutist: it occupies the *middle ground* excluded by oppositional categories. Theory is *relational* rather than relativist: it occupies a position (that of the sexed subject) and is connected to other practices, rather than, in relativism, having no fixed position. It is neither neutral nor indifferent to individual particularities (as the objectivist or absolutist maintains), nor purely free-floating, a position any subject can occupy at will (as the subjectivist or relativist maintains). Thus, it is neither a question of adopting ahistorical, universal criteria nor an 'anything goes' attitude for feminist theory in its problematisations of male knowledges. Absolutism and relativism both ignore the concrete functioning of power relations and the necessity of occupying *a position*, particularly a changeable one, with regard to the socio-political context of theory production. Feminist theory establishes its own criteria of validity rather than accepts those inherited from patriarchal tradition. Very briefly, these may consist, not in objectivity considered as substitutability of similar observers, but on intersubjective understandings between different subjects, a shared or collective response to new material. Feminist theory may subvert or reinscribe the theoretical traditions out of which it has developed, using the *intertextual* effects of misogynist discourses against their own aims.

3. Feminist theory is crucially engaged with the question of language and representation in their material and political effects. In challenging prevailing knowledges, feminists also tackle the question of the language available for theoretical purposes and the constraints it places on what can be said. Rather than ignore language as a material, active, productive system, feminists are clearly

concerned with creating new modes of expression, new discursive styles, new enunciative positions to experiment with a language that may be able to articulate women's specificity and avoid the strategic deafness hitherto common in male paradigms. As a material entity, language is seen as a borderline process, hovering between theory and practice, and the material and the ideal, being a form of theoretical practice, a practice involving labour and risk in analogous forms to the production of other material objects. This may help to reconceptualise the nature of intellectual labour, so that it is no longer considered a privileged reflection on practices, but is instead seen as one practice amid and in relation to others.

4. Instead of presuming a gulf or space between the subject and the object of knowledge, feminist theory accepts their continuity and interrelatedness. The gap between the subject and object is an effect of male interests. This enables theory to regard itself as purely conceptual and not as a material and institutional practice. The standard form of knowing subject is considered disembodied, non-historical, non-sexual and non-social, a subject divided from itself in forms of self-knowledge. The gulf separating the subject as knower from the subject as the object known is the gulf of male reflection and speculation, the space of meta-language and meta-theory. This idealised space, the prerequisite of the knowing. objective, rational subject, is the space based on the male disavowal of his body and his sex, and the assumption that he occupies a neutral position. Feminist theory on the other hand readily accepts the complicity of subject and object in knowledge-production. It openly accepts that different subjects of knowledge may produce different forms of knowledge. Feminism seems able to accept the *sexualisation of discourse*—that all discourses are produced from and themselves occupy sexually coded positions.

5. In recognising the implicit hierarchical structure in binary oppositions, which accord positive value to the primary term and regard the secondary term as its debased counterpart, feminist theory recognises the collusion of these dichotomies with the fundamental one underlying them and providing their context: the distinction between male/female or masculine/feminine. In questioning the implicit value and domination of the binary structure, feminists will attempt to occupy the impossible, paradoxical position of the middle ground, the ground left uncovered by the oppositional structure—being both subject and object, self and other, reason and passion, mind and body rather than one or the other.

Going beyond the problematic assumptions of patriarchal texts and phallocentric traditions (in so far as this is possible), feminist theory effects an entire 'transvaluation' of intellectual values. In posing the question of the inherent *sexualisation* of knowledges, discourses and representations, it upsets the ideals of a universalising rational consciousness by demonstrating its *sexually* particular masculine allegiances. Feminists of autonomy are not interested in developing a 'more universal' or overarchingly 'human' perspective but are content with a narrower scope and aspirations: these do not aim to develop neutral, general, position-less theory—which is simply theory that disavows its position—but theories to which such an acknowledgement poses no threat.

When patriarchal texts are able to accept their sexual limits and their representative relation to one sex only, feminist theory can embark on a more genuine interchange with it than has yet been possible. Until knowledges can make clear their limits and restrictions (in ways that do not necessarily limit their possibilities of autonomous representations) feminist theory must remain both a critical watch-dog, signalling patriarchal infringements into the domain of the universal, and a constructive yet provisional reclamation of the territory cleared from male domination, a territory which now needs to be explored from different points of view, with different methods and interests.

Feminists who concentrate only on the sexism of knowledges are limited in their effects: even if all overt expressions of woman-hating, all clear exclusions of women, all discriminatory proposals concerning women are eliminated, knowledges do not include women in the same ways they include men. Searching out and eliminating sexism will, at best, result in a more insidious and less easily identified form of exclusion or unfair containment of women. It may remove the *symptoms* or *manifestations* of misogyny, but not its operative causes. Investments in patriarchal power relations become thus less visible and possibly thus more powerful (this seems to be the problem with 'reformist' or bureaucratised feminism which seeks *only* equal opportunity, or only egalitarianism without questioning the positions women find themselves in as a consequence of their absorption into male-defined positions). Moreover, even an attempted 'androgenisation' of knowledges and methodologies—integrating masculine and feminine principles—leaves the character of these principles unquestioned. This remains problematic in so far as *both* male and female attributes are defined in patriarchal terms.

Combating the patriarchal commitments of knowledges, structuralist feminists, like liberal feminists, are also committed to transforming patriarchal into sexually neutral frameworks. In general, those feminists who make out the most convincing arguments for the problems with, say, marxism or psychoanalysis, also maintain that these knowledges can be reformulated in non-oppressive, nonpatriarchal terms. Once again, feminists remain intellectual 'house-keepers', clearing away the 'mess' produced by men in their attempts to present the Truth. While some of elements of the patriarchal discourses are criticised and rejected, their overall values are not questioned. Such feminists thus direct their energies towards bolstering and improving, correcting or reinterpreting knowledges so that they are genuinely neutral or universal, applicable equally to both sexes.

By contrast, it is only what I have described as a third, or autonomist position that questions the very framework and foundation of prevailing knowledges by developing thoroughgoing critiques and displacements. While remaining as concerned with misogynist theories, this mode of feminist analysis is *not* committed to the upholding of any particular elements of phallocentric knowledges. Phallocentric knowledges must be understood by feminists, even if only to adequately move beyond them. These feminist in(ter)ventions aim at establishing an *openly* sexualised body of knowledges, knowledges whose enunciative positions and political perspectives are capable of being directly articulated. Feminist knowledges, on this model, are *not* competing intellectual paradigms, vying with patriarchal knowledges for primacy. They are *different*, possibly even incommensurable, knowledges, knowledges which make contrary claims about truth, objectivity, confirmation, neutrality. They are knowledges which constitute not only Truth, but also autonomy and political effectivity.

It remains to be seen what will be articulated in this new space of enunciation cleared of masculine impingements. This much is clear: for men to take back what they have produced and for us to see that this is only half of the productive possibilities of knowledge, perception or practice, is in itself one of the most dramatic revolutions to have occurred in western knowledges. It is the acknowledgement of a limit and a foundational debt that has up to now remained un-spoken, that patriarchal knowledges must accept if there is to be any further development in the directions it may have initiated. In exploring the language of femininity and autonomy, feminist theory has introduced the possibility of a dialogue between knowledges now accepted as masculine, and the 'alien' or 'other' voice of women. If the theoretical past has up to now been men's, the future, the direction forward, is now up to women. Feminist questions in the future may then need to turn away from women's exclusion and submersion in patriarchal paradigms to turn instead to the question of the *ethics of sexual exchange* in knowledges, an ethics of exchanges between beings who are different, who occupy different positions, and take up different perspectives. Only when women are able to take up autonomously chosen and defined perspectives and positions can there be more encompassing knowledges, knowledges capable of including both sexes, not through their homogenisation, but in full recognition and acceptance of their heterogeneity.

> Sexual difference would constitute the horizon of worlds of a still unknown fecundity ... Fecundity of birth and regenerescence for amorous partners, but more the production of a new epoch of thought, art, poetry, language ... (Irigaray, 1984:1)

PART III
WOMEN IN AUSTRALIA

MARIE DE LEPERVANCHE

Introduction

Analyses of Australian society have changed considerably over the last 50 years. They needed to. Most commonly, Australia was represented as white, male and British. This image persisted even well into the 1960s, when popularised constructs of the bronzed Aussie/Anzac/bushman gradually gave way to a more suburbanised (but equally male-dominated) image, in which women (as well as migrants and aboriginal peoples) were ignored or absent. Australia was characterised as a classless (that is, a homogeneous middle-class egalitarian) society in which the ethos of mateship and the myth of 'the promised land' presented a rosy picture of an 'Australian Way of Life' that refused to find a place for the disinherited, the poor, blacks, migrants, women. In the 1970s class analyses began to question and challenge this myth of classless equality, and government policy changed during this period from integrationism to multiculturalism, giving migrants a voice. But women still remained largely absent from mainstream representations, relegated to mere appendages and helpmates for men and ignored as such in political and theoretical strategies and policies.

Feminist research, however, revealed women's usually unrecognised contributions to Australia's past and present. Furthermore, they explored and created new perspectives and frameworks, which question the most widespread and firmly held assumptions about Australian history and social life yet provide procedures and techniques, forms of analysis and research to actively include women where they had been ignored. No longer content to simply add women to existing agendas, feminist scholars problematised the ways in which Australia has hitherto been represented and analysed.

In the year of its bicentenary, there is all the more reason to further develop feminist perspectives on Australian culture, on the use of stereotyped representations of 'the Australian' (the ocker), and on the appropriation of these by implicitly masculinist ideals and values. In analysing and assessing an Australian 'national character' feminists have already begun to indicate that the ways in which Australia is theorised—whether historically, sociologically, anthropologically, politically etc.—are male-defined; they have also begun to indicate the possibility of developing new research methods, new theoretical questions and new sources of data that can take into account the specific effects of the sex-gender system on the way Australia is represented.

The essays in this section extend the work of two scholars who have been especially active in analysing the significance of gender in Australian social life. Both Cass and Curthoys focus on the material conditions of women's existence and the ways in which sex differences cross class boundaries to link women through their shared roles and functions in the family. In addressing the 'feminisation of poverty', Cass questions the research of feminists outside Australia who simplify women's particular experiences of poverty or reduce it to more conventional interpretations. Curthoys looks to women workers to ask why they have been paid at different rates from men. In doing so, she points to the specificities of Australian cultural history, that is, to why it is difficult to generalise from other contexts to gain an understanding of Australian economic and social practices.

There is nothing unusual about the inclusion of women in poverty statistics, but the debate initiated by feminists regarding the feminisation of poverty has revealed a previously unrecognised proportion or degree of female poverty. Instead of focusing on the particular impoverishment of female-headed families, as Anglo-American feminists tend to, Cass points to the increasing incidence of poverty among women and children in all kinds of households, including those headed by men. Instead of presuming the impoverishment of the single-parent (and thus sexually neutral) family, Cass demonstrates that it is being a female more than being the head of a single-parent family that affects job opportunities and the likelihood of poverty. She substantiates her arguments with supporting data on sex inequalities in Australia which challenge many methods and assumptions in more mainstream forms of class analysis. For example, the concept of household as an 'income unit' assumes that household members have equal access to income. But, as Cass argues, this methodological device all too easily hides the poverty of dependent wives and their children within male-headed households.

Extending her researches on women and labour, Curthoys looks at the equal pay campaign since the 1940s. In answering the question of why women were paid less than men, she considers explanations focusing on employer strategies for dividing the labour market to their own advantage, as well as on those of workers themselves clinging to the notion of the irreplaceability of their skills, with the result that hierarchies develop in the labour market, as do demarcation disputes. Neither type of explanation, according to Curthoys, gives a satisfactory answer to why women have been paid less than men.

Central to her argument is the analysis of women's roles in unpaid caring work which has, in turn, meant that women's relations to the labour market are very different from men's. Although women's wages have improved relative to the male rate more recently, these may well result from the interlocking of gender and class relations. Where class analyses tend to homogenise the working class and tend to assume a male worker, Curthoys notes the differences between men and women, and between right- and left-wing unionists, and within various women's organisations, all of which were active in the equal pay campaign. This reveals a complex set of relations between gender and class in Australian social life that require reconsideration of their prevailing norms and functions. The analysis of the movement for wage justice must recognise gender's role as a crucial variable in theoretical analysis and political struggle.

Cass and Curthoys both move beyond patriarchal accounts of work, wage justice and poverty; each underlines the necessity of understanding the significance of gender in both the experience and the analysis of social inequalities. In doing so, they signal major revisions that may need to be made to existing representations of Australia and Australian social and economic life if they are not only to include women but also to accommodate and change according to new principles that enable women to be more adequately theorised.

BETTINA CASS

8   The feminisation of poverty

The notion of the 'feminisation of poverty' has achieved a certain academic legitimacy and acquired some political recognition in recent years, largely as a result of English and American feminist scholarship (Scott, 1984; Rose, 1984; Nelson, 1984; Pearce and McAdoo, 1981). In Australian writing the language has been more cautious: the concern has been with the vulnerability of women and their children to impoverishment and the overrepresentation of women and their families among those excluded from full social, economic and political participation (Roe, 1975; 1983; Bryson, 1983; Montague and Stephens, 1985).

Are there advantages in the use of the more dramatic terminology, advantages for theoretical developments in poverty research, accurate measurement and informed social policy debate? Equally as pertinently, are there advantages for a more adequate comprehension of the position of women in the distributions of income, wealth and other resources? Posing the questions in these terms is predicated on two assumptions: that there is an essential interrelationship between theory, measurement and policy. The theory of poverty which I adopt has consequences not only for accurate measurement, but also for the formulation of policies which will combat the harsher manifestations of economic inequality (Townsend, 1979a). My second assumption is that only a relative deprivation conception of poverty is able to make the connections between, on the one hand, income which is insufficient to meet the needs of the unit dependent on it and, on the other hand, the unequal distributions of income, wealth, services and other resources in society (Townsend, 1979b; Tulloch, 1980; Allen, 1983). People suffer poverty when they have insufficient income, wealth, access to services and amenities to participate fully in the customary life of society. Poverty is a set of life circumstances characterised by economic, social and political marginality (Rose, 1984).

What then do we understand the 'feminisation of poverty' to mean? In a recent issue of the feminist journal *Signs* (Winter, 1984) devoted to the subject 'Women and Poverty', the concept is taken to mean first, that the rate of poverty among women-headed households has increased since the early 1970s and, second, that women-headed households now constitute an increased proportion of the poor (Nelson, 1984; Pearce and McAdoo, 1981). It is not merely that women and their dependants are overrepresented among the poor, but that this process has become more prevalent in the last decade as a result of recessionary labour market changes, changes in patterns of marriage, separation, divorce and family formation, and contractionary public policies which have eroded both job opportunities and the adequacy of income maintenance programs for women household heads (Kamerman, 1984; Smith, 1984; Zinn and Sarri, 1984).

This paper analyses the available Australian data to find out whether the proportion of women-headed income units in poverty has increased in the period 1972/73 to 1981/82, and also whether women-headed units constitute an increased proportion of the poor in the current period. However, while testing these propositions, it is important not to lose sight of two issues which are critical for adequate measurement and explanation. The first is that the 'feminisation of poverty' must not be taken to mean that women's poverty is a new phenomenon: rather, our attention has been directed to a recently *recognised* phenomenon, thrown into dramatic relief by a recessionary period and constraints on welfare expenditures.

Women's economic insecurity has sturdy historical roots in Australia, as a consequence of unequal wage structures, the reinforcement of dependency by industrial policies, marriage law and the assumptions embedded in social security provisions (Roe, 1983; Baldock, 1983; Bryson, 1983; Shaver, 1983). But the extent of the hardships borne by women have tended to be hidden in the daily domestic struggles and sacrifices which they have made to manage scarce household resources (Power, 1980; Travers, 1983).

This leads to the second issue which tends to be overlooked in discussions of women in poverty. It is conventional to contrast the poverty of women-headed income units with that of male-headed units (among whom married couples are included) (Commission of Inquiry into Poverty, 1975). But it then becomes possible to ignore the numbers and conditions of poor women in *married-couple* families, whose job it usually is to manage insufficient household income. As Hilary Rose has put it in respect of English evidence, 'Women carry the burden of poverty, the exhausting labour of the micro-administration of insufficient resources for their families and for themselves' (Rose, 1984:1). This observation is as pertinent for women in poor married-couple households as in single-parent households. To attribute women's poverty predominantly to single parenthood, separation, divorce and widowhood, as is often done (Kamerman, 1984), is to place too much emphasis on the apparent security of marriage and to ignore the *class* inequalities which have increased poverty rates for men and women and their children in a period of labour market downturn.

THEORETICAL DEBATES: CLASS, GENDER AND
LIFE-CYCLE EXPLANATIONS OF POVERTY

Although this paper focuses on gender inequalities that result in insufficient income for women to participate fully in the customary life of society, it is essential to consider gender inequalities with class inequalities and with life-cycle factors in order to construct a comprehensive analysis of the causes and characteristics of poverty.

While class theories of poverty have been well developed, at least since the early 1970s, poverty research tended to ignore significant gender inequalities until the early 1980s. It is the relevance of gender that I address particularly in this chapter. In Australia, critiques of the Commission of Inquiry into Poverty Reports of 1975 (Bryson, 1977; Tulloch, 1979; Halladay, 1975) and more recent research in England and Europe (Townsend, 1979b; George and Lawson, 1980) have emphasised the genesis of poverty in the unequal distribution of labour market power and wealth. People with the weakest market power suffer low pay and insecurity when in employment, a much greater likelihood of unemployment, of impoverishment in the event of sickness, accident and disability, and of accumulated disadvantage on retirement with no, or with inadequate, retirement benefits. The Poverty Commission's First Main Report (1975) noted that three-quarters of the poor in 1972/73 were outside the workforce because of old age, sickness, invalidity, single parenthood or, in a very small proportion of cases, because of unemployment. Poverty was therefore attributed mainly to receipt of inadequate government pensions and benefits, a condition exacerbated by the absence of private home ownership and, in the case of women (comprising three-quarters of the poor aged), discontinuous labour force participation and a lifetime of unpaid household work.

Despite the significant body of scholarship addressing the class-based genesis of poverty, linking it to the unequal distribution of income and wealth (Richardson, 1979; Wild, 1978; Atkinson, 1975), official poverty research in Australia and the OECD countries continued to use, either explicitly or implicitly, the concept of the 'disability group' to categorise the poor (Roberti, 1979; SWPS, 1981). This usage conflates demographic characteristics like old age and large family size with de facto labour force characteristics: sickness, invalidity, unemployment and single parenthood which entail full or partial exclusion from paid employment: it therefore confuses life-cycle and labour market theories of the causes of poverty. This usage also focuses attention on the characteristics of the 'poor', on their 'disabilities', as if these characteristics inhered in them rather than in the disabling market processes and public policies which exclude *certain* categories of workers, parents and the aged from full economic, social and political participation.

The increase in the rate and duration of unemployment since 1974 has drawn into joblessness those people with the weakest market power and who are much more likely than the employed to be low-paid when in work (Whiteford, 1982; Cass and Garde, 1983). This in turn has further reduced the income of families with an unemployed breadwinner or breadwinners, increasing their risk of poverty (Cox, 1982; Manning, 1985). Manning emphasises quite correctly that when the Poverty Commission reported, '"the dominant factor which determined poverty was whether or not the head of the income unit is able to work." Nowadays, with the end of full employment, we would say that the dominant factor is whether or not somebody in the income unit is able to find work' (Manning, 1985:131). The end of 'full employment' since 1974 has increased the rate of poverty of individuals and of families with children, those in the prime of working life. A large proportion of the labour force and of the population in general has been drawn into the ranks of pensioners and beneficiaries (Cass and O'Loughlin, 1983; Sheehan and Stricker, 1983). These processes have illuminated the class-based nature of poverty, which was as pertinent in 1972/73 as in the early 1980s, although it was not as immediately apparent when old age, 'misadventure' and 'injudicious fertility' were linked with inadequate income.

Identifying the income units most vulnerable to poverty in 1978/79, the Social Welfare Policy Secretariat (SWPS) named the long-term unemployed and single-parent families, both of whose chances for full-year, full-time work are thwarted by job shortages: the chances of work for single parents are also affected by the scarcity of childcare services (Cox, 1982). However, it is not sufficient to conclude, as the SWPS report does, that the employment of at least one adult in full-year, full-time work (or even better, two adults in employment) is the best safeguard against poverty, without also noting that the chances of job security are not randomly distributed. First, full-year, full-time employment is a typically male prerogative, and fits much less well with the typical labour force experience of wives and mothers (Eccles, 1984). Second, the experience of unemployment has been concentrated in working-class families, households and regions (Cass and Garde, 1984). That is, access to the major resource required for secure and adequate income, a full-year, full-time job, is restricted on the bases of gender, family responsibilities and market power. This perspective assumes that position in the labour market and the state of the labour market are the prime determinants of income security, and that we must look in the first instance to the primary distribution of earnings in any analysis of poverty.

This approach brings into focus the position of women who, because of their socially expected domestic and parenting responsibilities, tend to be excluded from access to full-year, full-time employment for a certain period of their vigorous adult lives, and who are expected to be either partially or totally dependent on another income-earner.

Gender-based explanations of poverty emphasise the 'disabling' outcomes of the inequalities resulting from women's dependency as household workers and childcarers. Non-market caring work is accorded no monetary value, but is used to legitimate women's industrial marginality, discontinuous labour force participation and relatively low pay in sex-segmented occupations and industries (Bryson, 1983; Baldock, 1983; Rose, 1984; Scott, 1984). These inequalities have their effect through the female life-cycle for single women, mothers who do not live with a male partner and for older women.

In Australia, official poverty research—the Commission of Inquiry into Poverty (1975, 1976) and the Social Welfare Policy Secretariat's *Report on Poverty Measurement* (1981)—provides data which, after re-analysis, show the continuing overrepresentation of women-headed income units among the poor. Yet, apart from categorising single women and mother-headed families as 'disability groups', the official reports provide no explanation of women's relative deprivation. But the benchmark figures are very useful. The Poverty Commission found that in 1972/73, before the onset of the recession and before the marked increase in the formation of single-parent families, women-headed income units constituted 22 per cent of all income units but 55 per cent of all units in poverty (Table 1). The

Table 1 Poverty in income units by sex of head, 1972/73 and 1981/82 using Detailed Henderson equivalence scale n = 1,000

Income unit type	1972/73 (excludes self-employed)			1981/83 (includes self-employed)		
	Below pov. line	Population	% in poverty	Below pov. line	Population	% in poverty
One-person						
Male	59.0	535.0	11	173.1	1,526.3	11
Female	171.0	725.0	24	157.4	1,435.9	11
TOTAL	230.10	1,260.0	18	330.5	2,962.2	11
Sole-parent						
Male-headed	4.5	28.0	16	7.1	37.6	19
Female-headed	49.5	132.0	38	119.2	237.6	50
TOTAL	54.0	160.0	34	126.3	275.2	46
Married-couple						
No children	14.0	736.0	2	72.8	1,439.3	5
1 child	26.7	921.0	3	46.0	594.4	8
2 children	26.7	921.0	3	82.3	822.8	10
3 or more children	30.7	423.0	7	103.7	538.7	19
TOTAL	71.4	2,080.0	3	304.8	3,395.3	9
All adult income units	399.4	3,916.0	10	761.5	6,632.8	11
All persons	781.2	9,527.0	8	1,905.7	14,536.8	13
All children	254.6	3,182.5	8	839.3	4,508.8	19

Sources: Commission of Inquiry into Poverty *First Main Report* 1975; P. Gallagher, *Work in Progress on Poverty in Australia* 1985

rate of poverty for women-headed income units was 26 per cent, compared with 5 per cent for male-headed units; the rate of poverty for female sole parents and their children was 38 per cent compared with 16 per cent for male sole parents. Women-headed families comprised 9 per cent of all families with children in the population, but 44 per cent of all families in poverty.

The critical issue is to find out whether this marked over-representation of women-headed income units among the poor in 1972/73 has been *reduced* in the decade which saw the implementation of several major reforms. These were the introduction of equal pay for work of equal value between 1972 and 1975; the introduction in 1973 of the Supporting Mother's Benefit (later the Supporting Parents' Benefit), and the introduction of family allowances in 1976. All these measures, particularly the equal pay decisions, have resulted in a greater share of overall income distribution to women, from 38 per cent of men's income in 1973/74 to 48 per cent of men's income in 1981/82 (see Table 2).

There have, however, been countervailing processes: between 1973/74 and 1981/82 the proportion of women whose principal source of income is pension or benefit increased from 41 per cent to 46 per cent of all female income recipients in that nine-year period. In the same period the proportion of men whose principal source of income is pension or benefit also increased substantially from 9 per cent to 18 per cent, but women remain 2.5 times more likely than men to be dependent on social security for their major source of income (Table 2). In respect of earnings from wages and salary, the share of women's average annual earnings compared with men's increased from 52 per cent to 64 per cent, following the implementation of the equal pay decisions. Women continue to receive on average only two-thirds of men's earnings, mainly because of their lower rates of full-year, full-time employment. However, even the proportion of women's to men's average weekly *full-time* earnings hovered around 76 per cent from 1975 to 1983, because of the impossibility of implementing equal pay in a sex-segmented labour market where women are employed in a narrow range of relatively low paid occupations (Jones, 1984).

There is very little recent information about the gender divisions of wealth holding, except in relation to private home ownership. In 1982 women household heads were less likely than male household heads to be home owners or purchasers (60 per cent compared with 75 per cent), while women were much more likely to be renting, particularly in the private market (36 per cent of women were renters, 26 per cent private tenants, compared with 23 per cent of men renters and 19 per cent private tenants). These gender differences were even stronger when household heads had responsibility for dependants: 47 per cent of women were owners/purchasers compared with 78 per cent of men, while a very high proportion (53 per cent) of women were renting, 30 per cent in the private rental market (ABS, 1984). There are demonstrated connections between low income, lack of home ownership, renting in the private market, and poverty (Vipond, 1986).

Because of women's unequal access to labour market participation, income and wealth, and because of the vulnerability of dependency associated with unpaid caring work, gender inequalities must be placed along with class inequalities at the centre of poverty analysis. These two components of explanation cannot be reduced or subsumed by the other.

The third element in a comprehensive explanation of poverty is concerned with age, with identification of the most vulnerable period of the life-cycle. Recent Australian research has noted a shift in vulnerability away from the aged and towards families with dependent children, resulting in a marked increase in children's poverty. This trend was first emphasised by the Social Welfare Policy Secretariat's *Report on Poverty Measurement* (1981) which found that the share of poverty borne by families with children increased from 34 per cent in 1973/74 to 41 per cent in 1978/79, while the share borne by single people without dependants also increased from 18 per cent to 34 per cent. It was the share of poverty borne by the old aged (i.e. those entitled to the aged pension) which *fell* from 42 per cent to 18 per cent.

Two processes have converged in increasing poverty rates for families with children: first, the increased number and proportion of single parents whose employment rates have fallen since 1974 and who are dependent on pension or benefit. The second is the impact of labour market downturn on married-couple families with children, and the consequent drawing of a greatly increased proportion of them into the social security system. In 1973 there were approximately 180 000 children of pensioners and beneficiaries, comprising 4 per cent of all dependent children; in 1984 this number had increased to approximately 765 000 children, comprising 18 per cent of children.

This increase took place in a period which saw a deterioration in the real value of all components of income support for children (particularly since 1976), while the real value of the base rate of pension for adults rose (Harding and Whiteford, 1985).

It is misleading to separate the life-cycle shift in the impact of poverty, which resulted in the increased poverty of children and their parents, from class and gender explanations. While poverty rates for older women without dependants have fallen and the poverty of female sole parents has increased, similar gender-based inequalities are operating. Another shift has been from older retired couples to younger couples where neither partner is in full-year, full-time work, but similar class inequalities in access to secure employment and income are involved. However, the life-cycle issue raises a *separate* consideration: the adequacy of income support for *children* through the tax/benefit system, that is, the adequacy of redistribution to that part of the life cycle when there is no social expectation of participation in the labour force.

FACTORS AFFECTING THE RATE AND THE IMPACT OF POVERTY: 1974–1984

I turn now to an examination of the economic processes and social policies which have tended to exacerbate the rate of poverty since 1974, and which have markedly changed the composition of the poor. There are five:

The increase in the rate and duration of unemployment

In 1974 there were 32 000 people in receipt of unemployment benefit, comprising 0.5 per cent of the labour force. By 1984 the number of beneficiaries was 584 500, comprising 8 per cent of the labour force. Of even greater consequence for the impoverishment associated with unemployment is the increased average duration of spells of unemployment: whereas in 1974 only 18 per cent of beneficiaries were receiving benefit for more than six months, by 1984 this proportion had risen to 53 per cent and a third of beneficiaries had been doing so for more than one year (Department of Social Security, 1985).

This is particularly significant in the light of the available data on the relatively low incomes of the unemployed when in work, and the concentration of unemployment in families. But the numbers receiving invalid and widows' pensions, sickness and supporting parents' benefit also increased more rapidly than in the previous decade, again as a result of the shortage of jobs in the recession (Sheehan and Stricker, 1983). In 1974 pensioners and beneficiaries comprised 11.5 per cent of the population; in 1984 they comprised 20.8 per cent (Department of Social Security, 1985).

The increase in the numbers and the proportion of single-parent families in receipt of pensions and benefits

Between 1974 and 1983 there was an increase of 62 per cent in the numbers of single-parent families, from 182 500 to 295 300, that is, from 9 per cent to 13.6 per cent of all families with dependent children. But there was a much greater increase, more than 100 per cent, in the numbers of single parents who were not employed.

Women sole parents' participation rate fell from 45 per cent to 39 per cent, men's from 95 per cent to 80 per cent. Although the substantial decline in participation rates for both women and men reflect the shortage of job opportunities in the economic downturn (and for men the introduction of eligibility for supporting parents' benefit), women's participation rate remains half that of their male counterparts. Similarly, although the rate of all sole parents' dependence on social security increased significantly between 1974 and 1983, from 65 per cent of women and 10 per cent of men to 84 per cent of women and 22 per cent of men, women remained four times as likely as men to be receiving pensions or benefits, accounting for 96 per cent of all sole-parent beneficiaries (Cass and O'Loughlin, 1984).

The disparity between male and female single parents' take-up of pension or benefit demonstrates that it is female gender, rather than single parenthood per se, which affects the job chances of single parents. Women with sole care of dependent children confront a sex-segmented labour market which offers a narrow range of jobs at relatively low rates of pay. In addition, women sole parents are much less likely than their male counterparts to have formal post-school job qualifications, and they are also responsible on average for more and younger children. These barriers to employment are reinforced by an ideology which prescribes dependency for women in a couple relationship and which does not facilitate independent full-time employment when a relationship ends (Montague and Stephens, 1985). Studies in the United States, the United Kingdom and in Australia show that women employed during marriage and before separation or divorce are much more likely to be employed, and much less likely to be poor, when they become heads of single-parent families compared with women who had little employment experience during their marriage (Rainwater, 1979; David, Mac-Leod and Murch, 1983; McDonald, 1985). These findings indicate that labour force participation during a couple relationship and after it ends is one of the critical safeguards against poverty for a woman and her children. However, the only Australian study on the economic consequences of divorce shows that it remains an atypical pattern for women to have a continuous employment history, and that time spent at home caring for children has a very strong capacity to depreciate income-earning potential (McDonald, 1985).

Increased housing costs, both of rent and of interest
rates which are particularly onerous in the period of
early family formation

Public housing has remained the 'Cinderella' of Australian housing policy. Long waiting lists for public authority housing in the States

Table 2 Principal source of income, gross mean annual income and ratio of female to male mean incomes, 1968/69, 1973/74, 1978/79, 1981/82

		Wages and Salaries	Own business trade, farm or profession	Share in partnership	Govt soc. sec. benefit or other transfer	Super-annuation annuity	Interest, rent, dividend	Other	Total
1968/69 (%) gaining principal source of income from:	M	76.2	6.3	6.7	7.3	1.2	2.1	0.2	100
	W	42.8	1.5	4.9	41.7	0.8	7.2	1.2	100
Mean annual income ($)	M	3450	4780	4480	860	2750	2880	3010	3390
	W	1670	2050	3080	400	1640	1160	1820	1130
ratio W:M	R	0.48	0.43	0.69	0.47	0.60	0.40	0.60	0.35
1973/74 (%) gaining principal source of income from:	M	75.1	6.2	6.3	9.3	1.0	1.9	0.3	100.1
	W	46.1	1.4	4.8	41.0	0.5	5.3	0.9	100
Mean annual income ($)	M	6060	7870	6500	1440	4310	4000	4130	5710
	W	3160	3950	4770	740	2470	1540	2430	2160
	R	0.52	0.50	0.73	0.51	0.57	0.39	0.59	0.38
1978/79 (%) gaining principal source of income from:	M	67.1	5.8	8.3	15.0	1.4	1.9	0.6	100.1
	W	41.4	1.3	6.6	43.2	0.5	6.2	0.7	99.9
Mean annual income ($)	M	11570	13580	10560	3040	9310	6910	6270	10170
	W	7050	8170	8640	1980	6760	3210	4830	4720
	R	0.61	0.60	0.82	0.65	0.73	0.46	0.77	0.46

133/82 (%) gaining principal source of income from:							
M	57.0	15.9	included on left	18.2	1.5	5.9	1.5	100
W	32.9	9.1	included on left	45.5	0.7	10.3	1.5	100
mean annual income ($) M	16 910	13 301	included on left	3 741	12 450	5 564	4 587	13 020
W	10 852	9 888		2 626	10 407	4 204	4 045	6 230
R	0.64	0.74		0.70	0.84	0.76	0.88	0.48

Sources: Commonwealth Bureau of Census Statistics, *Income Distribution, 1968–69*, Part 1, Ref. No. 17.6
ABS *Income Distribution, 1973–74*, Part 1, Cat. No. 6502.0
ABS *Income Distribution, Australia, 1978–79*, Cat. No. 6502.0
ABS *Income of Individuals, Australia, 1981–82* (Preliminary) Cat. No. 6501.0

Notes: *In 1981/82, the two categories, own business, trade etc. and share in partnership were aggregated.

Table 3 Labour force status and poverty rates, 1981/82

	Full-year, full-time employment, % below poverty line	Full-year, part-time employment, % below poverty line	Full-year unemployment, % below poverty line	Full-year not in labour force, % below poverty line	Over 25 weeks unemployed, % below poverty line	TOTAL, % below poverty line
One-person income units	2	17	33	18	15	11
Single-parent income units	6	31	62	66	55	46
Married-couple income units, husband's labour force status	6	14	64	13	45	9
Married-couple income units, wife's labour force status	5	14	18	11	14	9

Sources: Computer tables supplied by P. Gallagher from Policy Coordination Unit
ABS *Income and Housing Survey, 1981–82*.

have forced low-income households to remain in private rental accommodation (Paris, Williams and Stimson, 1985).

*Decreased real value of government income
support for children*

Inadequate and unindexed child-related components of pensions and benefits and unindexed family allowances have resulted in a decline in the real value of all income support for children. This has most adversely affected the position of pensioners and beneficiaries with children. In the same period the real value of the indexed base rate of pension rose. Between 1976–77 and 1984–85 the real value of

- additional pension and benefit for children fell by 9 per cent
- mothers/guardians allowance fell by 20 per cent
- family allowances fell by 23 per cent
- single base rate of pension rose by 8 per cent
- married couple base rate of pension rose by 9 per cent (Harding and Whiteford, 1985)

In this period the disposable incomes of pensioners and beneficiaries rose modestly in real terms, mainly because of indexation factors. In contrast, the real disposable incomes of pensioners and beneficiaries with children declined, particularly for those with greater numbers of children and for single parents because of the significant proportion of their total benefit payment (about one-third where there is one child) which is not indexed. In addition, failure to increase family allowances has resulted in a decline in the real disposable income of all families with children compared with individuals and couples without children in the same income group.

*Non-indexation of unemployment benefit
for single people*

A further major element of social security policy which has adversely affected the income situation of adults excluded from paid employment was the withdrawal from indexation in 1978 of the unemployment benefit for single adults without dependants. Although this payment again became subject to routine indexation and incremental catch-up increases from May 1984, its value declined in real terms by 13 per cent in the period 1976/77 to 1983/84.

PEOPLE IN POVERTY 1981/82

How have these factors affected the extent and characteristics of poverty in the early 1980s?

The analysis of poverty used in this paper is derived from income distribution data for 1981/82 provided by the Australian Bureau of Statistics, and from the use of the detailed Henderson Poverty Line (Appendix 1). Table 1 shows a small increase in the proportion of income units in poverty in the period 1972/73 to 1981/82 (from 10 per cent to 11 per cent), but a greater increase in the proportion of *people in* poverty, from 8 per cent to 13 per cent of the adult population, and an even greater increase in the proportion of children in poverty, from 8 per cent to 19 per cent of children. These changes have arisen because of the decrease in the overall rate of poverty of one-person income units, in effect older women, and the marked increase in the poverty of families with children. The proportion of women-headed sole-parent families in poverty increased from 38 per cent to 50 per cent; and the proportion of male-headed sole-parent families in poverty increased from 16 per cent to 19 per cent. Poverty rates for married couples with children also increased, particularly for those with larger families. As a result of the increased rates of poverty of their parents since 1972/73, children comprised 44 per cent of the poor in 1981/82 when children were one-third of all poor people.

The relationship between poverty and labour force status is demonstrated clearly in Table 3, which shows a relatively low rate of poverty for all income units where the adult is employed full-year, full-time (never higher than 6 per cent). In contrast, poverty rates increase substantially when the adult is employed full-year, part-time, especially in the case of single parents. Unemployment for a full year is associated with poverty rates of 62–64 per cent for single parents and married-couple families, and a full year spent outside the labour force has an even greater impoverishing affect on single parents (66 per cent in poverty). There is little doubt that recorded and unrecorded unemployment (for single parents this is usually categorised as being outside the labour force) are significantly associated with high levels of poverty.

THE QUESTION OF THE FEMINISATION OF POVERTY

This analysis provides strong evidence supporting one major aspect of the feminisation of poverty thesis. There *has* been a marked increase in the rate of poverty among female-headed single-parent families in the period 1972/73 to 1981/82. Using the Detailed Henderson Poverty Line, the increase is from 38 per cent to 50 per cent of female-headed single-parent families living in poverty. While male-headed single-parent families also become poorer, the increase has been much less marked (from 16 per cent to 19 per cent).

Demographic changes in single-parent family formation (largely resulting from increases in separation and divorce), coinciding with reduced job opportunities and erosion in the real value of income support for children through the tax/benefit system, have resulted in a significantly increased rate of poverty among female-headed families.

There is, however, no evidence for the proposition that female-headed income units, or female-headed families with dependent children bear a *greater share* of poverty in the current period. In 1972/73 female-headed families comprised 44 per cent of poor families with children and 9 per cent of families in the population; in 1981/82 they comprised 33 per cent of poor families and 11 per cent of families in the population. Thus female-headed families remain overrepresented among families in poverty, but not to the same extent as in the early 1970s, and their share of the total number of families in poverty has declined.

This has occurred because of the increased rates of poverty among two-parent families with children which have been associated strongly with unemployment, both of the husband and the wife. The rate of poverty for all married couple families with children has tripled (from 4 per cent in 1972/73 to 12 per cent in 1981/82) and the increase is dramatic where there are three or more children (reaching a rate of 19 per cent). The deterioration in labour market conditions from 1974 to 1982 has therefore had class effects as well as gender effects, resulting in a decrease in job opportunities for men and women and a shifting of the impact of poverty to the child-rearing stage of the life cycle.

However, in poor married-couple families there are also poor women (as noted earlier) whose joblessness (often hidden) is as critical to their families' well-being as is the joblessness of their husbands. Moreover, policies regulating the payment of unemployment benefit (usually paid to the husband as the former bread-winner who is looking for work, and income-tested on joint married-couple income) may exacerbate inequities of income distribution within the family and create disincentives to women's job-seeking.

Clearly, the feminisation of poverty thesis, as currently stated, is too simple if we look only at female-headed families and allow marital status to be the key variable in denoting the income situation of women. The thesis is partially upheld by the much greater proportion of female-headed single parent families in poverty compared with any other income units. This is testimony among other things to the strength of the ideology of women's dependency and its impoverishing effects when women care for children without a co-resident parent, and when they are jobless and dependent on pension.

The continuities between the circumstances of women in poor married-couple families and in single-parent families become clearer when the interaction between responsibility for children and joblessness is considered. Moreover, deterioration in the real value of income support for children through the tax/benefit system affects all families, and in particular it disadvantages the parent directly responsible for children's care. The much greater proportion of children in poverty in 1981/82 is a result not only of their parents' lack of a full-year, full-time job, but the failure of the tax/benefit system to redistribute adequately and consistently to families.

CONCLUSIONS AND IMPLICATIONS

Theoretical explanations of poverty will not be sufficiently comprehensive or adequate for policy debate unless gender inequalities are considered together with class inequalities at the core of the analysis. In addition, periods of vulnerability in the life cycle, in particular the needs of dependent children, must be highlighted. The feminisation of poverty thesis illuminates one of the two major processes affecting the rate of poverty and the composition of the poor, but the thesis must be expanded to take account of the situation of married women in poor families. In the same vein, the *similarities* underlying the two processes which have changed the face of poverty must be stressed, namely, the joblessness of sole parents and of the long-term unemployed which has been exacerbated by public policies that fail to redistribute adequately to the child-rearing stage of the life cycle. The three components of a comprehensive theoretical explanation converge in identifying appropriate policy responses.

The analysis therefore points to the condition of the labour market as well as to the tax/benefit system. In the mid-1980s it is not feasible to look predominantly to the social security system and the tax system to redistribute income to alleviate poverty (as the Poverty Commission did in 1975). High priority must be given to job creation and to associated job training and retraining programs for adults and youth excluded from the labour market. There is a further need to make wage justice for women a reality rather than a theoretical gain incapable of full implementation while the labour market is sex segmented.

In the field of social security, attention must be paid to increasing and maintaining the adequacy of all components of income support for children, and in particular the children of sole-parent pensioners and unemployment beneficiaries. Attention must also be directed at progressively eliminating the disadvantages suffered by unemployment beneficiaries, and towards examining the adequacy of benefits for the long-term unemployed.

Finally, the policy implications of hidden as well as recorded joblessness entail recognition of the interrelated need for job training, job placement and childcare services.

Comprehensive strategy would place consistent emphasis on the provision of enabling policies which treat men and women as equal breadwinners, by increasing their labour market qualifications and their job chances, by pursuing wage justice for women and by increasing income support and services for children.

Problems of measuring poverty: the definition of
income and the sensitivity of various equivalence scales

There are technical problems associated with the measurement of poverty: first, the definition of income; second, the choice of a measurement device (the poverty line and associated equivalence scales which compute the comparative needs of individuals, families and income units according to the size and composition of the unit, the age, sex and labour force status of its members).

These are not merely *technical* problems—there are also problems of adequate conceptualisation. First, the definition of income. In the absence of more comprehensive survey data on the inter- and intra-household distributions of income, wealth, non-cash benefits, community services and private amenities which would provide a measure of 'total income', I have used the Australian Bureau of Statistics Income and Housing Survey data for 1981/82. The shortcomings of this approach include the narrow definition of income which excludes most aspects of wealth except the nature of housing occupancy, and also excludes the imputed value of social services, non-wage employment benefits and home-produced goods. In addition, the concept of the 'income unit' (a co-resident group of individuals related by marriage—de jure or de facto—or by parenthood) assumes equitable sharing of the resources available to the unit and does not permit analysis of intra-family income and wealth distribution. This may obscure the hidden poverty of women and children which may be associated with dependency (Edwards, 1981).

Finally, Australian Income Survey data provide the basis for a 'snap-shot' approach to poverty, but do not provide information on the duration of time spent in poverty, the flows of various demographic groups into and out of poverty, or the likelihood of recurrent spells of poverty over the life-cycle (Allen, 1983; Duncan, 1984).

The next conceptual and technical problem of measurement concerns the choice of a poverty line. Phil Gallagher (1985) has demonstrated the sensitivity of various commonly used scales to different areas of social need. He concludes that the Detailed Henderson Scale (developed for the Poverty Commission) which differentiates on the basis of sex, age and labour force status of adults and the age and sex of children is most sensitive to the needs of children, particularly to the increased costs of adolescent children.[1] In addition, continued use of the Detailed Henderson Poverty Line allows for valid comparisons to be made with the Poverty Commission's findings for 1972/73. In order to do this, people under 21 and self-employed income units are excluded from his analysis, as they were by the Poverty Commission, on the grounds that both juveniles and the self-employed can draw upon resources which are not reflected in their stated incomes. Gallagher suggests that the exclusion of these groups may be inappropriate because a significant proportion is in poverty.

There are also problems with the use of the Detailed Henderson Scale, in particular the assumption that women incur lower costs than men (i.e. have lesser needs). As a result of this assumption, women in the same age group and the same workforce status as men are assumed to have lower costs. Even adolescent girls are assumed to have lower costs than adolescent boys (Commission of Inquiry into Poverty, 1975). The use of these equivalences can result in the underestimation of the numbers of women in poverty, particularly older women. The sensitivity of the Detailed Henderson Scale to the needs of women must be questioned. The Simplified Henderson Scale does not make these assumptions, but its use is less helpful in this paper because of lack of earlier comparable data.

It is essential that research proceed to establish equivalence scales which reflect the actual needs and costs of women compared with men. In the interim, I have adopted the Detailed Henderson Scale, in the interests of achieving a measure of continuity with data from 1972/73.

In order to identify changes in the rate and composition of poverty in the period 1972/73 to 1981/82, the analysis applies the Detailed Henderson Equivalence Scale to the 1981/82 income distribution figures for income units, supplied by the Australian Bureau of Statistics.[2] Because of the lack of comparable sex-differentiated data for 1981/82, it was necessary to use a population base which includes the self-employed for 1981/82, while this group is excluded from the 1972/73 figures. This makes strictly accurate comparison difficult, but the broad pattern is clear.

127

NOTES

1 The Detailed Henderson Poverty Line or Equivalence Scale computes poverty lines which vary according to the family status, age, sex and workforce status of individuals. The Simplified Henderson Poverty Line or Equivalence Scale uses some of the standard costs assumed in the Detailed Scale, but with age and sex differentials removed. Details are outlined in Commission of Inquiry into Poverty, *First Main Report* (1975) Appendix F.
2 I gratefully acknowledge the assistance of Phil Gallagher, Policy Coordination Unit, Department of Community Services who supplied the computer tables from the ABS Income and Housing Survey 1981–82, on which this analysis was based.

ANN CURTHOYS

9 Equal pay, a family wage or both: women workers, feminists and unionists in Australia since 1945

The questions I address in this paper include: why were women and men paid differentially in the past? and why has there been a closing of the gap between men's and women's pay rates? I approach these questions in two stages: first, by looking at some key theoretical considerations; and second by sketching some of the conclusions from my research into Australian equal pay campaigns since the 1940s.

Historians and economists have tackled the problem of how to explain the disparity in the past between male and female wages, both in the sense of differential payment for the same level of skill and in the sense of the concentration of women in unskilled low-pay jobs. It is the second source of disparity which has been seen as the most important and the harder to explain. It is usually accounted for in either of two ways: one is to affirm that women's cheapness lays the basis for their exclusion from the male trades and thus for job segregation by sex; alternatively it is alleged that the separation of men and women into different jobs enables employers to pay men and women differently.

An example of the latter view is the theory of labour market segmentation, expounded most notably in the USA by Edwards, Reich and Gordon (1975), who see job segregation as the product of employer strategies designed to increase profits by employing particular types of workers in distinct jobs at low rates. That is, certain kinds of workers have been identified with certain kinds of jobs, thus preventing various groups from focusing on their common exploited condition. But there is nothing in this theory to explain why it is especially likely to be *women* (along with men of certain ethnic groups) who are confined to the low-pay jobs. The theory has in any case been criticised in recent years for asserting that job and pay structures are products of capitalist initiative rather than of class struggle between employers and workers. Although the theory recognises that these structures arise as a result of class conflict, when for example employers use divide-and-rule tactics to combat trade unionism and working-class organisation generally, the emphasis in this theory, strengthened by the influence of Harry Braverman's *Labor and Monopoly Capital*, has been on *capital*'s ability to structure and divide the labour market, to fragment, routinise, and stratify the labour process.

In subsequent debate, the emphasis has moved to stress how working-class action in the struggle to maximise returns for labour has resulted in a stratified labour market. Jill Rubery (1970), for instance, has argued that in the course of such struggle any group of workers will adopt tactics that try to narrow the supply of labour for a particular job. Of paramount importance in restricting labour supply is the ability to assert the need for skill; entry is then confined to those who have acquired those skills, and the greater the skill claimed the stronger the bargaining position of the worker in relation to the employer. The implication, though Rubery does not spell it out, is that employers would on the whole prefer to maintain a large pool of homogeneous labour, whose members are easily interchangeable and all low-paid. It is therefore the different degrees of success by various sections of the working class in their fight with employers that has led to the erection of hierarchies in the labour market. Workers rather than employers insist on the irreplaceability of their skills and on the specialisation of labour, as evidenced in part by demarcation disputes.

But this is not the whole story. The ability of a particular group of workers to claim skill is not related only to their industrial success in controlling entry and in bargaining with the employer. It is related also to the organisation of work in a particular industry, the degree of fragmentation on the one hand and to specialised knowledge on the other. This organisation is in part an outcome of past class struggles in that industry, and in part an outcome of the degree to which it has suited employers in particular industries to retain broadly rather than narrowly trained workers. That is, some industries are inherently more conducive than others, economically and technologically, to specialisation and fragmentation.

We can therefore see job and pay structures as products both of industrial struggles and the economic and technological character of particular industries. Why, then, did women workers receive low pay? How was it that male wages, at least for skilled and semi-skilled workers, reached a level sufficient to support a family, while female wages were nearly always barely sufficient to support the female worker herself? The answer from the foregoing argument would appear to be that women's wages were especially low because of female concentration in industries exhibiting a high level of job fragmentation, and because of women's lesser industrial organisation. We then need to ask why this was so. Here I can only sketch some elements of the argument.

Within an industrialising capitalist economy only part of the population is in a direct wage relationship as either employer or employee. Others remain dependent on a wage earner through the institution of the family. Despite the incursions of capital and the state, a great deal of the work of personal caring is done privately in the family, traditionally and most commonly by women. This constitutes a major social asymmetry which I cannot discuss further here, except to argue that it is closely connected to the fact that men and women relate to the labour market differently. Women's participation is lower, and this has several major consequences for the nature of their participation. A working-class family will generally rely on the male, not the female wage. Men will attempt to maximise their wage by defending the male trades against incursions by women, or indeed by any outsider group whom employers can engage at lower than the agreed rate. Women may therefore be paid less by virtue of their weak industrial organisation, because of a preindustrial tradition in agricultural wage-payment or, in a great many cases, by virtue of their greater youth and inexperience. This initial cheapness has then laid a basis for their continued exclusion from male trades, and so both job segregation and wage inequalities have been perpetuated.

There has of course been considerable debate over the role of male trade unionists in this history. Some writers emphasise their restricted options in the attempt to maximise return for their own labour (Jane Humphries, 1977; Johanna Brenner and Maria Ramas, 1984). Humphries also stresses working-class women's support for the idea that working-class housewives should not have to enter the labour market, in preference to a situation where all family members have to work and where labour would consequently be in greater supply and therefore cheaper. In contrast, feminists such as Heidi Hartmann (1976), Michelle Barrett and Mary McIntosh (1980) argue that male trade unionists have acted not on behalf of the working class as a whole, but on their own behalf and against the interests and desires of working-class women, whose labour in the home has been exploited.

For whatever reasons, an unequal pay structure developed between the late eighteenth century and the 1930s depression. The next problem is to explain why it gradually crumbled thereafter. Because many feminists have been reluctant to acknowledge just how substantially women's wage rates have come closer to those of men, far more theoretical energy has been devoted to explaining why pay differences by sex persist than in explaining why there has been a very significant closing of the gap. Contributing factors to women's increased pay must include: the growth in demand for women's labour, particularly during the Second World War and the late 1960s and early 1970s; the rapid supply of that labour, strengthening women's industrial organisation; the increase in women's years of education at a rate faster than men's, which created both a supply of skilled female labour and a body of angry, articulate white-collar and professional women fighting as a distinct lobby group for equal pay from both within and without the union movement; and the growing significance of white-collar unions which have contained the mass of, and the most industrially active, women workers.

I turn now to concentrate on the immediate postwar years 1945 to 1953, the period of the Cold War. During this time there was considerable activity over the issue of women's wages, as the effects of wartime disruption of job allocation by sex and of the wages structure were felt and addressed (see Ryan and Conlon, 1975; Encel and Tebbutt, 1974).

At the end of the war there was an astonishing range in women's wage rates: not only the usual variety resulting from differing rates between occupations, classifications and industries, but also unusual disparities resulting from the fact that during the war women had entered a wide range of jobs previously reserved for men. These included both blue-collar jobs, such as those in munitions and aircraft manufacture, and white-collar administrative jobs in the public service and in private industry. This entry of women into men's jobs posed severe problems for wage determination and the arbitration system: if women were paid at low rates the status of the job was undermined, the chances of men getting the job back at the end of the war lessened, and the chances of getting women to do the job at all during the war diminished. Yet if women were paid at high rates, the principle of a needs-based wage, a family wage, was jeopardised. To resolve these problems the Women's Employment Board (WEB) was set up in 1942 (Larmour, 1985). The board rejected needs as a basis for wage determination and determined women's wage rates in male occupations purely on the basis of women's productivity as compared with men's. But this was clearly open to highly subjective judgment, and women gained between 70 and 100 per cent of the male rate, although generally around 90 per cent.

This set up huge disparities between women in male and women in female jobs which had little to do with skill or labour supply. For a period the Curtin government tried to deal with these problems through the Manpower legislation, which could simply direct women from the high-pay male jobs to the low-pay female jobs. Eventually, in response to female workers' expressions of extreme dissatisfaction, including several strikes especially in the textile industry, the government declared under the National Security (Female Minimum Rates) Regulations that certain industries were vital to the war effort, and in these industries women doing traditional female jobs should have their wage rates upgraded from the old 54 per cent of the male rate to 75 per cent. Furthermore, women in the textile and rubber industries managed to have this 75 per cent rate incorporated in their award. But women who worked in non-vital industries remained on the old 54 per cent in terms of their awards, although many were actually getting the 75 per cent rate.

In other words, women's wage rates and wage relativities between men and women were in a mess. Although after the war many women left or were forced out of male jobs under the exigencies of the WEB's 90 per cent rate, some remained. Many were on 75 per cent, while others were on 54 per cent of the male rate. A major debate ensued, involving employers, the union movement, arbitration authorities, the Commonwealth and State governments and various women's organisations. Here I concentrate on two of these groupings, the trade unionists and the feminists. I am interested particularly in the divisions within each grouping, and the connections and hostilities between them.

The union movement was deeply split during the Cold War period as the rightwing ALP Industrial Groups and the Communists struggled for control of particular unions. Communist support for any issue in the union movement therefore attracted both militant support and violent opposition. The argument over women's wages was very much affected by this internal conflict, as it was by other sources of cleavage in the union movement—between skilled and unskilled, white-collar and blue-collar, all-male or mixed-sex membership. Yet despite the very deep conflicts within the union movement, there was one matter on which there was little or no disagreement: the need to support the concept of a family wage. Everyone saw this as the guarantee of family support and basic social security, as a wage which had been achieved only after great struggle with employers and which would continue to form the basis of union wage claims.

Where differences occurred within the union movement on this matter, these were over whether women should be paid a family wage as well. The pro-equal-pay position was that there should be a shift in national income from capital to labour: that is, women's wages should rise to the level of men's, and the employers' overall wage bill would therefore have to rise. This was the position of the Communist Party and the communist-led unions, and also of certain non-communist female trade unionists such as Muriel Heagney.

The right-wing in the union movement, led by the anti-communist, often Catholic, Industrial Groups, was more cautious. One of its main arguments in this period was that wage levels should be based on productivity, on capacity to pay. It saw communist demands for equal pay as motivated more by a desire to confront employers, and thereby seize leadership of the union movement, than by a desire for sexual equality. Furthermore, the Groupers were militant in arguing that the position of single-income families had to be protected, and they opposed married women working. In their opinion, young single women, the only women who should work at all, did not really require a family wage. For all these reasons the right wing of the union movement was not active in equal pay campaigns.

In contrast to this right-wing union support for a family wage, and to the generally left-wing and communist support for equal pay *and* a family wage, stood the women's organisations of the period: the United Associations of Women (UAW), the Professional and Businesswomen's Clubs (PBC), the Housewives' Association, the Australian Federation of Women Voters (AFWV), and the National Council of Women (NCW). These groups ranged from being quite left-wing, as were the United Associations, to quite conservative in the case of most of the others. Although they supported and campaigned for equal pay, these organisations did not support it on the same basis as the union-based equal pay movement, for they rejected the notion of a family wage. They differed from one another on whether the basic wage should cover a spouse, but all agreed it should not cover children. The problem that all feminists perceived was that the family wage, fought for so hard by unionists to maximise their returns on their labour and to enable the provision within the household of basic caring and domestic services, not only enabled the support of a working-class housewife, but also sanctioned an enforced dependency for working-class and indeed middle-class women. Female dependence on a male wage may have been a happy enough arrangement where family life was harmonious and secure; but it was disastrous where it was not. Feminists have always been concerned about the desperate plight of those falling outside the support of a family wage—battered wives, deserted wives, single mothers, single girls on a pittance and so on. They point to those instances where the family either falls apart or becomes most pointedly oppressive. In opposition to the powerlessness and dependence characteristic of women's place in the single-income family, feminists have long sought individual autonomy such that no woman should ever again have to offer her services, sexual and other, to a man purely in order to survive in a comfortable fashion.

This search for autonomy implied a completely different conception of a wage structure from that built up as a product of class struggle over the previous century and a half. The feminists of the late 1940s did not usually argue, as some unionists did, for any overall shift from capital to labour. As middle- and upper-class women with conservative political ideas, they were very much able to see the employers' point of view. But they did want equal pay, and to achieve it they wanted a redistribution from male to female wage-earners, and openly advocated wage cuts for men to allow equal pay for women. They also wanted the sources of child support transferred from wage-earners to the state in the form of a family allowance. For the feminists, an increase in state support for children was essential if women were to gain equal pay, and with it the source of economic independence and thus of personal and bodily autonomy.

To the trade union movement of whatever political complexion, this idea was anathema. It meant a lowering of hard-won wage levels for men and an increased reliance on the state. While unionists were interested in achieving social gains through the state, more precisely through Labor governments, they generally saw these as additional to wage gains, not substitutes for them. Essentially, then, there were three positions: a family wage (supported largely by trade unions); equal pay (the feminist position); and a mixture of both (advocated by the communist-led equal pay committees and some female trade unionists).

In 1946 a lively debate broke out on the equal pay issue. Several women's organisations—the United Associations of Women, the National Council of Women, and the Federation of Women Voters—wrote letters to the *Sydney Morning Herald* advocating equal pay. Towards the end of the year a number of women trade unionists decided to set up a Trade Union Equal Pay Committee consisting of representatives of unions with women members. This committee met throughout 1947, and its members raised equal pay issues at the monthly meetings of the New South Wales Labor Council. In response to this pressure, in August 1947, the Labor Council called a special conference on women's pay and conditions. Twenty-five unions were represented, resolutions were passed and the Labor Council decided to set up its own equal pay committee.

Very similar resolutions were submitted to the ACTU Congress in September. As this year represented the peak of communist and left-wing influence in the ACTU, the resolutions were carried.

With the general swing to the Right in the union movement after 1947, effective support from the ACTU diminished, but certain left-wing unions and the women's organisations continued the fight. During 1948 the issue became more urgent, as the wartime Regulations were due to expire on 31 December. Once these ended it was possible that many women might suffer wage cuts, from the 75 per cent rate to the old 54 per cent, unless the 75 per cent was inserted into new awards. It was in this climate that the Metal Trades Case of 1948 was seen as critical. The left-wing unions in the industry asked for equal pay. Particularly significant was the Sheet Metal Workers Union led by Tom Wright, a consistent supporter of equal pay who argued for both wage justice and for the protection of male metal workers from replacement by cheap labour. The union lost its case, which was a real blow, for as Tom Wright told the Trade Union Equal Pay Committee in October 1948, the metal trades unions had as good a case as any. Wright concluded that little could be expected from the court, and the only solution would come from industrial action. There was some such action in the following three years on women's wages, but overall it was isolated and sporadic. The argument continued, mainly in the Arbitration Court, but rather futilely, as Wright had warned.

In December 1948 an amendment to the arbitration legislation, allowing it to set a separate female basic wage, cleared the way for a major court hearing on women's wage rates which began soon after in February 1949. Various interested parties began preparing cases, generally attempting to show that existing female wage rates were not enough to live on. Feminist organisations worked hard to prove that many women needed the male basic wage, and that it was not true that all women workers had male wage earners on whom to rely. The Australian Women's Charter and the United Associations of Women conducted a survey designed to prove this point, and the Business and Professional Women's Clubs (BPWC) began preparing their case for the unit basic wage plus family allowances.

At a Trade Union Equal Pay Committee conference on 1 April 1950, which criticised the ACTU for its inaction since 1947, a note of caution about the usefulness of these surveys was sounded. Mr Baker, the union advocate in the Basic Wage Case, said that the unions could not win the case on the basis of an argument about needs, as the feminist organisations and the equal pay committees were hoping to do. Further, the BPWC case for a unit basic wage plus wife and child allowances cut right across the union case, which was based on the family wage concept. He pointed out that reliance on state-provided support for children was a tactic generally used by governments and court judges to keep male wages down.

Baker's analysis of the incompatibility between the union and the feminist case was supported by the court. The Basic Wage Decision came down on 12 October 1950. The key judgment was given by Justice Foster, who said the court could not grant equal pay as this would disturb the traditional pay structure based on the fact that men supporting families needed more than did single women. Equal pay would cost too much and the effect would be that if single women got more, then married men with families would have to get less. Since the court knew there was a difference in the level of need, but had no basis for determining exactly what that difference was, it had to fall back on the capacity-to-pay principle, which current practice showed to be that women's basic wage needs were 75 per cent those of men. This view was carried by two to one, with the dissenting judge wanting an across-the-board return to 54 per cent. The court therefore decided that it could not disturb the whole basis for wage-fixing in Australia unless it was politically encouraged to do so through, for example, the provision of substantial family allowances for single-income families.

The government in its turn took the easy way out by affirming the principle of equal pay in the House of Representatives on 10 July 1951, and by voting for the International Labour Organisation (ILO) recommendation on equal pay, at the same time saying that it would not act because wage-fixing was a matter for the court and not the government. So the equal pay advocates found themselves confronted with a classic catch-22—the courts said change was up to the government while the government said it was up to the court.

In 1952 the equal pay cause was confronted by the threat of a step backwards rather than forwards. On 24 June the employers lodged a claim for a 44-hour week, a lower basic wage, and for women to receive 60 per cent of the male rate. Their argument was that labour was too expensive; it promoted inflation and prejudiced Australia's industries in comparison with those overseas. In this renewed round, the women's organisations again put their case to the court. The BPWC argued for a unit basic wage and were supported in this by the Western Australian Women's Services Guild. Their emphasis was that the present system was grossly unfair to widows and large families, and that the wage should be supplemented by state allowances paid for from general taxation. The Australian Federation of Women Voters joined in with similar arguments.

The newly formed, communist-led Union of Australian Women opposed the BWPC and Housewives' Association case for a unit basic wage plus allowances, and wrote to the United Associations of Women on 5 October 1952 seeking their support in opposing such a case. The United Associations replied that the argument for a unit basic wage was indeed a dangerous one, and asserted that the basic wage should be computed on the basis of the needs of two people, that is, it should include the costs of domestic labour. Thus the United Associations was midway between the Union of Australian Women and the BPWC position. Flo Davis of the Trade Union Equal Pay Committee, also tried to persuade the BPWC to change its case, but to no avail; indeed it gained further support from the National Council of Women. In May 1953 Amy Wheaton argued to the court for the Australian Federation of Women Voters that support for children should be a state responsibility: any attempt to provide this support through the wages system was inequitable as so many adult males did not have child dependants. What was needed was a system which paid out only to those who had such dependants and not to those who had none.

The court did not accept this view. It reiterated its belief in the needs principle as this applied to the difference between male and female wages, and it also rejected the employer's application for a reduction to 60 per cent, arguing that 75 per cent had proven reasonable in that it had not led to female unemployment or to massive wage bills. Thus we can see that the court maintained a slightly strange argument. Its reason for a differential was the socially different needs of men and women; but the amount of the differential was to be based on capacity to pay.

The equal pay movement in 1954 realised that it had convincingly lost the battle in the courts. Indeed it was not to win a major court victory until 1969 and more importantly, in 1972. As a result of these defeats, the equal pay forces developed the strategy of turning their attention to the State governments. The idea was that if these governments could be pressured into bringing in equal pay legislation, then the courts would have the legislative guidance they said they needed. And indeed this was to prove in the long run a correct strategy, for the 1969 judgment was influenced by the fact that four States had legislated for equal pay for equal work.

Taking a great leap forward in the narrative, I conclude with a brief look at the 1969 and 1972 cases, to see how the unions and the women's groups argued. It is somewhat ironic that it was pressure from employers that paved the way for equal pay. In 1964 employers' representatives argued to the Arbitration Commission that the basic wage plus margins approach should be abandoned and replaced by a total wage related to skill and to capacity to pay. The Commission adopted this approach in principle in 1966 and applied

138

it in 1967 in the national wage decision. The Commission pointed out that while for the moment it would set the total wage differently for males and females, it considered that the concept of the total wage 'has allowed us to take an important step forward in regard to female wages'. It invited the unions to make an application for equal pay (Encel, MacKenzie and Tebbutt, 1974:160).

The unions proceeded to do so. The principal union advocate was R.J. Hawke, who argued that the question of wage equality was ever more pressing owing to the rising female proportion of the workforce. The economy could no longer do without women. Wages were no longer set on the basis of needs; indeed the needs criterion for wage-setting had first been disregarded in 1931 and then consistently after the war, and its retention as a basis for setting women's wages was anomalous. Hawke explicitly rejected the argument that women be given equal pay to protect men's jobs; he argued on the basis of economic justice and said that wage-fixing procedures should contain no needs element. The ACTU case was supported by the Australian Council of Salaried and Professional Associations and by public service and white-collar unions.

The main difference between 1969 and 1949 is that the unions no longer argued on the basis of the needs of a family, that is, for a family wage. Nor were they anxious about women replacing men, at least overtly, presumably because they were arguing in a climate of labour shortages. In particular unions, especially white-collar ones, there seems to have been a view that equal pay was necessary to protect men's jobs, to inhibit a process of using women to replace men through technological change and deskilling. The union movement as a whole was able to back equal pay because under conditions of general prosperity and labour shortages wage increase for women did not imply wage cuts for men. Further, the bitter divisions between Left and Right within the union movement had diminished by 1969 compared with 1949 and 1952. And again, while many may have still privately believed married women should not work, and that skilled jobs should be preserved for men, they found that it was their own wives and daughters who were working for what now seemed unnecessarily low pay.

If the official union position with its abandonment of needs criteria brought it closer to the feminist position, the feminists also came closer to the unionists. The year 1969 was just before the emergence of the women's liberation movement which was to transform the face of Australian feminism, and the organisations who presented submissions were the same as those in 1952: the Australian Federation of Business and Professional Women's Clubs, the National Council of Women, the Australian Federation of Women

Voters, and the Union of Australian Women. They all supported the submissions made by Hawke for the ACTU, although their emphasis was more on economic justice for women and less on the question of capacity to pay. The AFWV, for example, like Hawke but to a greater extent, invoked the equal pay resolutions of the United Nations and the ILO as well as the US equal pay legislation of 1963. It was they, not the unions, who argued that 'the disappearance of many jobs and the creation of new ones makes the early introduction of equal pay imperative if women are not to be used to undercut men in competition for new jobs as they are created' (AFWV Submission, 1969:6). It was the women's organisation, too, which continued to argue in terms of need, pointing to the fact that women were often in the position of breadwinners and needed a wage sufficient to support not only themselves but also their children. But they retained the emphasis they had developed in the late 1940s and earlier, namely, that it was not the wages system but the state, through measures such as tax rebates and child endowment, that should redistribute from the childless to those who were parents.

The 1969 equal pay decision affected only 20 per cent of women workers, and it was the 1972 decision which removed the very restrictive 'equal work' criterion and replaced it with that of 'equal pay for work of equal value', thus enabling women working in all-female occupations to claim, and subsequently receive, significant wage rises. It was the 1972 decision also which in principle introduced the notion of 'comparable worth': that this has not been fully applied is more a matter of precedent, existing wage relations, and subjective judgment than of principle. It is because the 1972 decision was a comparable worth decision in principle that the wage differences, in terms of rate for the job between men and women, have been reduced so much more effectively for women in Australia than in the US.

The note I sound in conclusion, then, is one of the complexity of the social changes I have been discussing. This complexity arises fundamentally from the fact that wages are paid to individuals for work done, while people do not generally subsist as individuals. As long as this remains the case the relationship between wages and the attainment of either social security or economic equality remains inherently problematic.

PART IV
FEMINISMS, FEMINISTS AND FORGOTTEN WOMEN

BARBARA CAINE

Introduction

For the last ten years, feminist historians have been engaged in
extensive debate about the history of feminism. The very limited
interest in earlier feminist movements which was evident among
those interested in women's studies in the early and mid-1970s (see
e.g. Lerner, 1969), has given way to an intense and constantly
increasing interest in every aspect of the theory and the politics of
all known feminists and all known women's movements. Scholars
working in the field have greatly expanded the range of questions
and issues which are encompassed in discussion of the history of
feminism, so that it has now become central to the study of women's
history. Until the late 1970s, those historians engaged in the study of
feminist movements concentrated on the various campaigns which
were mounted in the nineteenth and early twentieth centuries to
achieve political and legal rights for women. Feminism within this
framework was actually defined simply as 'the deliberate attempt to
achieve equality between the sexes in the political, economic and
domestic spheres' (Banks and Banks, 1965). While this framework
continues to exist (e.g. Evans, 1979), it is increasingly coming to
occupy a marginal position within the field, while the question of
feminist theory and feminist analyses, of women's support networks
and independent activities have been given much greater promin-
ence. As a result, the scope of discussions of feminism within an
historical framework has become much broader, while its subject
matter has been greatly enriched. Feminist political goals and
strategies have been recognised as simply one aspect of a very much
more complex phenomenon and are now studied in relation to
broader questions about the ways in which women have organised
their lives, analysed their experiences, and coped with the many
situations and problems which they face.

As a result of this renewal of interest, the history of feminism now encompasses a vast field with very disparate aims, objectives and ideas about how the subject should be approached. While the importance of understanding the history of feminist theory is universally accepted among feminist scholars, there is no general agreement on what precisely this theory is or how it should be discussed. One major area of difference which is addressed in this volume concerns the question of whether or not feminism should be studied in relation to other political movements. A number of scholars working in the field argue that feminism is ultimately a product of the Enlightenment, and that it shares certain basic assumptions and values with some of the other political theories which have dominated political and social debate since the eighteenth century, particularly liberalism and socialism (Bankes, 1983; Randall, 1985). In accordance with this view, the appropriate frameworks for studying the different nineteenth- and twentieth-century feminisms are established by relating each brand of feminism to a broader political movement from which, or so it is argued, feminists derived their analyses and objectives. Here, concern has mainly been focused on the differences between socialist and liberal femininism, although there has also been interest in conservative feminism, anarchist feminism, evangelical feminism—and even in Nazi feminism (Banks, 1984; Eisenstein, 1984; Koonz, 1977).

This approach to feminism, seeing it as the offshoot of another political theory, is one with a long history of its own. Many nineteenth-century feminists carefully linked themselves to already existing political movements and parties as a way of legitimising their demands, and the earliest histories of the various women's movements in turn adopt this approach. While this approach to the subject continues, scholars currently working in this field have tended to take a far more critical approach and one which explores the inadequacies of the analyses of women offered by male-centred political movements (e.g. Eisenstein, 1983). Within this volume, Carole Adams offers an example of this approach. In Chapter 10, Adams offers a critical analysis of German socialist feminism in terms of the inadequacy of its explanation of the oppression of women. Its attempt to explain gender asymmetry in class terms led, in her view, to the failure of the German Social Democratic Party and of the Free Union movement either to establish a program for emancipating women or to integrate women fully into their own organisations.

An alternative viewpoint has been presented by a number of other scholars who argue that the incorporation of feminism into essentially male political discourse has involved the subordination of feminist aims and objectives to those of the male'master discourse'. The central concerns of feminists and the coherence of their critiques are ignored or denied by incorporating them within a set of objectives defined by the needs of men. Recent feminist scholars argue that the very question of whom we should include within the category 'feminist' has been framed in such a way as to include only those who belong to feminist organisations which have a definite connection with male political groups. Thus those women who have concentrated specifically on issues pertaining to the sexual oppression of women have often not been seen as feminists because they did not take part in campaigns like that of gaining the vote (Jeffreys, 1982; 1985).

Although there has not been any attempt to enlarge the overall catalogue of late nineteenth-century feminists within this volume, strong arguments are put forward about the need to reread and to reevaluate the ideas of certain well-known feminists. Barbara Caine takes up this question in regard to Millicent Garrett Fawcett, one of the English women's suffrage leaders. Fawcett's reputation as a moderate and pragmatic liberal feminist has led to a complete disregard for her intense and passionate concern about the sexual exploitation of women and young girls. Her activities in these areas, her involvement in the social purity movement of the late nineteenth century and her intervention in specific cases of sexual abuse are little known. Even less recognised is the extent to which she explained her own interest in the women's movement in terms of her concern about the sexual oppression and exploitation of women. Fawcett's own writings offer a very clear expression of her feminist convictions and of her feminist theory and these need to be read in order to understand her.

Judith Allen argues a similar case in regard to Rose Scott, a leading Australian feminist. In Allen's view, it is necessary to see Scott's critique of masculinity as the centre of her feminism. This is all the more important because of the way in which Scott's view ran counter to the many scientific discussions of the late nineteenth century which defined sexuality in male terms, thus reinforcing the dominant masculine viewpoint and excluding women from any active role in the analysis of sexuality. Once one does this, Scott's whole career, especially her interest in questions such as the age of consent for girls, the fate of women convicted of infanticide and the question of sex reform, can be seen as a coherent whole. This provides a new version of Scott—as a feminist rather than as a woman interested in many worthy causes.

The discussions of both Fawcett and Scott raise another issue which is very pertinent both to feminist history and to the history of feminism: the problem of forgotten women. For while both these women are well known, important aspects of their lives and of their ideas have simply been ignored or regarded as unimportant. One could well argue that they are both forgotten women in the sense that both have consistently been presented as unproblematic political activists with little to contribute to a broader study of women's history. The importance of retrieving women's forgotten past and of bringing to light the stories, the experiences and the ideas of unknown women has played a major part in, indeed it has been one of the central concerns of women's history. This endeavour is important, not just because it adds more names to our historical record, but because it enables us to grasp the full range and diversity of women's experience and at the same time enables us to see how women have experienced historical events and conflicts which are usually only studied through men. Judith Keene's study of Aileen Palmer, which is the most moving and poignant essay in this collection, highlights many of these themes. Now permanently confined to a nursing home, Aileen Palmer has been deprived of her own past; her recollections of driving an ambulance in the Spanish Civil War have been taken as yet another sign of her delusional state by young medical men. Her story is interesting and important in itself. Her battle to deal with the expectations that she would inherit the literary mantle of her famous parents, Vance and Nettie Palmer and her discomfort in Australia, her desire to immerse herself in the life, the politics and the culture of Europe raise interesting questions about Australian social, political and cultural history in the twentieth century. But while these themes have often been discussed in regard to men, here we see their distinctive form for a woman for whom all of these broader issues are fought out alongside the particular familial concerns and expectations and the conventions demanded of an unmarried daughter. Aileen Palmer's story is a tragic one, but that it should be entirely forgotten would be even more tragic.

CAROLE E. ADAMS

10 Pre–World War I socialist feminism in Germany: homo economicus

In the period before World War I, the German Social Democratic Party was viewed as a model by socialists throughout the world, and by the socialist women's movement as well. German socialist feminist theory predicated women's emancipation upon their entry into the proletarian work force and their participation in socialist revolution. However, although some socialist leaders firmly believed in equality for women, German socialists in and outside the Free Union movement were, as Jean Quataert has remarked, 'reluctant feminists'. They missed a striking number of opportunities to work constructively for the equality for women in which they fervently believed. Moreover women remained subordinate and largely unheard in both the Party and the unions.

It is the argument of this chapter that the socialists' failure to grasp clear opportunities to take steps to carry out their own theoretical positions—to work with employed women, to encourage unionisation and to foster equality between the sexes—was a direct result of a theory that attempted to explain gender asymmetry in class terms. This paper is a case study based on the experience of one socialist union before World War I, the Central Alliance of Male and Female Commercial Assistants. The union was small but is of particular interest because half its members were women, who 'stood shoulder to shoulder' with the men.

GERMAN SOCIALISM AND WOMEN BEFORE WORLD WAR I

Rapid urbanisation and industrialisation in Germany in the late nineteenth century led to the rise of a powerful socialist movement and an affiliated network of Free Trade Unions; by 1912 the SPD had approximately one million members and the socialist Free

Unions had over two and a half million (Schorske, 1955:13). From the beginning, proletarian women made real efforts to share equally in the struggles of their working-class brothers and to achieve an equal place in society. Against the opinions of working men, German proletarian women both organised their own groups and fought for their right to join working men's associations. When anti-socialist legislation drove socialist movements underground in 1878, women worked in alliance with men in underground labour groups and founded unions and self-help organisations on a local basis, and a number of female 'trustees' maintained links among different groups (Losseff-Tillmanns, 1982).

Because of their underground contribution, the Social Democratic Party became more actively engaged in women's issues, and when the Party again became legal, male leaders worked with a semi-autonomous women's group (Quataert, 1979) and its platform now demanded both 'universal, equal, and direct suffrage, with secret ballot for all citizens ... without distinction as to sex' and the 'abolition of all laws which discriminate against women as compared with men in the public and private legal sphere' (quoted in Thoennessen, 1973:47). In 1906 about 10 per cent of Party members were women; by 1912 that figure had risen to about 14 per cent. Men in the socialist trade unions were also more willing to accept women members after the lapse of the anti-socialist laws. Union membership had declined sharply, and the recession of 1891–95 led to a mood of pessimism in which any new members were welcomed. Further, the 1895 census had revealed the great extent of female participation in the workforce. The proportion of female members in the Free Unions increased to 8.8 per cent by 1914 (Losseff-Tillmanns, 1982).

GERMAN SOCIALIST FEMINIST THEORY

Socialist feminist theory was formulated at the same time that women were participating in the growth of socialist economic and political organisations. Clara Zetkin, the head of the German socialist women's movement and a leading radical socialist, defined orthodoxy on women's issues, even though her ideas derived to a great extent from August Bebel's best-selling 1878 book *Woman and Socialism* and from Friedrich Engels' 1884 *Origin of the Family, Private Property, and the State*. Zetkin's positions as a feminist were often taken in reference to larger socialist debates, particularly that concerning revisionism, rather than in the light of a careful analysis of the circumstances of women (Quataert, 1979). Zetkin's 1889 book *The Contemporary Question of Women Workers and Women* followed Bebel's argument; where he had chosen a rather scholarly form of discourse, however, hers was combative.

In Bebel's eyes, 'all social dependency and oppression has its roots in the *economic dependence* of the oppressed upon the oppressor' (Bebel, 1904:9; italics in original). Women suffered twofold oppression: they were economically and socially dependent on men in marriage, and working women, like working men, were exploited and oppressed wage labourers. Owing to this dual oppression, Bebel contended that only revolutionary change could truly liberate women by granting them social and economic independence. Like men, they would live largely in the public sphere, freed from domestic tasks because of the end of monogamous marriage, of technological inventions such as modern and centralised kitchens, and of universal childcare and education (Bebel, 1904).

Zetkin followed Bebel's argumentation, tracing woman's role in the contemporary family back to the sexual division of labour occurring in primitive cultures. Woman was the productive worker in the home, where she functioned like a proletarian in 'sex slavery'. Like Bebel, Zetkin believed that modern society had created the conditions for women's liberation, for new technology freed women from domestic labour and laid the basis for the women's movement. Further, capitalism, with its drive to reduce wages, made paid work outside the home essential for an increasing number of married women, and 'woman herself gained from this ability *to live without the man*, it gave the *woman for the first time the ability for a completely independent life.*' Zetkin remained within the marxist tradition too with her contention that employed women lost any gender distinction and took on the same class position as men. 'From that day when woman threw off the yoke of economic dependence on the *man*,' she wrote, 'she fell under the economic sway of the *capitalist* . . .' (Zetkin, 1889).

These analyses had in common a certain reductionism in which woman's subordination to man, in the family and in the workplace, arose from economic factors. In the home as well as the workplace, her subordination could be explained in class terms. Women's oppression would therefore end with the advent of socialism. And as Zetkin implied, the end was in sight, for women were by 1900 already leaving the domestic sphere and seeking paid employment. For Bebel and Zetkin and for German socialists in general, the conclusion was clear. Women's paid employment was to be encouraged, as was public intervention in domestic tasks. Working women and men were to struggle together to overthrow capitalism and establish socialism, which alone would free them of both.

It is not the case that these theories ignored the home and family.

An analysis of the domestic sphere was undertaken, as the striking phrase 'sex slavery in the home' attests. The problem, rather, was that men and women were defined as essentially economic beings. A determinist and economist marxism assured that there would be no theoretical concern with divisions of labour other than by class, no solution to domestic 'class' relations except the mechanisation of household tasks, and no analysis of the interaction of the economic base with culture or ideology. As a result, no language, no conceptual framework existed for discussing psychology, socialisation, or power relations except in terms of narrowly defined relations of production and reproduction.

Socialist feminists thus held that female wage labour alone would free women from family dependence, end female 'sex-slavery', and place women in a common position with male workers, whence they would recognise their class interests and press for revolution. Socialist feminists relied on a sort of industrialisation of domestic life, through which its routines and responsibilities would be removed to the public sphere. Like monogamy, the family would wither away after the revolution. Therefore, although both Bebel and Zetkin insisted that women had been educated and socialised to play a subordinate role, neither they nor other theorists analysed the problems faced by proletarian women except in terms of the division of labour.

This left socialist feminists with no basis for analysing the second-class status of working women. The fact that working women did not face problems identical to those of working men was implicitly recognised when leaders discussed the difficulty of organising working women and women's desire to marry and leave the workforce. However, leaders invariably assumed that the problem stemmed from women's 'slavery in the home' and expected the difficulty to disappear with socialism. Socialists contended that women accepted domestic slavery because they saw themselves as women rather than as workers. The solution therefore was to agitate and organise them as workers in unions; developing their sense of class consciousness and solidarity would encourage personal independence and self-assertion (Zetkin, 1898–1901; Altmann, 1905; Ihrer, 1896 and 1905).

However, since socialist feminists urged the transformation of woman into proletarian, they were unwilling to offer union women special services (such as women's columns in union papers or all-female union schooling) although that might have fostered independent and assertive behaviour. When Else Lueders—a left-liberal radical feminist—offered a series of educational proposals to socialist feminist unionists, she met withering criticism. She proposed special discussion courses for competent trade union women, to be taught by a woman with solid socio-economic knowledge and skilled in 'the tools of running an association' and including small group involvement. Lueders also suggested a 'women's corner' in union papers to increase female interest in union affairs, written in a 'popular—but by no means insipid' manner (Lueders, 1905).

For socialist women leaders, such an approach threatened permanent second-class status. Ida Altmann, head of the women's secretariat of the Free Union General Commission, responded with sarcasm and hostility toward any hint of separatism within the unions: 'Union women's courses are supposed to be necessary to overcome the shyness of working women. The wonder of this logic! ... Exactly because the separation of human communities on the basis of sex has made women shy, shyness will be fought by again practising separation on the basis of sex ...' Zetkin, during a similar dispute, maintained that 'the task of the socialist women's movement should be to awaken female proletarians to class consciousness' (Zetkin, 1897:154).

Party and Free Union women were to work in solidarity with male colleagues and to attempt to raise the level of class consciousness among women, enlisting them in the ranks of the socialist movement. This alone would lead to human—including female—emancipation. Thus socialist feminists failed to perceive the interaction between the public and the private, between women's lives at home in the family and abroad at the workplace. They expected the transformation of the public sphere to end female subordination at all levels, and were optimistic about the possibility of that public transformation occurring. Organisations of working women were an obvious place to turn theory into practice, yet in the case of white-collar women, the chance was missed.

SOCIALIST FEMINISM AND WOMEN CLERKS

The limits of socialist feminist theory emerge clearly in studying the Central Alliance of Male and Female Commercial Assistants of Germany. The union was very small; it had only 16 000 members out of the more than two million members of socialist Free Unions in Germany before the First World War. It was unique in that half its members were female, making it especially apt for a study of the degree to which socialist precepts of female equality were carried out in socialist organisations (Zentralverband, 1904 and 1906; anon., 1910; Stehr, 1926; Urban, 1949).

Although the leadership of the Central Alliance remained firmly male, the organisation made serious efforts to recruit women, to address issues important to them, and to work toward women's equality. As early as 1896, the union coordinating committee demanded that women should receive pay equal to that of men (Zentralverband, 1904; Stehr, 1926). In part, the response to female issues was a pragmatic tactic, for leaders were aware of the increase in female employment in clerking and of male hostility to women's lower pay and to their 'dirty competition'.

But it was not pragmatism alone that led the Central Alliance to include women's issues. For the organisation accepted Bebel's and Zetkin's analysis of economic development and believed that the degradation of clerking and increased female participation in the white-collar workforce could not be hindered (Zentralverband, 1904). They therefore encouraged female clerks to organise as a part of that general politicisation of all workers that would lead to human emancipation.

Under the guidance of Max Josephsohn, earlier the Hamburg chair, the national Central Alliance embarked upon active recruiting of women, primarily using the tactic of 'plant meetings' developed by other Free Unions. Local unions invited sales staff at a single department store or all saleswomen in a particular retail branch to attend meetings to discuss grievances or poor work conditions, at which a woman often spoke (Stehr, 1926; Hamburg Staatsarchiv, PP V676; Zentralverband, 1906 and 1908).

Plant meetings for saleswomen were important for recruiting, but they served to support female members as well. Women at the meetings learned about work and pay conditions, the history of women's work and the importance of female organisation solidarity (Hamburg Staatsarchiv, PP V676; Zentralverband, 1910 and 1912). It is quite likely that an informal network existed for women on the job where the Central Alliance was active, for without some community network, women would not have continued to participate. Attending meetings sponsored by the Central Alliance, young saleswomen could meet their colleagues, discuss grievances and perhaps establish a workers' committee to draw up demands. They would sometimes also have the opportunity to work with a female leader. These activities would encourage women somewhat in assertive and independent behaviour and would aid in developing a female support network.

In addition, many union educational activities were designed to bring both sexes to a better understanding of issues of female employment and of the 'woman question' in general. Lectures traced the history of sales work and explained trends within capitalism tending toward concentration; others described the poor conditions faced by sales workers, especially women, and insisted that only organisation could bring justice to employed women (Hamburg Staatsarchiv, PP V676). The Central Alliance held meetings addressed to all female clerks, not just saleswomen. Other meetings attempted to reach men as well, emphasising the economic circumstances that drove women to seek employment and the need for both sexes to express solidarity and work together in the same union (*Handlungsgehilfen-Zeitung*). They countered male prejudices and stereotypes, placed women's issues within the framework of socialist theory, and showed the necessity of a joint male-female clerks' organisation.

Some individual locals of the Central Alliance also tried to involve women in the local leadership. They pressed women to attend meetings, agitate for new members and hold executive positions, and a number of them elected women to their committees and executive boards (*Handlungsgehilfen-Zeitung*; Hamburg Staatsarchiv, PP V676). Individual male leaders also recognised that women needed particular encouragement to join the organisation and to stand for office.

However, it is also clear that many national and local leaders did not truly believe in female equality or were at best unwilling to take active measures to ensure equity for women. Yet that fact sufficiently explains neither the lack of interest in women's issues nor women's lack of full participation in a union half composed of women, especially given the good will that was evident in the actions of many of the male leaders. In addition to prejudice, discrimination, and notions of what was gender-appropriate behaviour, it was the limited nature of socialist feminist analysis that kept women subordinate in the union and women's issues secondary in consideration.

THE SECONDARY POSITION OF WOMEN IN THE CENTRAL ALLIANCE

Since union leaders accepted the theoretical position of socialist feminism, the issue of discrimination against women inside the union was ignored and women played a passive role within the Central Alliance. The emphasis on class struggle in the entire Free Union movement made leaders unwilling to establish any separate female activities in the locals or any 'woman's corner' in the journal. As a result, women members found it difficult to develop an effective female support network or to attain responsible positions. There was therefore no female equality within the organisation, despite the fact that by 1910 male leaders themselves seem to have felt uncomfortable about the low level of female involvement in the group.

Few delegates to Central Alliance conventions were female, and protocols indicate that the female delegates often failed to speak throughout the sessions. A man, Max Josephsohn, was even selected to represent the Central Alliance at the 1904 Bremen Conference of Social Democratic Women (Zentralverband, 1906). On the local level women held only approximately 10–30 per cent of the offices. The single woman to sit on the national executive, Regina Krauss, was elected only in 1914 despite her national reputation as a recruiter (*Handlungsgehilfen-Zeitung*, esp. 18, 1914:41). Not only could women continually be outvoted, but male predominance quite likely resulted in women acquiescing in decisions and voicing few opinions at all.

Male leaders were apparently ambivalent about the role they wanted and expected female members to play. They recognised that female leaders were essential to an organisation half composed of women and desiring to recruit more. But giving women responsible positions was still an uncomfortable novelty. The women evidently sensed this. In all the reports of discussions at meetings throughout the years, there were few occasions on which women ventured any opinions, and the women who did speak were those same few women who held office. Sometimes when they spoke, they were dismissed patronisingly. When Frl. Storch criticised the executive board in Hamburg in 1908 for failing to support members in a dispute, the chair denied her charges in a manner suggesting that she was at fault. A month later, a chastened Storch explained that she had not meant to attack the board, 'she had only intended to explain the benefits of a workers' committee' (Hamburg Staatsarchiv, PP V676). Rather than seizing its opportunity to involve Storch in organisational efforts, the board embarrassed her.

The general insensitivity of male Central Alliance leaders is underscored by events at its 1912 convention, where the decision was taken to omit the word 'Female' from the title. A delegate had offered the proposal once before in 1908 in order to shorten the title, but then the motion was easily rejected (Zentralverband, 1908). In 1912 the proposal came from the executive board and no women sat as delegates to the convention. The board argued that it would shorten the title and be a 'radical modernization'. There were a number of opponents. One man pointed out, in a bit of an understatement, that 'things are different with us than other organizations that take no women, for we have a very large number of women members'. Other delegates asserted that it was important for agitation purposes 'that female clerks are also named in the title' and that the change would make the group sound all-male. One suggested that if the name were too long, the word 'Germany' should be struck out. By a small majority, however, the change was approved (Zentralverband, 1912).

Furthermore, the proportion of speeches and articles pertaining to women was not very high. A 1910 survey showed that the journal, which ran to 40000 lines, devoted only 1021 lines to 'women's issues'. Approximately the same number was given to historical topics or to discussions of political parties, while 'professional questions other than pay' received 15 121 (*Handlungsgehilfen-Zeitung* 14, 1910:109). When the subject of a talk or essay was not specifically addressed to women, they were usually ignored. A journal article entitled 'The Suppression of the People in Prussia' attacked the state's limited franchise, but was silent about women's lack of voting rights (*Handlungsgehilfen-Zeitung*).

Since socialist feminists rejected female separatism, there were no particular supports for women members of the Alliance outside of the informal support networks that probably existed in conjunction with the plant meetings. This was a real contrast to the all-female clerks' associations founded in the same period with the support of middle-class feminists. Those organisations, with a much larger membership than the Central Alliance ever achieved, provided many opportunities (such as women's discussion groups) for women to learn skills essential to advancing in the public sphere: the ability to speak in public, to express opinions authoritatively, to formulate policies, to assume authority, or to hold office. Enough female clerks learned assertive behaviour to lead clerks' groups throughout Germany (Adams, 1984; Nienhaus, 1982).

The all-female groups' emphasis on teaching job skills and behaviour, such as preparing properly for a job interview or assuming responsibility on the job, also benefited women. The Central Alliance did not see its task as teaching individual self-improvement, but as a consequence, neither the Hamburg local nor the national union offered women a chance to learn effective work behaviour. Some locals offered 'cheery evenings' at members' meetings, but no evenings were held for women alone (*Handlungsgehilfen-Zeitung*). Discussion evenings as well were open to all members, with no opportunity for women to develop their speaking skills or assertiveness in debate in an all-female environment. Since socialist feminists expected economic independence alone to liberate women, there was no attempt made to encourage women to develop personal assertiveness or independence through travel, education, or leisure activities. A woman's consciousness was to be raised concerning employment issues, the need for organisation and solidarity, and the importance of class struggle and socialism. Beyond that, politicisation did not occur. Women were urged to vote in state insurance elections, and lectures were given on the importance of female civic rights, but abstract rights were never connected to the political activities (or lack of them) undertaken by women in the union.

What does all this signify? One might argue that the situation described above was bound to occur in a male-female union. Yet, given the oft-stated goal of equality for women—and awkward male attempts to achieve it—that is clearly not the whole picture. I would argue that socialist feminist theory contributed to the subordination of women and of women's issues in the Central Alliance.

First, there was no means for getting women into leadership positions in large numbers. Owing to the rejection of separatism as a strategy, there was no training ground for women, and even little opportunity for women to develop support networks. Second, since women's emancipation was expected to flow from female employment in the short run and from socialist revolution in the long run, there was little discussion of women's issues unless an explicitly 'woman's topic' was raised.

Most important, since employment offered the solution to female oppression, there was no interest in non-employment issues. Socialist feminist theory posited women and men workers as the same and therefore failed to analyse differences between them such as women's different life cycle (then typically paid employment followed by marriage and work in the home, ending with a return to paid employment) or the double burden faced by all employed women, who had responsibility for both paid and domestic work. As a result, no strategies could be developed to deal with the oft-cited facts that women were harder to organise and had less sense of solidarity than men. Nor could leaders recognise that within the union male and female members shared their class situation but not that of gender.

The evidence of this case study indicates not that male leaders in the Central Alliance failed to practise socialist feminist theory, but that that theory was impracticable. The theory assumed that class analysis alone could account for female subordination. However, as we have seen, class analysis without parallel gender analysis could neither explain reality in a satisfactory way nor point to policies that could aid in women's emancipation.

JUDITH ALLEN

11 Rose Scott's vision: feminism and masculinity 1880–1925

What sympathy at present have men and women in the affairs of life? Even in love, which brings them most together, what sympathy? To the highest type of man, the consummation of love is the indulgence of an animal passion. To a woman, physical manifestations of any kind deteriorate rather than enhance the beauty and spirituality of love. The gulf between them is bridged by women's self sacrifice and man's self indulgence—but for how long? Man's selfish animalism is driving women further and further away into the opposite direction and these unsympathetic relations have more to do with conjugal misery than anything else.

—Rose Scott, n.d. unpublished notes entitled 'Marriage'[1]

Rose Scott (1847–1925), an Australian feminist and social reformer, was unusual in that she left an enormous collection of diaries, private papers and correspondence.[2] These papers were unsorted when I began research on her political career in 1977; and a considerable proportion of them were what any cataloguer would identify as scraps of paper, written in pencil, almost illegible, and often crossed out. Their form varied, but the subject of most of them concerned sexual mores, marriage and the degradation of women through sexual relations with men. A journal which I have failed to relocate in the now sorted collection referred at length to the 'animal in man' which Scott likened to a snake which coils itself around woman, suffocating her spirit. In the same passage, she declared that all 'woman' wanted from the physical side of marriage was to lie in man's arms and feel his warmth and strength. For this pleasure, however, she had to endure 'the snake'.[3] Elsewhere she commented on the repulsiveness of the male anatomy in a notebook entry entitled 'Revolt against the organs'—'Revolting, hideous, beauty forbids to enhance them ... poor souls [are] brought into the world not for their own sakes but for the enjoyment of animal lust through which woman, the slave, retains her power over the animal in man'.[4] In some undated scrawled handwriting, partly crossed out Scott wrote: 'It is for men that street women live and die. Oh would that some amongst them might strive to live and die if need be for women. Oh friends, if these words I could say ... could make woman as dear to woman as man is now dear to her ...'[5]

My first work on Scott substantially ignored her writings on masculinity and sexuality. Instead, by splitting the public and the private, I focused on those of her activities generally accepted as giving Scott her importance to the history of feminism. These activities included: her work in the Womanhood Suffrage League of New South Wales concluding with women's enfranchisement in 1902; her founding of the Women's Political and Educational League in 1903 (a prototype for the current Women's Electoral Lobby) which worked for reforms in women's and children's situations, especially that of women prisoners; her work on feminist legal issues in affiliation with the National and International Councils of Women; and her presidency of the New South Wales Branch of the Peace Society from 1908 (Allen, 1977; 1979a; 1979b).

Later work on crimes involving women entailed my reexamining Scott's papers. This reexamining of her papers alongside other material on women's social conditions 1880–1925 raised a number of questions. What was the relationship between the writings on masculinity or sexuality in Scott's private papers (that I and other historians had ignored) and the public campaigns of sexual politics she undertook? Do these writings provide grounds to significantly alter interpretation of her work in particular, and of first-wave feminism in general? Why did Scott herself, and why have others since, minimised the abundant evidence of her critique of male sexuality?

This question in turn gives rise to a broader one which underlies the whole question of the evaluation and the assessment of 'first-wave' feminist ideas on sexuality. An implicit or explicit libertarianism has often informed historians' interpretations of the ideas of nineteenth- and early-twentieth-century feminists. In so far as they have shown themselves to be uninterested in, unaware of or unpersuaded by the importance of sexual pleasure for women, feminists like Scott have been characterised as puritanical, conservative, and as fatally flawed social critics.[6] Their writings on sexuality have been ignored and they have been seen as interested only in questions pertaining to the public sphere. In general women like Scott have been seen as less important and certainly as less interesting than those feminists like Margaret Sanger in the United States or Stella Browne in England who fought for women's access to sexual freedom and to sexual pleasure. This latter group has tended to be seen as the 'good' feminists whose ideas remain relevant today because they identified the 'right' sexual issues—contraception, abortion, free love—and offered critiques of the family and expressed enthusiasm about the emancipatory potential of rapturous adult sexuality (Weeks, 1977:166–67; Rowbotham, 1977:11–13; Gordon, 1982:43–47). In this process, the critique of masculinity and of the ways in which male definitions of sexuality contribute to the oppression of women which was offered by Scott and other early feminists has been substantially ignored.[7]

A MASCULINIST CONTEXT

Feminism of the late nineteenth and early twentieth centuries coexisted with other radical knowledges which were strongly linked to the emerging sciences and the professions. Within this context, the important radical positions were libertarianism, biological determinism, and socialism. These radical knowledges were believed to be in the forefront of social inquiry and critique; they interacted with each other and generated theoretical work and political movements such as social Darwinism, sexology, eugenics and radical nationalism. All of these were antithetical to feminist objectives.[8] Initially, the works of such influential Australian and international cultural figures as Lindsay, Lawson, Ellis, Stopes, Van der Velde, Pearson, Carpenter, Freud, Wells, Shaw appear to share little in common. Disparate as their preoccupations were, taken together they established a framework which suppressed feminist social inquiry. There were ever more scientific rationalisations for the then current form of male dominance, sexuality and desire (Rosenberg, 1982). While materialists and environmentalists might posit the social order as a construct and therefore manipulable, masculinity was exempted from discussion. This exemption was not a decision made after debate; it was an omission by men whose subjective experience gave them no reason to consider masculinity and its mores anything more than what nature dictated. Fish did not know that the water was wet.

Late-nineteenth-century feminists, as women, were formally and informally excluded from the sciences, the professions, and research levels of humanities that presided over knowledges relating to sexual differences (Rosenberg, 1982;178–206; Alic, 1985; Fausto-Sterling, 1985; Fox-Keller, 1985). As critics of the deleterious male rule, feminists in this intellectually hostile context from 1880 to 1930 faced few opportunities to express themselves. They could become trenchant environmentalists and insist that men could change, or they could believe the different offerings of these other knowledges and employ them, subvert them to negotiate more favourable conditions for women as a sex (Rosenberg, 1982:54–83). Scott's writings include jokes about biological determinism such as 'the brains of women are smaller than men because they inherit them from their fathers' and 'old maids: the survival of the fittest'.[9]

To offer serious and public criticism of masculinity and male sexual practices per se was to court marginality and intense defamation. This was because of pervasive assumptions about the characteristics of men and their sexuality, so pervasive as not to require justification. Foremost among these was what Vicinus (1982) identifies as a hydraulic energy release model of male sexual drives, and accompanying characteristics such as aggression, phallocentrism, pursuit of orgasm via penetration of, or stimulus by, other objects—women, children, horses, fowls or whatever (see also Jackson, 1984). Whether one examines the writings of sexologists, scientists, moralists, pornographers, or novelists of the day, masculine sexuality is unrelated by them to interaction, mutuality, or to reciprocal desire. Moreover there was a widespread masculine resort to prostitution before, within and outside marriage, to rape, to sexual harassment, and to the use of what was called in Scott's day indecent publications and materials, nowadays labelled pornography.

We cannot be surprised then if feminists like Scott who died only 50 years ago, were not candid in publicly expressing their feelings about prevailing theories and practices of masculine sexuality. Perhaps the more surprising matter is that Scott wrote her thoughts down at all, even if she often did cross them out. The feminists who spoke publicly and who were influential were those with an optimistic picture of male sexuality, who sought freedom from inhibition for women; to be more like men, as long as they could have certain aids for problems associated with heterosexuality—contraception, abortion and men better skilled in the act of love (Gordon and Dubois, 1983; Jeffreys, 1985; Trimberger, 1983). I refer here to the disparate group including Dora Russell, Stella Browne, Marie Stopes, Emma Goldman, Alexandria Kollanti, Jessie Street and Ruby Rich—the cluster of women periodised after Scott as interwar feminists. The price of their influence was the acceptance of masculine experience as the norm. As Ellen Dubois and Linda Gordon have observed (1983), this was the condition of allegedly greater sexual freedom—a point to which I return in my conclusion.

ROSE SCOTT'S VISION

Scott's pessimism about the character of 'the physical side of marriage', male animality and the degradation of women through 'carnal relations' substantially reorients interpretation of her reform work, especially the explanation of her targets and priorities.

The first public campaign to engage Scott as a feminist concerned seduction of girls and the age of consent. Her involvement in work with philanthropists and charitable and public institutions showed an intense concern for 'fallen women', prostitutes, unmarried and deserted mothers, most of whom had been adolescent live-in domestic servants. Scott believed their position of economic and social dependence made them vulnerable to sexual demands. She advocated measures to discourage men from exerting the power they possessed, almost systemically, as residents of servant-employing households. Domestic service was then the largest registered occupation of women, except for marriage.[10] Once pregnant women tended to be sacked without references, and if their own families rejected them, charity or prostitution might be their only options. In principle Scott also opposed the state regulation of men's use of women prostitutes in so far as this meant the removal and treatment of venereally diseased workers, but not their clients—she saw this as in effect supplying clean women for profligate men (Golder and Allen, 1980). She was later to be prominent in campaigns against such regulation, introduced in New South Wales in 1908 (Allen, 1984).

Nothing could be done about these aspects of the sexual exploitation of women by men until women had the vote. Supporters and opponents of women's suffrage alike believed that women's estate was sufficiently similar to mean that despite class, ethnic, age, and religious differences, women would vote as a sex. Scott was confident that all women needed was the vote in order to place legislative obstacles to the unchecked operation of masculinity. In other words, contrary to the prevalent liberal and left interpretation that suffragists simply sought bourgeois liberal rights as ends in themselves, feminists like Scott sought the vote to arm women to achieve their own interests.[11]

Despite the official picture of Scott's involvement in worthy activities and associations, a survey of her public work from 1902 until 1922—when she retired from public life aged and in ill health— shows that the bulk of it was concerned with discouraging exploitative masculine sexual practices. For instance, the British age of consent became sixteen in 1885 (Gorham, 1978). In New South Wales it took a long 25 years after that date, and bitter campaigning by Scott and others to have it raised from fourteen to sixteen (Allen, 1979). This was the major battle Scott undertook, one that sought to make men responsible for 'the ruin' of young women instead of accepting that the onus be placed only on the women. Other campaigns to which Scott directed considerable energy included that in 1903 for the release of Ethel Herringe, a young rural domestic servant, who was convicted for shooting her ex-employer. He had deserted her when she fell pregnant to him.[12] Cases of young women who had committed infanticide after being seduced and abandoned and received heavy terms of imprisonment also engaged Scott's energy, under the shadow of the 1903 New South Wales Royal Commission into the Decline in the Birthrate, before which she declined to appear.[13] Instead, during 1903–1904, she worked on legislation to extend the rights of unmarried mothers to extended financial maintenance for themselves and their children from the man responsible.[14]

The kind of 'ruin' Scott addressed in this was was not just in terms of bourgeois morality. It was material. She was concerned about the way unchecked exercise of masculine sexual power and prerogatives consigned women to poverty, dependency and prostitution. For Scott, anything that enlarged women's options for economic autonomy so that they did not have to sell sexual services to men in order to live was to be encouraged. Women's dependence and the view that selling sexual services was the inevitable and defining feature of women's estate encouraged the exercise of men's sexual power and prerogatives. Men's animality was thereby enlarged. It was in this spirit that Scott fought discriminatory laws surrounding women's work, employment opportunities and citizenship rights. She was not interested in simply pursuing bourgeois, liberal equality for itself.

By skilful use of the available rhetoric, Scott sought the control of men. While privately she held a 'demonised' picture of male sexuality, and an idealised one of female sexuality, publicly she worked to demystify and disempower men, charmingly describing them as silly little bully boys.[15] In her pacifist work she would cite the ways these boys had messed up the world, and suggest it was time the boys let women do some national and international housekeeping.[16] Taking up the scientific discourse of her time, Scott utilised the one great legitimated site of womanly power—instinctive motherhood—and made terrifyingly large claims for the political ramifications of an electorate of mothers, enshrining the respect due women as mothers. Less overtly, by the combination of her then famous jokes about marriage as 'friendship under extremely adverse circumstances' and positing women as wise, all-knowing mothers, and men as little boys, Scott was subverting heterosexual scripts in a way that potentially empowered women to contain masculine animality, to hold it at arm's length. As mothers, women were enjoined to place their children as shields against conjugal demands; and implicitly to reduce male experience of heterosexuality to an incest relationship in which men were infantilised with diminished power.

In this connection, Scott's instrumental role in the public defence and propagandising of W.J. Chidley, Sydney sex reformer 1912–16 is most illuminating. Chidley claimed that the penile erection and penetration of the female *homo sapiens* was a violence to women and an affront to nature, that all other species showed that instigation and control of heterosexual intercourse resided with the female, exercised by her usually only when she was fertile and sought to reproduce. Chidley's work expounded other sexualities and sexual variations in all animal species, including humans; the reproductive heterosexual model was only one. According to conventional interpretations of Scott as either the worthy liberal or the repressive, 'wowser' spinster, the aiding and abetting of an unpopular sexual radical like Chidley should not have been part of her brief of appropriate public activities (Finnane, 1981). But if she is viewed instead as a *feminist*, that is to say, one opposing the systematic oppression of women by men, by masculinity as constituted in this particular historical context, then her defence of Chidley belongs with the campaigns described above, although these are usually described as minor in her career. Yet all of them were struggles against masculine sexuality and its power to coerce women— including the campaign for women's suffrage. Without this interpretation of Scott, her public career makes no sense; its parts lack interconnection.

Late-twentieth-century libertarian assumptions that sexology and the so-called 'sexual revolution' have changed everything, by reforming heterosexuality in women's favour, allow Rose Scott's pessimism about male animality to be dismissed as ignorant, misguided or cavalier on the question of women's sexual pleasure. Recent work that reexamines the texts and contexts of sexologists from Havelock Ellis to Shere Hite, however, casts substantial doubt on libertarian claims for the equity and health of modern reformed heterosexuality. Some British historians even make a plausible case for the connections between anti-feminism and sex reform; showing how phallocentric and male supremacist were the sexual scripts of Ellis, Kinsey, Masters and Johnson (Jackson, 1984; Bland, 1983). Others criticise the crudity of libertarian and feminist understandings of 'the problem' in defining it merely as the access of women to equal sexual pleasure *via* the orgasm—that is to say, by making men better lovers. This is what Segal (1983) calls the 'technicist approach', one that reduces the issue to men giving women orgasms apparently unlike the bad old days. Such reductionism seriously underestimates the profundity of first-wave feminist awareness that male dominance was not only mirrored in heterosexual mores, but that heterosexuality as men enforced it was central to the oppression of women. All the orgasms in the world bestowed by men could not alter the essential dynamic of this oppression.

NOTES

1 R. Scott, Marriage, n.d. unpublished notes, *Rose Scott Papers* ML.MSS. 38/22/2
2 The Mitchell Library published an annotated description of her papers with their *Guide to the Scott Family Papers in the Mitchell Library*, Sydney, Library Council of New South Wales, 1979, Part I. Rose Scott's Papers are Vols/Boxes 20–76. *The Rose Scott Correspondence* is a separate collection. ML.MSS. A2270–84
3 This journal is mentioned in the entry under 'Rose Scott' in Daniels, Murnane and Picot, 1977:192. It was in Item I of the unsorted collection.
4 R. Scott, 'Revolt Against the Organs', n.d. unpublished notebook entry, *Rose Scott Papers* ML.MSS. 38/22/4
5 R. Scott, Untitled speech, n.d. unpublished, *Rose Scott Papers* ML.MSS. 38/25, p.295
6 For Australian work of this kind, see Dixson, 1976; Summers, 1975:255–59; Mackenzie, 1960. Other instances of this historical tendency include Gordon and Dubois, 1983; Bland, 1983; Mitchell, 1977:226–31; Weeks, 1981:88–92.
7 For a forceful critique of this neglect see Jeffreys, 1982:629–45; and 1983:177–202
8 For analysis of their anti-feminist aspects, see Easlea, 1981:105–23; Fee, 1974:86–102; Jackson, 1982; Bleier, 1984:49–57; Bacchi, 1980:132–56; Modjeska, 1981:16–29
9 R. Scott, untitled notes, n.d. unpublished, *Rose Scott Papers* ML.MSS. 38/22/14, pp.16 and 23
10 Her analysis corresponds with that advanced in MacKinnon, 1979
11 R. Scott, 'Why Women Need a Vote,' unpublished speech, 1903, *Rose Scott Papers* ML.MSS 38–41, pp.173–249
12 See letters regarding this case in the *Rose Scott Correspondence*, ML.MSS. A2276–7, 'Women's Work and Women's Movements' and ML.MSS. A2278, 'Women's Political and Educational League' (binders' titles). Herringe was tried at Young Circuit Court, 15 April 1903
13 Letter to Editor, *Daily Telegraph* 19 May 1903
14 C. Mackellar to Rose Scott, 17 July 1903, *Rose Scott Correspondence* ML.MSS. A2278, p.45
15 R. Scott, untitled notes on men, n.d. unpublished, *Rose Scott Papers*

ML.MSS. 38/22/4; c.f. her speech delivered at the Sydney School of Arts in 1903, 'Why Women need a Vote', *Rose Scott Papers* ML.MSS. 38/41, pp. 173–249
16 See for example R. Scott, Peace and arbitration, 1904, unpublished speech, *Rose Scott Papers* ML.MSS. 38/54, pp.353–433

BARBARA CAINE

12 Millicent Garrett Fawcett: a Victorian liberal feminist?

Millicent Garrett Fawcett (1847–1929), was one of the leaders of the English women's suffrage movement. The longest-serving worker in this campaign, she began her participation as a very young member of the first Women's Suffrage Committee in London which formed in 1867, emerging formally as its leader in 1897, when she became president of the National Union of Women's Suffrage Societies. She finally retired from this position in 1918, feeling that the movement should now be led by younger women—and that her advanced age entitled her to indulge her hatred of the committee work in which she had been immersed for decades (Strachey, 1931:330). In the light of this, it is not surprising that the memorial to her in Westminster Abbey describes her as having 'won citizenship for women' (Oakley, 1983:184). But Fawcett was not only a suffragist: she was active as a lobbyist, a lecturer and a propagandist in several other campaigns as well. She worked in the campaign to extend higher education to women, in the battles to gain entry for women to medicine and to the other professions and to prevent the exclusion of women from a number of industrial occupations. She was particularly active in a number of campaigns to prevent the sexual exploitation of women and young girls and to establish an equal moral standard for women and men.

Despite her enormous importance within the women's movement, Millicent Fawcett has been the subject of remarkably little scholarly attention. Her biography was written shortly after her death by her friend and colleague, Ray Strachey, and is only now in the process of being revised.[1] She figures necessarily within most studies of the women's suffrage movement, but her role is often played down, especially in those studies which concentrate on the early twentieth century and highlight the dynamic actions of the Pankhursts and the

WSPU (see Liddington and Norris, 1978:13; Morgan, 1975:23–51). Fawcett was personally responsible for much of this lack of posthumous interest in her life and ideas: the care with which she culled her papers, removing anything of personal significance and leaving only public documents and formal letters, has preserved after her death the privacy she sought during her lifetime. Only the public figure remains. But the public figure itself has received less attention than one might have expected. Moreover the attention she has received has been directed only in very limited ways: notably towards her role as leader of the National Union of Women's Suffrage Societies. Little attention has been paid to her extensive published writings, to her interest in the work of the National Vigilance Association or to her constant concern about the situation and the problems of women (but see Jeffreys, 1985:72–75).

Indeed the one thing which seems absent from almost all existing accounts of Millicent Fawcett is her continuous and overriding concern with the sufferings of women and of young girls in the economic, social, legal and particularly in the sexual sphere. The failure to recognise this central informing interest is largely a result of the emphasis that is given to Fawcett's suffrage work at the expense of her other interests and activities. Discussions of her as a suffrage leader tend to concentrate on her pragmatism, her detachment and her lack of passion rather than on her ideas. Anecdote tends to serve in place of analysis where Millicent Fawcett is concerned—and one particular anecdote is frequently used to encapsulate her whole approach. This is a story taken from Helena Swanwick's autobiography, involving a petition for women's suffrage which referred to the petitioners as 'passionately desiring' the suffrage. When Fawcett was asked to sign, she paused to ask, 'Must I be passionate? ... oh very well' and duly added her name (see Swanwick, 1935; Rover, 1967:58). But to be passionless is not to eschew feminism. Moreover, as we will see, Fawcett's lack of passion in regard to the suffrage was more than counterbalanced by her intense anger and total emotional commitment to some other campaigns, notably those involving the age of consent and the protection of young girls from sexual exploitation and abuse.

Neglect of Fawcett's ideas and of her range of interests cannot be ascribed to lack of material. She left many published speeches as well as a number of articles in a wide range of well-known Victorian journals which covered almost every aspect of her interest in the situation of women. Her writings and speeches are not only accessible, but also to an unusual degree lucid, witty and enjoyable. She was a skilled controversialist who enjoyed doing battle, although she chose irony rather than anger as a literary mode. One cannot but admire her treatment of the ideas of such self-confident and prestigious opponents as Frederick Harrison and Fitzjames Stephen (Fawcett, 1873; 1891; Harrison, 1891; Fitzjames Stephen, 1873). Where Josephine Butler was wrought to fury by Harrison's assumption that all women married—and that those who did not should be induced to follow their true path by economic need, Fawcett contented herself with gently commending his insights while she humorously exposed his ignorance, his inconsistency, his presumption—and his unconscious brutality towards women.[2] She agreed with Butler that economic need and lack of employment drove women not into marriage, but into prostitution—and that it emphasised the similarities between marriage and prostitution (Fawcett, 1891:678). But she retained throughout her discussion a detachment and an air of amusement from which anger and despair were carefully removed. Her articles are no less telling for this, indeed she seems to have pitched them in such a way as to gain maximum support from an indifferent readership—but they have rarely been read by twentieth-century scholars. Fawcett continues to be seen as a pragmatic liberal who worked for women's suffrage because she saw it as her duty, but who neither added anything of significance to feminist theory nor engaged in those nineteenth-century battles which are still able to inspire contemporary feminists (see for example Spender, 1982:354–55).

I do not wish to claim that some radically different version of Fawcett is immediately evident if we read her writings with care. What I want rather to argue is that the unproblematical version of Fawcett which is offered in almost all discussions of the nineteenth-century English women's movement is a false and oversimplified one, achieved only by ignoring certain major areas of her interests and activities. This version seems to have an important function within the whole construction of the nineteenth-century English women's movement in recent scholarship and hence has not been subject to challenge. Millicent Fawcett continues to be seen as the embodiment of a particular kind of Victorian bourgeois feminism, opposed on the one hand to campaigns dealing with sexual politics and on the other to any approach which involves radical social or economic criticism (Banks, 1983:66; Davis, 1982:309; Spender, 1982:345). But this view of Fawcett ignores both her profound involvement in some campaigns centring on the sexual exploitation of women and her very cogent reasons for opposing certain socialist and trade union approaches to the woman question. Her opposition to protective legislation for women, for example, was based on an understandable belief that such legislation was really designed to limit women's occupational opportunities and that it was supported by trade unions not to protect women but rather to restrict them to unskilled and low-paid jobs and to reinforce the view that their place was in the home (Fawcett, 1898; Hartmann, 1979:206–274). Recently Fawcett's involvement in the social purity campaigns which developed in England in the 1880s has been recognised (Banks 1983:68; Bristow, 1977:120–21; Jeffreys, 1985:72–75), but this later activity has not been given detailed analysis nor has it been studied in relation to her other feminist activities.

In this chapter, I want to relate Fawcett's involvement in the suffrage campaign and in the other campaigns for legal and social reform to her fundamental concern about the sexual exploitation of women and young girls, a concern which was part of her original reason for becoming involved in the women's movement. This focus serves immediately to point to tensions and conflicts within Fawcett which dispel the idea that she was simply a pragmatist. That significant tensions exist within Fawcett's ideas about and approach to the woman question is immediately evident to anyone who looks beyond her suffrage work and takes note of her involvement in the campaigns directed at the 'double standard' in sexual morality. Edward Bristow deals only cursorily with Fawcett in his study of social purity movements, but notes that while she was a moderate on the suffrage question, she became a militant in the social purity movement in 1885 (Bristow, 1977:121). In a much more sympathetic treatment of Fawcett, Ann Oakley has recently commented on the complexity and inaccessibility of her moral values and on the fact that her behaviour occasionally appears hard to understand. She cites, as an example of this, Fawcett's personal campaign to prevent the election to Parliament of a man whom she believed to have seduced and then abandoned a young girl (Oakley, 1983:194). Oakley is right to point to the importance of this episode. But she is incorrect, in my view, to see this as the only exception to the rule of Fawcett's 'single-minded and life-long devotion to the suffrage cause'. It seems to me, by contrast, that there are other episodes which also deserve attention and that these in turn serve to raise the broader question of the importance of the sexual exploitation of women in Fawcett's feminism.

The episode cited by Oakley is an interesting one, but it has at least one companion. This is the story of the way in which Millicent Fawcett, accompanied by W.A. Coote, the secretary of the National Vigilance Association, and a couple of friends, embarrassed and upbraided a man who was pursuing a young servant girl and forcing upon her his unwanted attentions.

The girl was followed by the man on her day off and subsequently complained to her mistress about him and about the fact that he had followed her home. She then received a note suggesting that she meet him on her next day off work. It is worth continuing the story in Fawcett's own words.

> He told the girl to meet him on Saturday the 11th at one o'clock outside the British Museum. The servant brought the letter at once to her mistress, her mistress to me, and I to Mr. Coote, . . . No answer was sent to the Beast's letter. At 12.45 on the appointed day, we stationed the girl at the gate of the British Museum. The mistress's sister waited out of sight, just inside the rails; Mr Coote and a 'rough friend' lounged in a doorway opposite and the mistress and I walked up and down. Punctually at one the Beast arrived, dressed up to the nines and extending his hand to shake hands with the little servant. Before he could touch her Mr. Coote seized him and bellowed 'Scoundrel' and other appropriate epithets. The rough friend seized him and pinned him to the spot. Instantly a crowd of about fifty persons was on the spot. Mr Coote shouted the Beast's name and explained his evil intentions. I never saw a man so taken aback. (Strachey, 1931:117–18)

And well he might have been. Mrs Fawcett would have liked to give the man a thrashing and regretted that this would have been illegal. Indeed, as she said, 'The worst of it is that it is illegal for a woman to solicit a man for immoral purposes, but not for a man to solicit a woman'. She had to be content with a moral victory—and presumably with a feeling of great personal satisfaction.

These acts of confrontation suggest not only that Fawcett was concerned about moral standards, but also that certain actions directed by men towards women elicited from her intense and even violent anger. Where Josephine Butler always argued that one should not pursue the individual, but should concentrate on the organised trade of prostitution, Millicent Fawcett sought both legal redress and the more personally satisfying avenue of direct intervention. In the view of some recent historians, this makes her an exemplar of some of the worst aspects of Victorian repression and prudery (Weeks, 1981). But one can equally see Fawcett as demonstrating her recognition that the unrestrained exercise of male sexuality could be and often was exploitative of women. Alongside a large number of other nineteenth-centry feminists, she campaigned for the protection of women from the unwanted sexual advances and from the sexual victimisation which they too often suffered at the hands of men (see Jeffreys, 1985:1–9).

Millicent Fawcett's concern about the sexual exploitation of women was not confined to these singular instances. Indeed one could well argue that it was a fundamental part of her interest in the women's movement generally. It is evident throughout her life—and is stated quite clearly in her own account of her reasons for becoming involved in the suffrage movement.

Fawcett's autobiography, *What I Remember*, offers no startling revelations and was clearly intended to be part of her wider propaganda for the women's movement. She follows the general pattern of nineteenth-century feminist autobiography by offering us a specific personal explanation for her interest in and commitment to the social and political equality of women. But her personal explanation is nonetheless fascinating—and all the more so because it has been almost systematically ignored in later writing about her. For most later writers, two anecdotes serve to explain Fawcett's interest in and her entry to the women's movement. One is the story told by Ray Strachey, of how Emily Davies, sitting in the Garrett House one night, took for herself the fight for higher education for women while giving to Elizabeth Garrett that of gaining entry for women to the medical profession. '"After these things are done," she added "we must see about getting the vote." And then she turned to the little girl who was still sitting quietly on her stool and said, "you are younger than we are, Millie, so you must attend to that."' (Strachey, 1931:101; Kamm, 1966:132; Spender, 1982:349). To this rather charming story is sometimes added one told by Fawcett herself about the horror she felt when, having charged a young man with the theft of her purse, she heard that purse described in court as the property of her husband, Henry Fawcett (Strachey, 1931:83–84).

But while these two stories are often repeated and one, at least, was told by Fawcett herself, neither of them was used by her to explain her interest in the women's movement. Her account is a very different one. Fawcett began her chapter entitled 'Early Suffrage Work: Sowing Seed' in an altogether more dramatic fashion by describing an incident in a biography of Abraham Lincoln. It concerned his visit to a New Orleans slave market where a young girl was being inspected by prospective purchasers. 'He saw a young mulatto girl exposed naked before the buyers and handled by them as if she were an animal . . . [O]ne of his companions declared that Lincoln burst out "My God, boys, let us get away from this. If ever I get a chance to hit that thing, I'll hit it hard"' (Fawcett, 1924:116). Fawcett of course disclaims any intent to compare herself with Lincoln or to liken 'the legal and social subjection of women in England in the nineteenth century with the gross horrors of the slave trade in its most terrible aspect'. But the powerful image of the slave girl remains and it is reinforced by her recounting of 'two small accidentally heard conversations' which moved her to devote herself to gaining political and social equality for women. The first conversation occurred at her parents' home while she and two guests were waiting for a dance to begin.

> My two companions were talking, and presently took up the subject of the failure of a recent marriage in our immediate circle. The young husband and wife were estranged, and no one exactly knew the reason why; after pursuing this interesting theme for some time, one said to the other, 'I cannot see what she has to complain of. LOOK HOW HE DRESSES HER!' I fumed inwardly, but said nothing. I thought I would like to make that sort of talk impossible. I kept on thinking about it, and the shame and degradation of it, which seemed to be accepted by my companions as a matter of course. I did not know anything at that time about 'kept women', but 'Look how he dresses her' was of its essence. (Fawcett, 1925:117)

As this story makes clear, Fawcett did not see the marriage ceremony itself as sufficient to sanctify a sexual relationship or to differentiate between marriage and prostitution. It was the spiritual and emotional element in marriage which did this. True marriages would only become prevalent when women were free not to marry, i.e. when celibacy and careers were not only possible for women, but widely accepted and respected. Hence for Fawcett, legal and social reform was essential in order to remove some of the most degrading aspects of the sexual subjection of women.

The second conversation which Fawcett records is at first sight very curious. It is a much more trifling story than the first and does not directly relate to the theme of sexual exploitation or the ownership of women's bodies by men. This story centres on an overheard conversation involving the wives of two clergymen discussing which items sold best at the parish fairs which were held to raise money for parish schools.

> 'What do you find sells best?' said No. 1 to No. 2, who instantly replied, 'OH! THINGS THAT ARE REALLY USEFUL, SUCH AS BUTTERFLIES FOR THE HAIR!' Of course there was a comic aspect to this which I did not fail to appreciate, but I hoped a time would come before very long when intelligent and active-minded women would cease to regard 'butterflies for the hair' as 'really useful'. (Fawcett, 1924:117)

These stories provide Fawcett's introduction to the women's movement which she then went on to describe. It is worth emphasising her insistence that it was a many-sided movement in which political freedom was only one aspect:

> Speaking generally, its most important departments dealt with 1) education, 2) an equal moral standard between men and women, 3)

professional and industrial liberty, and 4) political status. My special experience and training fitted me best, as I thought, for work on behalf of the fourth of these, but I recognised that this was only one side of the whole question, and I was likewise convinced that whoever worked for any of the branches of our movement was, whether he liked it or not, really helping the other three. (Fawcett, 1924:117–18)

Fawcett's inclusion of the butterfly episode, demonstrating as it does the trivialisation of women's lives and activities within Victorian society, provides a useful introduction to her insistence that the women's movement was a many-sided one and that the situation of women required improvement through education, and through legal, political, social and moral reform. But it is also clear that while these changes would broaden the scope of women's lives and increase their self-determination, they offer only an indirect means of dealing with the specifically sexual degradation evident in both the story of Lincoln and the mulatto girl or in Fawcett's own response to the way married women were kept. Fawcett did not ever discuss this question directly, but throughout her career as a suffragist and feminist campaigner there is a distinct tension between her calmness and detachment as a political and legal campaigner and the fury which was aroused in her by specific incidents of sexual exploitation. Fawcett is not usually seen as similar to Josephine Butler in her feminism or her concerns about the oppression of women. But although she lacked Butler's charismatic appeal and her religious faith and sense of herself as called by God to fight the sexual oppression of women, she shared Butler's sense that every question about the economic or legal situation of women involved also the question of prostitution and of sexual abuse.

That this should be so comes as something of a surprise as Fawcett held aloof from the campaign led by Butler against the Contagious Diseases Acts in the 1870s. Indeed she is still sometimes seen as the leading figure in the attempt made by the London National Society for Women's Suffrage in the early 1870s to 'keep the suffrage struggle separate from a campaign ... which, because of its subject might impair or tar the suffrage claims' (Davis 1982:309). Millicent Fawcett did keep aloof from the Contagious Diseases agitation, but it cost her dearly to do so and it was a position she accepted only after considerable internal struggle (Strachey, 1931:52–53). She was always privately a supporter of the Contagious Diseases agitation and spent some time deciding whether or not to involve herself in it. John Stuart Mill regarded her as one of the people on the executive committee of the London National Society for Women's Suffrage who was likely to be hostile to his attempt to keep that society, of which he was president, completely separate from the Contagious Diseases agitation. However, he knew her husband did not sympathise with it and hoped that this would sway her (Caine, 1978:66). Millicent Fawcett was at this stage a recently married woman in her early twenties and she was persuaded by the combined influence of Mill and of Henry Fawcett to eschew the Contagious Diseases agitation and to devote her energies to the suffrage campaign. Unlike Mill, however, she never criticised the motives, the abilities or the conduct of those who combined their suffrage work with the campaign to abolish the Contagious Diseases Acts and in later years she too became active in abolitionist campaigns.

The discussion surrounding the Contagious Diseases Acts in the 1870s and 1880s brought to the fore a number of questions about prostitution and sexual commerce. The existence and extent of the white slave trade became an issue of public debate particularly in relation to the question of young girls. The age of consent for girls was then twelve and little was apparently done either to enforce this or to protect young girls from becoming ensnared in prostitution. Fawcett became deeply involved in these questions. In a way that seems highly uncharacteristic, if one looks only at the model offered by her suffrage work, she catapulted herself into the midst of these debates by her articles and by her strong private and public support for W.T. Stead. In 1885 Stead published a series of articles on child prostitution entitled 'The Maiden Tribute of Modern Babylon' which exposed the existence of widespread child prostitution and the lack of care and protection which many children experienced. To demonstrate the ease with which a girl could be obtained for sexual purposes, Stead purchased a young girl for £5 and took her to France. He was subsequently arrested—for paying the money to her mother and not to her father—and imprisoned. Stead's articles caused a great public outcry, with many people insisting that the matters which he raised were not a fit subject for general discussion. Although Fawcett believed strongly in reticence and decorum and could not, for example, condone the widespread dissemination of birth control material, she insisted that on this particular matter silence was neither acceptable nor desirable. Her first short article on the question entitled 'Speech or Silence' stated her conviction that speech was imperative. Stead's articles in the *Pall Mall Gazette* had exposed a

> hideously perverted state of morals running through, so far as one sex is concerned, the whole of Society from the highest to the lowest; while so far as the other sex is concerned, it condemns the poorest, most ignorant and most helpless to a living death of unspeakable

degradation, and drags down certain others, through appeals to their cupidity to a much lower depth of infamy and shame, that of living in luxury on the trade of decoying and selling children and their fellow women.

Silence about this state of affairs has existed for too long and even 'the most optimistic can scarcely claim that it has succeeded' in reducing the evil. Speech should now be tried to force action. She rejected totally the idea that Stead was revealing matters that had not been known in polite society. He had 'not so much told us what we did not know before as whipped and lashed us to a sense of our dastardly cowardice in knowing these things and making no effort to stop them' (Fawcett, 1885:327).

This article, and indeed all the others that Fawcett wrote about prostitution or about the exploitation of young girls, are markedly different from those she wrote about women's suffrage, education, professions or about the general question of the emancipation of women. They are as different in tone as in content. The cool, amused detachment which could relish the absurdities of opponents like Harrison or Fitzjames Stephen, and could welcome the emergence of an anti-suffrage league as a means of reviving the flagging energy of the pro-suffrage camp is all gone. Instead one has an earnest tone and an urgent insistence on the need for immediate action. No one had to urge Mrs Fawcett to be 'passionate' when it came to denouncing the sale and exploitation of women and young girls.

For Fawcett, the horrors of child abuse and child prostitution revealed by Stead demonstrated yet again the need for women's suffrage. She was convinced, and not without reason, that once women had some say in parliament, legislation dealing with their protection would be dealt with in an altogether more adequate and expeditious manner (Fawcett, 1898:6–7). At the same time, she was aware of the limits of legislative reform and saw economic, social and moral change as necessary to supplement it. Like Butler she saw the economic and social subjection of women as the root cause of their engaging in prostitution. Hence in her suggestions of a solution, she stressed—again like Butler—the economic hardships faced by women and the need for the moral transformation of men.

> Deep down at the bottom of the questions that have been raised by the recent agitation is the economical and political subjection of women; their miserably low wages in the poorest classes, wages on which life can hardly be supported unless recourse is had to the better paid trade of sin. If a real remedy is to be found it must be sought in two ways, both full of difficulties and needing patience, enthusiasm, courage, and faith. The demand for victims must be diminished by a growth of

unselfishness and of purity of heart among men; the supply of victims must be diminished by giving the poorest women more opportunities of fairly remunerative employment, by insisting on an extension to women of the trades-union doctrine of a fair day's pay for a fair day's work, by improvement in the dwellings of the poorest classes, and by endeavouring to form in every girl's mind a worthy ideal of woman-hood. (Fawcett, 1885:331)

Her concern about the exploitation of young girls led Millicent Fawcett to do more than utter passionate words. She became an active member of the Vigilance Association in 1885 and served on its executive committee for a number of years. She chaired the Preventive and Rescue Sub-Committee and this involved her in a number of different campaigns. She led the National Vigilance Association campaign to bring further changes to the 1885 Criminal Law Amendment Act in order to increase the time available to girls to bring an action against a man for rape or seduction, to bring incest within the scope of this legislation and hence to make it a punishable offence; and to get more severe punishments for men who abused positions of authority. Fawcett's work on this committee greatly extended her awareness of the nature and the extent particularly of the sexual abuse of children. She was appalled by the number of girls under twelve who came into the homes and refuges set up by the Association, already exhausted by years of pro-stitution. She saw the employment of very young girls in theatres and entertainment centres as a major source of child prostitution and attacked the practice—and the parents who allowed and encouraged their daughters in this way of life. Fawcett's discussion of theatre children and child prostitution, like all her discussions of prostitution, combines anger and an insistence on the need for the effective moral policing of those who profit from the sale of women with enormous compassion for the women themselves.

Questions about the sexual exploitation of girls and about pros-titution came to occupy more and more of Fawcett's time in the late 1880s and 1890s. She did not let up on her suffrage activity: indeed it was during this time that she became president of the National Union of Women's Suffrage Societies and was constantly exercised by the need to steer the suffrage movement away from the direct party affiliation which was sought by many of her colleagues. At the same time, she was both active and recognised within the overall abolitionist campaigns. In 1896, for example, Josephine Butler re-commended Fawcett as a speaker to the Westminster Committee of the Abolitionist Federation. Fawcett, in Butler's view, was superior to any of the other suggested speakers. 'She lacks warmth rather, but she is clear and deeply convinced of the vital character of the abolitionist movement.'[3]

Precisely why Millicent Fawcett became actively involved in the campaigns centring on prostitution and sexual morality in her later years, having held aloof from them earlier, is something on which one can only speculate. It is interesting to note that she did so in 1885, the year not only of Stead's campaign, but also of the death of Henry Fawcett. Throughout their married life, Millicent had looked after and assisted her blind husband in his academic and political work, regarding her public role as a secondary matter. With his death, she emerged as a public figure herself in a much more significant way. It is interesting, however, that she should have done so through focusing her attention on those very campaigns about sexual matters which Henry Fawcett had earlier dissuaded her from entering. He was himself an opponent of the Contagious Diseases Acts and had apparently recognised the power of the movement for their repeal,[4] but he had never given his support to them. Now, after his death, it was Stead and the furore created by his 'Maiden Tribute' which, in Strachey's words, 'roused Millicent entirely, and which brought back all her old fighting spirit'. Strachey herself noted that the revelations made by Stead roused Millicent Fawcett 'as she had never been roused before', and that she 'burnt and flamed with rage against the evils he described' (Strachey, 1931:108). Shortly after this, Fawcett met Josephine Butler and was instantly smitten by the Butler charm and presence. She felt herself to be in the presence of greatness, and her comments on Butler are essentially those of a follower describing a cherished and revered leader. There is nothing in them of the irony which is present in her descriptions of Emily Davies, for example, or of the detachment with which she discussed J.S. Mill (Fawcett, 1881:4–5; 1924). Butler was to her 'one of the very great people in the world', and she expressed her reverence at length in the biography she wrote of her with Ethel Turner (Fawcett and Turner, 1927).

Fawcett's comments about Josephine Butler are in themselves enough to give one pause before accepting the view of her as a pragmatist interested only in the suffrage question. But even when extolling Butler's virtues, she continued to hide some of her own interests and activities in the very campaigns in which she praised Butler's role. The most interesting instance of this relates to the question of the debate about the Contagious Diseases Acts in India. In her biography of Butler, Fawcett devoted a chapter to this, out-lining the history of the Acts in India from the time of the 1859 Royal Commission into the Sanitary State of the Army to the extension of the Contagious Diseases Acts to India in 1869. She noted that these acts were not applied to the entire native civil population, but were used rather to provide 'clean' Indian women for the British army. Their use for this purpose was explicitly stated in a memorandum issued by the Commander-in-Chief of the British Army in 1886 who stated that the Cantonment Acts, as the C.D. Acts were called in India, were needed 'to arrange for the effective inspection of prostitutes attached to regimental bazaars whether in cantonments or on the line of march'. It was essential, he added, 'to have a sufficient number of women, to take care they are sufficiently attractive, to provide them with proper houses' (Fawcett and Turner, 1927). This memorandum, which was made public in England in 1888, aroused a storm of protest and led to a renewed mobilisation of abolitionists. The abolitionists were appalled by the fact that some people who had opposed the C.D. Acts in England were quite prepared to support their operation in regard to Indian women. They mounted an attack, however, in exactly the same terms as they had earlier used in England, pointing to the futility of these acts as a means of reducing venereal disease and stressing the ways they violated the rights of women. As they had done earlier, abolitionists also urged the government to show greater care and concern for the army by providing better accommodation and by making more provisions for the mental and physical well-being of soldiers. Fawcett stresses Butler's involvement in this campaign, regretting only that she did not live to see its final success with the end of the regulation of prostitutes coming to India during the First World War.

But while detailing Butler's role, Fawcett says nothing either here or anywhere else about her own involvement in this campaign. Strachey, who follows Fawcett's own lead in playing down her involvement in campaigns around sexual morality, refers to her making a 'fine speech' in 1898, 'upon the continuance of the C.D. Acts for the Army in India' (Strachey, 1931:181), but offers no hint of the content of the speech. A year before this, in 1897, Frances Power Cobbe wrote to Fawcett expressing her 'satisfaction at seeing you take up this side of the terrible question'—in opposition to Millicent Fawcett's sister, Elizabeth Garrett Anderson, who had always supported the Contagious Diseases Acts (see Caine, 1976:24; Manton, 1966). Cobbe offered £10 to help Fawcett in her work.

Fawcett's actions within the National Vigilance Association and in regard to the International Federation of Abolitionists clearly warrants more investigation. What seems evident immediately, however, is the need to broaden the focus which is applied to her ideas and to her activities and to see her involvement in campaigns about sexual exploitation and about the need to protect young girls as central to her concerns and to her feminism. Once one does this, it is possible to see the tension between her feminism and her ideas on strategy. Faced with the enormity of the sexual, legal, economic and political subjection of women, she followed the lines of other nineteenth-century reform movements in seeking political remedies first of all. Her pragmatic stance on the suffrage question was part of a strategic plan. She sought the suffrage as a means to an end. Hence her clearly expressed view that women's suffrage, when it came, would not bring a revolution, but would rather 'have the effect of adjusting the political machinery of the country to the altered conditions of its inhabitants' does not add up to the sum total of her involvement in the problems of women (Fawcett, 1898:3). It rather stresses her recognition that this issue was only one among many and would not in itself bring an end to the oppression of women.

NOTES

1 A biography of Millicent Garrett Fawcett is at present being written by David Rubinstein of the University of Hull.
2 For Josephine Butler's response to Harrison's views, see Butler Papers, Fawcett Library, Josephine Butler to Frederick Harrison, 9 May 1868, and Josephine Butler to Albert Rutson, 12 May 1868.
3 Butler Papers, Josephine Butler to the Miss Priestmans, 15 October 1896
4 Butler Papers, Josephine Butler to the Miss Priestmans, September 1871

JUDITH KEENE

13 Aileen Palmer's coming of age

Aileen Palmer has spent, off and on, a good third of her life in a mental asylum in Melbourne. The care is professional if perfunctory. Over the years she has survived the rigours of treatment designed to jolt stragglers back to the ranks of the sane; and daily she weathers the petty tyrannies of life in an institution: rationed cigarettes, evening meals served in mid-afternoon, and being constantly in the company of others with whom there is no connection except the tenuous link of propinquity.

Aileen Palmer's other life, outside the institution, has passed into obscurity. It is not the familiar obscurity which is the lot of many Australian women where individuality becomes blurred by the ordinariness of existence, the commonplace of jobs, marriage, homes and childrearing. Quite the contrary. Aileen Palmer's real life was atypical, even extraordinary in comparison with her peers. She remained single in a world which was relentlessly married; a poet, an intellectual, and a formidable linguist in a society smugly indifferent to such qualities; a communist who supported progressive and often unpopular causes; and a nationalist but one who only truly felt at home away from Australia, and who after eleven years abroad felt despair on returning to 'this dreadful steak and eggs country'.

In large part it is not Aileen Palmer's uncommon qualities which account for her invisibility. The detail of her life has been eclipsed by the figures of her famous parents, Vance and Nettie Palmer, and any impact she may have had on the Australian cultural landscape has been swamped by the mark of their distinguished careers. It was indeed in the wash of her parents' considerable wake that Aileen Palmer tried to create an independent identity for herself. She has called this her 'coming of age', a process in which she sought her own autonomy, an integral part of which was the establishment of herself as a serious writer.

This paper examines Aileen's perception of the process of her coming of age, and because her parents were so inextricably involved, it is concerned with Vance and Nettie too. It deals however only with a fragment of their lives and quite unabashedly presents Aileen's version of events. The paper has no pretensions to rewrite the Palmer story but, rather, only to illuminate a small part of it, and from a quite particular perspective.

My own introduction to Aileen Palmer came through research on the Spanish civil war. She was an interpreter and medical records officer with the International Brigades and has left an absorbing record in her diaries and letters, and the manuscript drafts of the novel which she wrote based on her experiences in Spain.[1] Her writings about herself and Spain are literate, graphic and unsentimental. As I read her papers I felt a great sympathy for the woman, and a strong interest in her as a person. She considered the Spanish civil war to be central in her own development. Spain was the rock on which her political life was grounded. It was also the stage when she made a conscious decision to separate from her parents and lead her own life. From 1936 until 1946, first in Spain and later in London during the Second World War, Aileen moved in a different orbit from that of her parents, on a trajectory which had its own distinct focal points. It was in the act of writing about her experiences, however, that she was drawn back into her parents' sphere, and, however unintentionally on the part of Vance and Nettie, was unable to break away from their intellectual domination.

Kay Iseman has discussed what she calls 'the problem of filiation' among young Australian women whereby their attempts to become autonomous writers often founder because they are based on a rejection of their mothers and an inability to disengage themselves from their fathers (Iseman, 1981). Aileen Palmer's coming of age may be part of a more general conundrum of filiation though in her case it was a more complex phenomenon than that which Iseman described. Vance and Nettie were a more complex couple than the simple dichotomy of powerless mother in the domestic sphere and father as agent in the outside world. Both Vance and Nettie were highly productive and creative, prizing the life of the artist above all else.[2] Since her childhood they had confidently expected Aileen to follow their path. They had instilled in her from an early age that creative writing was the most worthwhile endeavour. In becoming a writer Aileen was not having to break new ground in opposition to one or other parent, but rather was attempting to carve out a place for herself in a field in which her parents were already well established. Vance and Nettie were among the very few Australians whose lives were entirely devoted to writing. For Aileen it was a matter of doing in her own way what her parents already did extremely well, and in which their standards represented those of the objective world of published literature. Writing for them as well as for herself was a difficult task and one on which Aileen Palmer's coming of age eventually came unstuck.

Aileen was Vance and Nettie's elder daughter, born in London in 1915 several months before her parents' departure from Europe where they had lived since their marriage in the preceding year. Her childhood was shared between the bush at Gembrook outside Melbourne and long sojourns on the Queensland coast, at Vance's house in Caloundra. Nettie taught Aileen at home for the first years, and considered her a gifted and highly intelligent child. There are frequent references in Nettie's letters to Aileen's intellectual exploits: her story writing in French, her amusing observations, and the precociousness of the child's poetry. Finding that Aileen shared her own facility for languages, Nettie had taught her French, German and Latin. The 'methodicalness' of the latter Aileen found absorbing and 'took to it like a duck to water'.[3]

When the family moved permanently to Victoria in 1929 Aileen was enrolled at PLC, Nettie's old school. She matriculated to Melbourne University where she graduated in 1934 with first-class honours in French and German language and literature, presenting what Nettie described as 'an astoundingly original thesis on Proust'.[4] She also studied Spanish and Russian as 'extra subjects'. During her student years she was active in left-wing politics: prominent in the Victorian Writers' League; in the University Labor Club, editing *Proletariat*, the club's paper; and in her final year one of the organisers of the campaign for Egon Kisch. She had joined the Communist Party in April 1934[5] and though her parents had not opposed her decision there was some friction. During the Melbourne campaign for Kisch Aileen berated her parents for their self-absorption and their unwillingness to give politics all their time in contrast to Katharine Susannah Prichard's unstinting work for the cause.[6]

In March 1935 the Palmers left for England so that the girls could have some exposure to European culture and languages while Vance and Nettie renewed old friendships and literary acquaintances. Aileen had come with an introduction to the Communist Party of Britain[7] and eschewing her mother's rounds of the galleries, joined London Left campaigns, selling the *Daily Worker* and attending anti-fascist rallies. From November 1935 until March 1936 she lived in Vienna with an Austrian family, improving her German and

supporting herself by translations. On the streets and from the
family's Jewish friends Aileen saw at first hand the workings of
National Socialism.

The Palmers moved to Spain in May 1936, renting a house on the
beach at Mongat, a fishing village three train stops North of Barcelona where they settled down to live cheaply and simply. Through
the mails Vance and Nettie maintained contact with English and
Australian literary affairs. Nettie kept up a busy reviewing schedule
while Vance revised Furphy's *Such Is Life*, the drafts of which were
typed by Aileen.

In Spain Aileen was connected to their immediate surroundings
in a more direct way than was either of her parents. The family's
principal Spanish speaker, she shopped in the market and dealt with
the minutiae of passports, papers, and stamps required of foreign
residents. Through the Communist Party of Catalonia she met up
with young people, moving particularly in the circles of German-
speaking exiles, of whom at this time in Barcelona there were a
great many. A number of times Aileen took Nettie with her to
political meetings. In early June Aileen arranged tickets for them
both to attend a rally to hear La Pasionaria, at this time known only
as the recently elected communist woman deputy for the Asturias.
In the same month Nettie accompanied Aileen and her friends to a
meeting of the PSUC, the Communist Party of Catalonia, to rally
local support in the nearly village of Masnou. Confessing to understanding little of the proceedings, Nettie was fascinated by the
assembly and impressed at the intelligence of Aileen's observations
on what was taking place.[8] Early in June Aileen began work as a
typist and translator with the Olympiad Popular, the anti-fascist
games planned to open in Barcelona in mid-July in opposition to
Hitler's Olympics in Berlin in August. Henceforth she spent most of
her time at the Barcelona Stadium, coming home on days off,
frequently bringing friends with her to Mongat to spend the day.
She managed to obtain a pass for Vance to the press enclosure so he
could mix with the foreign journalists when the games began.[9]

On the fateful night of the Spanish generals' attempted coup
against the Republican government, Aileen was in Barcelona in
friends' digs. A number of her comrades joined the street fighting
which defeated the insurgents' attempts to take control of the city.
Vance and Nettie, hearing the sound of cannon fire along the coast
and assuming it was 'salutations to the Olympiad', only learnt of the
aborted coup the next day from the postman. Unable to get to
Barcelona they were 'comforted' that Aileen was 'with people of her
own sort'.[10] In the village all sorts of wild accounts of a revolution
in Barcelona were circulating, and Vance and Nettie became in-

creasingly concerned for Aileen's safety. When they could get to the city they eventually found her heading off, in high spirits, in a procession of Olympiad people to celebrate the defeat of the *pronunciamiento*.

Vance was extremely worried that the foreign mails would be held up in these chaotic conditions, and was alarmed by reports that foreigners were having difficulty cashing cheques. The staff at his English bank prophesied an anarchist revolution in Barcelona any day and the English consul impressed upon him the urgency of removing his family to the safety of Britain. Nettie gave away their household belongings and prepared to depart immediately. Aileen, summoned home, was horrified at the suggestion that they were leaving. Her efforts to reassure her parents were to no avail, as was a testimonial to their safety which she obtained from the head of the Mongat militia. Nor could she convince them to allow her to stay in Barcelona without them. Though Vance admitted to Nettie that if he were in Aileen's place he would feel the same way, he insisted that his daughter must leave with them.[11] With a good deal of bitterness Aileen joined her parents on the British warship which had come to rescue all British subjects in Spain.

In Paris Aileen left her parents, visiting friends from Nettie's student days, and travelled to London where she found herself a room and offered her services as a typist to the British Spanish Relief Committee. A few days before the members of the first British Medical Aid Unit were to leave for Spain Aileen was invited to accompany them as their secretary and interpreter. After some hard words between Vance and Aileen, her parents accepted the *fait accompli*, and Nettie rallied around, buying underwear and clothes to fit out Aileen's Spanish pack.[12]

The first British Medical Unit arrived in Barcelona at the end of August and Aileen was delighted to be back in the city. In letters home she emphasised that the city was calm and that Vance and Nettie's departure had been precipitous and ill considered. Her parents had sailed for Australia soon after Aileen had left for Spain and did not see their daughter again for ten years. Aileen was in Spain for almost the entire duration of the civil war and remained in London throughout the Second World War working as an air-raid warden and an ambulance driver during the blitz.

Writing years later, Aileen described her decision to separate from her parents after leaving Barcelona in July 1936 as her 'first coming of age': the first decision she had made independently of her parents. It had been precipitated by their insisting that she leave with them though her political instinct and personal preference was to stay. At that time she had become convinced that she 'had lived for too long under the August and all pervasive shadow' of her parents.[13] The depth of her political commitment to anti-fascist Spain probably gave her the courage to take the step, one which would have considerable ramifications for her future and her relationship with the family.

The British Medical Aid Unit first set up hospital in a small village in Western Aragon, handling casualties from the Huesca and Zaragossa fronts. In early 1937 the hospital staff was transferred to Albacete to became part of the Medical Services of the newly organised International Brigades with whom Aileen served continuously until mid-1938. She recorded details and statistics of the wounded and translated for the military and medical command where communication between the great number of different nationalities in the International Brigades was essential. During the Jarama Campaign in early 1937 she was with the XIVth, a French-speaking battalion, whose medical unit consisted of a German superintendent, French doctors, Spanish nurses and French-, English- and Spanish-speaking troops. During the punishing Republican offensive at Brunete in July 1937 she was stationed in the reception wards of the theatres set up within the Escorial. After a month's leave in London in August she joined the 35th Brigade in the snows of Teruel where in sub-zero temperatures the Republicans took the town which had been in Nationalist hands since the first days of the war. In early 1938 with a convoy of wounded she was part of the terrible retreat eastwards across Aragon before the advancing Nationalist forces. When Franco reached the coast in March 1938, cutting Republican Spain in two, Aileen was working in a base hospital near Barcelona. Exhausted and having lost her pack and all her possessions she was sent to London for prolonged rest and recuperation.

Throughout this time Aileen had kept up constant, if irregular, contact with her parents. To their mild admonishments for scrappily written letters or long gaps without news, Aileen explained that conditions were scarcely congenial to letter writing or receiving. Her unit was constantly on the move, frequently sleeping in the open while the field hospital worked from camouflaged tents. Even in commandeered houses there was uncertain light, little privacy, and the constant coming and going of drivers, ambulance bearers and medical staff in a daily regimen that was governed by the erratic rhythm of rushes of wounded from the front. There was also the obstacle to communication with the family that Aileen's 'horizons were entirely bordered by people and events' with whom they, in Australia, were unfamiliar.[14]

Since their return to Australia Vance and Nettie had worked

tirelessly for the Spanish Republican cause, Nettie as the president of the Spanish Relief Committee in Victoria, and Vance as a frequent speaker on Spanish affairs. In her letters Nettie frequently asked Aileen for news of the other Australians in Spain and for quotable copy and Spanish memorabilia that could be used in the Australian Committee's publicity campaigns. Apart from John Fisher, a journalist and the Australian committee's de facto representative in London, Aileen had very little contact with her fellow countrymen in Spain. She provided her mother, however, with an insider's commentary on political events taking place in Spain and often gave advice on matters that were of concern to the Spanish Relief Committee in Australia. Presumably their daughter's observations were useful to Vance and Nettie in their rather daunting task of drumming up support in Australia for the Republican side.

From Aileen's first days in the civil war Vance and Nettie had urged her to use the experience in Spain as material for a future novel. In August 1937, during her leave in London, Vance had cabled suggesting that the family would send funds for her keep, if she remained in England and wrote a novel. When she came back to London in mid-1938 she sent a short story, 'The Olives Must Be Picked', to her sister Helen for the *Melbourne University Magazine* (October 1938) and Vance, who liked the story, recommended that she send a polished version of it to the English weeklies. Under a pseudonym she also offered a couple of poems to John Lehmann for *New Verse*. All her time however was given over to political work for Spanish Aid and to settling down to the novel about the Spanish civil war, using the notes and jottings she had brought back from Spain.

Vance and Nettie were entirely supportive, sending money, encouragement and endless good advice. It was an enterprise close to Vance's heart. Since returning to Australia, he had spoken a number of times of his intention to write a novel about Spain which would alert Australians to the dangers of fascism.[15] Aileen's draft was completed in early November 1938 and she sent it to her parents asking for critical comments and 'hoping that they would not be too disappointed in it'.[16] Vance made a great many recommendations for revisions and Aileen rewrote accordingly while commenting wryly on 'the practicability' of 'trans Pacific criticism' whereby sections that Vance had recommended cutting were exactly those that people in London had considered necessary.[17]

The drafts of the novel, 'Last Mile to Huesca', are with Aileen and Helen Palmer's papers in the National Library of Australia. In its earlier forms the novel traces the fortunes of a group of men and women serving in a medical unit with the International Brigades from the battle of Brunete to Teruel. The backgrounds and tensions between the members of the group unfold as the novel progresses. Not surprisingly many of the incidents described are drawn from Aileen Palmer's own experiences. The writing is graphic, the portrayal of the characters sensitive, and the story is engaging, in places quite riveting. The later versions bear little resemblance to the earlier ones. At Vance's suggestion that a single protagonist was a more effective literary device than having a group of people on whom the narrative centred, Aileen rewrote the story around a single character. In later drafts the central character has become a young man from Queensland who in the course of the Spanish civil war is reunited with the father from whom, some years before, he had been separated.

There is no indication in the Palmer Papers of which version of Aileen's manuscripts was submitted for publication. In any event it was read by Gollancz who compared it favourably with a novel by T.C. Worsley, but declined to publish. There was discussion of a French translation and of a copy to be sent to Texas in case Hartley Grattan might be able to place it somewhere. Nothing came of these ventures.

It is unfortunate that the manuscript was never published. The novel is at least as good as a number of similar works based on personal recollections of Spain that appeared at this time. The main reason for its not being taken up probably had less to do with the novel itself than with the fact that by this time Franco had won the Spanish civil war, a much larger European war was imminent, and public interest in reading about the Spanish International Brigades had waned.

Aileen apologised profoundly to her parents for the manuscript's failure, explaining that it was as much for them as for herself that she had wanted it to appear.[18] She had hoped that a novel in press would have provided them with 'something tangible to show' for the years she had been away.[19] In an autobiographical piece written twenty years later Aileen reiterated that her disappointment had been stronger for Vance and Nettie. For herself, once the initial disappointment had passed, the episode with the Spanish novel had 'seemed to be one piece of mullock to add to that large heap into which [she] would delve in years to come'.[20]

By mid-1939 Nettie and Vance were anxious to have Aileen return home. In each letter to London they asked about her future plans and expressed concern that she would be cut off in Europe if, as seemed increasingly likely, there was another world war. It was arranged that she should board the *Stratheden* in Marseilles for Australia at the end of 1939 after reporting for the Australian

Spanish Relief Committee on the conditions of Spanish refugees in the camps in Southern France. In Biarritz Aileen visited a children's colony run by an Australian, Esme Odgers, and at Gurs, on the east coast, she managed to contact some of her Austrian International Brigade comrades, now interned by the French authorities.[21] On the trip to France she was overwhelmed with 'nostalgia' and a 'sense of tragedy': for the Spanish Republicans and their supporters reduced to the most pitiful condition; for the Europe which she had come to know and which most certainly would be engulfed in war before she saw it again; and for the friends and the life she had made for herself and was about to leave. Her 'sense of oppression' lifted only with the news that ships to Australia were no longer travelling through the Mediterranean and the *Stratheden* with her boxes on board was steaming around the Cape to Australia without her.[22]

Nettie worried a great deal about her elder daughter. In March 1935 she noted in her diary that a job at the Mitchell Library might be the solution to Aileen's uncertain future. While Aileen was in Spain Nettie asked always for more personal news, and gently chided her in London for letters that were remote and vague, providing no intimate detail of her daughter's daily life. It is ironical, perhaps, that Nettie, famous for lack of interest in her own appearance, manifested her maternal concern for Aileen in terms of the latter's wardrobe. After a parcel of corsets had arrived on the Aragon front Aileen complained to her sister that in future people should 'send something sensible' like cigarettes.[23] Communication between mother and daughter often degenerated into a catalogue of what Aileen called 'this footling business of dress': clothes sent and received; lists of underclothes; assurances of 'presentable accessories, hats and gloves'. After leaving Spain Aileen explained to her mother that her 'aim in life' was to have 'nothing more than her typewriter and what [she] could pack in her Fordite' but added reassuringly that she possessed 'two decent tea dresses' resurrected from Vienna days.[24] In September 1939 to her mother's insistent requests for news of her wardrobe Aileen informed Nettie that she owned two costumes, one made in Spain by the ex-King's tailor and though in it she looked a 'bit lady policemanish' it was hard-wearing and quite respectable. Aileen reassured Nettie too that when she returned to Australia she 'would look her size (whatever that means)'.[25]

Nettie confessed to her daughter that it was 'terrifying to be a mother and always in the wrong',[26] and apologised that her own letters to Aileen were 'makeshift' and 'never perfectly free' on the page, unlike 'the imaginary ones written lying awake at night'.[27] Towards the end of 1942 Nettie described a disturbing dream she had had about Aileen. It symbolises, perhaps, the source of the difficulties in their relationship as it suggests that Nettie perceived Aileen's political life as a cause of their separation. In Nettie's dream Aileen had returned unannounced to Australia and had hidden under her parents' bed. As Nettie put out her hands in welcome Aileen had drawn herself up and said very sternly, 'I don't approve of Australia's non-intervention'.[28]

Aileen agreed with Nettie that 'the mother–daughter relationship is a crook one'.[29] A number of times she reassured Vance and Nettie that they had been good parents and had given 'a difficult brat' 'a wonderful start at Caloundra', a houseful of books and tolerant surroundings. According to Aileen if she had 'suffered anything in her home environment it had been of feeling intellectually and generally inferior to my parents', and which had made her decide that she 'would never develop into anything until [she] got out from under [their] wing'. After years of separation however Aileen was sure that 'if we knew each other now we'd get on much better' and would not 'quarrel over basic things'.[30]

At the end of 1945 Nettie had an attack of coronory thrombosis and Aileen was summoned home in great haste. Nettie wrote to Miles Franklin at the end of October, 'Yes, be praised: Aileen is with us again'.[31] It was however a difficult time for all the Palmers. In London Aileen had been accustomed to a bohemian existence surrounded by a circle of her own friends, 'Spaniards and ex-Spaniards' and left-wing activists. She had been free to come and go as she chose, typing all night if it suited her, and sleeping late in the day. In Melbourne she returned to her parents' quiet house in Kew and attempted to fit back into their life and routine. With Vance's assistance she was found a job in a Melbourne library, and in her spare time began writing an autobiographical novel. *Pilgrim's Way* is a bleak story about the Pilgrim family, the scarcely disguised Palmers, who inhabit a place called Chilbrook. Blake and Noni, the parents, live with their two daughters, Gwen and Joan; the latter– Aileen– is the elder, and the story's narrator. In real life Aileen was as unhappy as her Pilgrim alter ego. She felt herself increasingly in 'a world of strangers' and within the family her sister Helen was the only one for whom she 'could find words'.[32] In 1948 Aileen entered a psychiatric clinic in the first of a number of such episodes, which over the years came to be of longer and longer duration.

There are a number of different versions, including several accounts she later wrote herself, of what triggered Aileen's first breakdown. These explanations are highly subjective and the discrepancies between them are unimportant. One will never know whether her illness was the delayed effect of war nerves from Spain

189

and the London blitz, or was caused by feelings of loneliness on returning to Australia, or from family tensions, or from all these combined with other longstanding factors. What is clear, however, is that Aileen felt a growing despair and isolation from her surroundings. The latter she found intolerable but was unable to alter. Equally, her condition placed Vance, Nettie and Helen under a profound strain. They were immensely distressed by Aileen's progressive withdrawal and their own powerlessness to halt her deterioration.

Between these bouts of illness Aileen lived with Nettie until the latter's death in October 1964, and has written a good deal about her and her parents' relationships which, as she described it, operated 'on an alternating current'. She perceived herself in a curious predicament. Her parents had profoundly impressed upon her as a child that writing was the thing above all others to which it was worth devoting her life. Nettie had 'treasured' her daughter's childhood stories and had 'carted from pillar to post the exercise books filled with novels written at the age of 9 or 10'.[33] As an adult, however, Aileen felt that her literary abilities had been discounted and Vance and particularly Nettie were entirely uninterested in what or how she wrote.[34]

It undoubtedly has been a tragedy that with the exception of some short pieces and a volume of poems published in 1964 by Overland Press none of Aileen's work has appeared. A novel in print would have provided objective proof of her abilities as a writer. She herself considered that publication would have constituted her 'second coming of age' after which she could have been recognised by her parents as an equal. Aileen's writing and her identity appear to have been closely linked. She believed that in Vance and Nettie's eyes her personal worth was inextricably tied to the value of her writing. As a proven writer she would have been part, on her own terms, of Vance and Nettie's sphere. Without such validation she remained always only her parents' daughter.

When I met Aileen Palmer she was in a crowded hospital day room, a large woman waiting for dinner. Aileen's contemporaries from the thirties had told me that she had been 'a troubled young woman', in many cases even 'difficult'. I had heard also the story from family friends of the young doctor at the psychiatric clinic who had told Helen that Aileen's grasp of reality was irreparably damaged, the proof of which was that she spoke often and unshakeably about her part in a war in Spain. She sat at a table with three other women, one of whom rocked continuously, and another kept up a cheerless dialogue with an invisible companion. Aileen was puzzled by my presence but sat graciously through a garbled explanation of my own attachment to the Spain of Lorca and that I had wept on first reading her poem on the poet's death. As I left the ward I asked the nurse on duty if he knew that the old lady with whom I had sat was a fine poet, and intrepid in her youth, had fought in the Spanish civil war, and was the daughter of one of Australia's leading literary families. He said no, as far as he knew, she was just Aileen Palmer.

NOTES

1 See, National Library of Australia, Manuscript Collection, Aileen Palmer Papers MS 6759; Aileen Palmer's letters and manuscripts in Helen Palmer Papers MS 6083; and Aileen Palmer's Spanish wartime diary for access to which I am indebted to Mrs Thora Craig, Powys, Wales.
2 This is not to suggest that there was no separation of roles based on gender between the Palmers. Drusilla Modjeska (1981) has shown that the division between Nettie the critic and Vance the novelist was based on a patriarchal view which worked to Nettie's detriment. Both, however, shared a belief in the value of creative work.
3 'Portrait of the Artist's Father', TS, NLA MS 6759, Box 5, Folder 37
4 Nettie Palmer's Diary 25 February 1935, National Library of Australia, Palmer Papers MS 1174, Series 16, Box 25
5 Australian Archives, Australian Security Intelligence Organization, File, Aileen Palmer, A6119/XRI, Item 111
6 AP to V&NP, 4 October [1938?] NLAMS 6759, Box 1, Folder 10
7 ASIO file Aileen Palmer
8 Nettie Palmer's Diary, 22 June 1936
9 Nettie Palmer's Diary, 18 July 1936
10 Nettie Palmer's Diary, 19 July 1936
11 Nettie Palmer's Diary, 25 July 1936; 26 July 1936; 28 July 1936
12 Nettie Palmer's Diary, 16 August 1936; 22 August 1936
13 'Coming of Age', TS, NLA MS 6759, Box 5, Folder 38
14 AP to NP 16 December 1936, NLA MS 6759 Box 1, Folder 7
15 See VP to NP, 12 October 1936, Palmer Papers, NLA MS 1174/1/5124
16 AP to V&NP 13 November 1938, NLA MS 6759, Box 1, Folder 7
17 AP to V&NP 13 February 1939, NLA MS 6759, Box 1, Folder 3
18 AP to V&NP 16 July 1939, NLA MS 6759, Box 1, Folder 7
19 AP to V&NP 14 May 1939, NLA MS 6759, Box 1, Folder 7
20 'The End and the Beginning', TS 'DL/21'. NLA MS 6759 Box 5, Folder 36
21 See the report of the visit in *Spanish Relief Bulletin*, November 1939, and the letters in Spanish and German from comrades at Gurs in the Saffin Collection, La Trobe Library, State Library of Victoria.
22 Fragment of AP's diary 1939, NLA MS 6759, Box 6, Folder 45
23 AP to HP 25 June 1937, NLA MS 6759, Box 1, Folder 10
24 AP to NP 15 July 1938, NLA MS 6759, Box 1, Folder 10

25 AP to NP, 14 September 1939, NLA MS 6759, Box 1, Folder 7
26 NP to AP, 20 November 1942, NLA MS 1174/1/6233–35
27 NP to AP [n.d.] NLA MS 1174/1/6240
28 NP to AP 6 September 1942, NLA MS 1174/1/6189
29 AP to NP 14 December 1941, NLA MS 6759 Box 1, Folder 3
30 AP to V&NP 20 December [1941?], NLA MS 6759, Box 1, Folder 3
31 Mitchell Library Manuscript Collection, Miles Franklin Collection, MS 364, Vol 24, p.317–318
32 'Pilgrims' Way', Chapter 4, NLA MS 6758, Box 4, Folder 34
33 'The Old Lady Takes Off', TS NLA MS 6759, Box 5, Folder 35; AP to Katharine Prichard, 17 August 1963, Box 5, Folder 36
34 'Coming of Age'. See also Helen Palmer's letters to Nettie on the importance of the latter's accepting Aileen as a writer, January 1963; NLA MS 6759, Box 1, Folder 1; 8 September 1963, Box 1, Folder 3

Bibliography

Abray, J. (1975) 'Feminism in the French Revolution' in *American Historical Review* 80

ABS (1984) *Social Indicators No.4* Canberra

Adams, C.E. (1984), Germany's Women Clerks: Class and Gender Conflict, 1890–1914, PhD thesis, Cambridge, Mass.

Addelson, K.P. (1983) 'The Man of Professional Wisdom' in S. Harding and M.B. Hintikka (eds) *Discovering Reality*

Alaya, F. (1977) 'Victorian Science and the "Genius" of Woman' *Journal of the History of Ideas* 38,2

Alexander, M.C., compiler (1934) *William Patterson Alexander in Kentucky, the Marquesas, Hawaii,* privately printed, Honolulu

Alexander, R.D. (1979) *Darwinism and Human Affairs* London: Pitman

Alia, M. (1985) *Hypatia's Heritage: Women in Science from Antiquity to the Late Nineteenth Century* London: The Women's Press

Allen, J. (1977), Aspects of the Public Career of Rose Scott: Feminist, Social Reformer and Pacifist, 1890–1925, unpublished BA thesis, University of Sydney

—— (1979b) 'Breaking into the Public Sphere: the Struggle for Women's Citizenship in New South Wales 1890–1920' in J. Mackinolty and H. Radi (eds) *In Pursuit of Justice: Australian Women and the Law 1788–1979* Sydney: Hale & Iremonger

—— (1979c) 'The Feminisms of the Women's Movement in Britain, America and Australia 1850–1920' *Refractory Girl* 17, pp.10–17

—— (1984) 'The Making of a Prostitute Proletariat in Twentieth Century New South Wales' in K. Daniels (ed.) *So Much Hard Work: Women and Prostitution in Australian History* Melbourne: Fontana

Allen, P. (1983) 'Poverty Policy Issues' in R. Mendelsohn (ed.) *Australian Social Welfare Finance* Sydney: Allen & Unwin

Altmann, I. (1905) 'Die Arbeiterin in der Gewerkschaftsbewegung' *Correspondenzblatt*, reprinted in G. Brinker-Gabler (ed.) *Frauenarbeit und Beruf,* series Die Frau in der Gesellschaft: Fruehe Texte, idem, ed., Frankfurt a.M.: Fischer Taschenbuch Verlag, 1979

Anon. (1910) 'Aus feunfundzwanzigjaehriger Geschichte' *Handlungsgehilfenzeitung* 14, pp.67–69

A.P.U. (Assessment of Performance Unit) (1982) *Mathematical Development*, Secondary Survey Report No.3, London: HMSO

Atkin, L. (1984), Sex Differences in Mathematics Attitudes and Expectations in England and Wales, paper presented at the Fifth International Congress on Mathematical Education, Adelaide

Atkinson, A. (1975) *The Economics of Inequality* Oxford: Clarendon

Australian Federation of Women Voters 'Intervention in Equal Pay Case, 1969' in *Archives of Business and Labour*, Canberra, N43/39

Bacchi, C. (1980) 'Evolution, Eugenics and Women' in E. Windschuttle (ed.) *Women Class and History* Melbourne: Fontana

Baldock, C.V. (1983) 'Public Policies and the Paid Work of Women' in C.V. Baldock and B. Cass (eds) *Women, Social Welfare and the State* Sydney: Allen & Unwin

Banks, O. (1981) *Faces of Feminism* Oxford: Martin Robinson

Barnes, M. (1983) 'Sex Differences in Mathematics Learning: How Can we Explain Them?' *Curriculum Exchange* Trinity Term, Sydney: Catholic Education Office, pp.53–78

Barnes, M., R. Plaister and A. Thomas (1984) *Girls Count in Mathematics and Science* Sydney: Commonwealth Schools Commission

Barrett, M. and M. McIntosh (1980) 'The Family Wage: Some Problems for Socialists and Feminists' *Capital and Class* 11, pp.51–73

Barthes, R. (1979) 'From Work to Text' in J.V. Harari (ed.) *Textual Strategies* London: Methuen

Beach, F.A. (1971) 'Hormonal Factors Controlling the Differentiation, Development, and Display of, Copulatory Behaviour in the Ramstergig and Related Species' in T. Tobach, Aronson and Shaw (eds) *The Biopsychology of Development* New York: Academic Press

Beaglehole, J.C. (ed.) (1967) *The Journals of Captain James Cook* 3, parts 1 & 2, Cambridge: Hakluyt Press

Bebel, A. (1904) *Women under Socialism*, trans. from the 33rd edn by Daniel de Leon. Reprinted from the 1904 American edn of New York Labor News Press. Studies in the Life of Women, New York: Schocken Books, 1971

Benbow, C.P. and J.C. Stanley (1980) 'Sex Differences in Mathematical Ability: Fact or Artifact?' *Science* 210, 12 December, pp.1262–64

—— (1982) 'Consequences in High School and College of Differences in Mathematical Reasoning Ability: a Longitudinal Perspective' *American Educational Research Journal* 19, 4, pp.598–622

Birke, L. (1979) 'Is Homosexuality Hormonally Determined?' *Journal of Homosexuality* 6, 4, pp.35–50

—— (1982) 'Cleaving the Mind: Speculations on Conceptional Dichotomies' in S. Rose, (ed.) *Against Biological Determination* London: Allison & Busby

Birke, Lynda and Sandy Best (1980) 'The Tyrannical Womb: Menstruation and Menopause' in *Alice Through the Microscope* The Brighton Women and Science Group, London: Virago

Blakemore, C. (1977) *Mechanisms of the Mind* London: Cambridge University Press

Bland, L. (1983) 'Purity, motherhood, pleasure or threat: changing definitions of female sexuality 1900–1970' in S. Cartledge and J. Ryan (eds) *Sex and Love* London: The Women's Press

Bleier, R. (1984) *Science and Gender*, New York: Pergamon

Bott, E. (1981) 'Power and Rank in the Kingdom of Tonga' *Journal of the Polynesian Society* 90, pp.7–81

Bowling, J. and B. Martin (1985) 'Science: a Masculine Disorder? *Science and Public Policy* 12, p.6

Bradshaw, J.L. and N.C. Nettleton (1983) *Human Cerebral Asymmetry* New Jersey: Prentice Hall

Brady, I. (ed.) (1976) *Transactions in Kinship. Adoption and Fosterage in Oceania* Honolulu: University Press of Hawaii

Braun, L. (1897) 'Forschlaege zur Agitation' *Gleichheit*, reprinted in G. Losseff-Tillmanns (ed.) *Frau und Gewerkschaft*, series Die Frau in der Gesellschaft: Fruehe Texte, G. Brinker-Gabler, ed., Frankfurt a.M.: Fischer Taschenbuch Verlag, 1982

Braverman, H. (1974) *Labor and Monopoly Capital: the Degradation of Work in the Twentieth Century* New York: Monthly Review Press

Brenner, J. and M. Ramas (1984) 'Rethinking Women's Oppression' *New Left Review* 144, March/April, pp.33–71

Brighton Women and Science Group (1980) *Alice Through the Microscope* London: Virago

Bristow, E.J. (1977) *Vice and Vigilance* Dublin: Gill & Macmillan

Bryson, L. (1977) 'Poverty' *Current Affairs Bulletin* 54, (October), p.5

—— (1983) 'Women as Welfare Recipients: Women, Poverty and the State' in C.V. Baldock and B. Cass (eds) *Women, Social Welfare and the State* Sydney: Allen & Unwin

Buerk, D. (1985) 'The voices of women making meaning in mathematics' *Journal of Education* 167, 3, pp.59–70

Buffery, A.W.H. (1981) 'Male and Female Brain Structure and Function: Neuropsychological Analyses' in N. Grieve and P. Grimshaw (eds) *Australian Women: Feminist Perspectives* Melbourne: Oxford University Press

Buxton, L. (1981) *Do you Panic About Maths?* London: Heinemann

Caine, B. (1976) 'Frances Cobbe and "the Little Health of Ladies"' *Refractory Girl* 11, pp.19–24

—— (1978) 'John Stuart Mill and the English Women's Movement' *Historical Studies* 18, 70, pp.52–67

Caplan, A.L. (1978) *The Sociobiology Debate* New York: Harper & Row

Carroll, Vern (ed.) (1970) *Adoption in Eastern Oceania* University of Hawaii Press

Carter, A. (1982) 'Unhappy Families' *London Review of Books* 16 Sept.–4 Oct., pp.11–13

Cass, B. et al. (1983) *Why So Few?* Sydney University Press

—— (1984) The Changing Face of Poverty In Australia: 1972–1982, paper delivered at Feminization of Poverty Conference, University of Michigan, Ann Arbor, USA, April 1985

Cass, B. and P. Garde (1983) 'Unemployment and Family Support' in A. Graycar (ed.) *Retreat From the Welfare State* Sydney: Allen & Unwin
—— (1984) 'Unemployment in the Western Region of Sydney: Job Seeking in a Local Labour Market' in R. Hooke (ed.) *54th ANZAAS Congress SWRC Papers*, R & P No.47, University of New South Wales
Cass, B. and M. O'Loughlin (1984) *Social Policies for Single Parent Families in Australia*, SWRC R & P No.40, University of New South Wales
Chalmers, A. (1976) *What is This Thing Called Science?* Brisbane: University of Queensland Press
Charlot, J. (1983) *Chanting the Universe. Hawaiian Religious Culture* Hong Kong: Emphasis International
Chipman, S.F. and D.M. Wilson (1985) 'Understanding Mathematics Course Enrolment and Mathematics Achievement: a Synthesis of the Research' in S.F. Chipman, L.R. Brush and D.M. Wilson (eds) *Women and Mathematics: Balancing the Equation* Hillsdale, New Jersey: Lawrence Erlbaum & Associates
Chodorow, N. (1978) *The Reproduction of Mothering. Psychoanalysis and the Sociology of Gender* Berkeley: University of California Press
Cixous, H. (1980) 'The Laugh of the Medusa' in E. Marks and I. Courtivron (eds) *New French Feminisms* Sussex: Harvester Press Ltd
—— (1981) 'Castration or Decapitation?' in *Signs* 7:1
Clancy, L. (1981) *Christina Stead's 'The Man Who Loved Children' and 'For Love Alone'* Melbourne: Shillington House
Clarke, J.H. and E.J. Peek (1979) *Female Sex Steroids: Receptors and Function* New York: Springer Verlag
Coleman, M. (1985) Targetting Welfare Expenditures on the Poor Is Targetting Needed?, paper presented at NSWCOSS Seminar, Sydney, 25 June
Commission of Inquiry into Poverty (1975) *First Main Report* Canberra: AGPS
Connell, R.W. (1985) 'Theorising Gender' *Sociology* 19, 2, pp.260–72
Corballis, M.C. (1983) *Human Laterality* New York: Academic Press
Coward, R. (1984) *Female Desire* London: Paladin
Cox, J. (1982) 'Equivalent Income Distribution' *Social Security Journal* (December)
Craney, J. (1985) Women, Maths and Science in TAFE, TAFE Women's Coordination Unit, Sydney
Culler, J. (1983) *On Deconstruction* [1982] London: Routledge & Kegan Paul
Curthoys, A. (1986) 'The Sexual Division of Labour: Theoretical Arguments' in N. Grieve and A. Burns (eds) *Australian Women: New Feminist Perspectives* Melbourne: Oxford University Press
Daniels, K., M. Murnane and A. Picot (1977) 'Rose Scott' in K. Daniels et al. *Women in Australia: An Annotated Guide to Records* Canberra: AGPS
Darwin, Charles (1922) *The Descent of Man* London: John Murray
Davis, G., A. McLeod and M. Murch (1983) 'Divorce: Who Supports the Family?' *Family Law* 13

Davis, T. et al. (1983) 'The Public Face of Feminism: Early Twentieth Century Writings on Women's Suffrage' in R. Johnson et al. (eds) *Making Histories. Studies in History Writing and Politics* London and Birmingham: Hutchison, in association with the Centre for Contemporary Studies, University of Birmingham

de Beauvoir, S. (1972) *The Second Sex* [1949] Harmondsworth: Penguin

Dekkers, J., J. Malone, J.R. de Laeter and B. Hamlett (1983) 'Mathematics Enrolment Patterns in Australian Secondary Schools: Course Trends' *The Australian Mathematics Teacher* 39, 1, pp.2–5

Denenberg, V.H. (1981) 'Hemispheric Laterality in Animals and the Effects of Early Experience' *Behavioural Brain Research* 4, pp.1–49

Dening, G. (ed.) (1974) *The Marquesan Journal of Edward Robarts, 1797– 1824* Canberra: ANU Press

—— (1980) *Islands and Beaches. Discourse on a Silent Land: Marquesas 1774–1880* Melbourne: Melbourne University Press

Department of Social Security (1985) *Ten Year Statistical Summary 1974– 1984* Canberra: Dept Social Security, Statistics Section, Development Division

Dick, A. (1981) *Emmy Noether: 1882–1935* Boston: Birkhauser

Dixson, M. (1976) *The Real Matilda* Ringwood: Penguin

Dorner, G. (1979) 'Hormones and Sexual Differentiation of the Brain' in *Sex, Hormones and Behaviour* Ciba Foundation Symposium, 62, pp.81–112

Driessen, H. (1984) Pers. comm., material from PhD. thesis-in-progress, Australian National University, Canberra

Duncan, G. (1984) *Years of Poverty, Years of Plenty* University of Michigan: Institute of Social Research

Durden-Smith, J. and D. de Simone (1983) *Sex and the Brain* London: Pan Books

Easlea, B. (1981) *Science and Sexual Oppression* London: Weidenfeld & Nicolson

Eccles, S. (1984) 'Women in the Australian Labour Force' in D. Broom (ed.) *Unfinished Business* Sydney: Allen & Unwin

Edwards, M. (1981) *Financial Arrangements within Families* Canberra: National Women's Advisory Council

Edwards, R.C., M. Reich, and D. Gordon (eds) (1975) *Labor Market Segmentation* Lexington, Mass.: D.C. Heath

Ehrenreich, B. and D. English (1979) *For Her Own Good: 150 Years of the Experts' Advice to Women* London: Pluto Press

Eisenstein, H. and A. Jardine (eds) (1980) *The Future of Difference* Boston: G.K. Hall

Eisenstein, Z. (1979a) 'Developing a Theory of Capitalist Patriarchy and Socialist Feminism', in *idem* (ed.) *Capitalist Patriarchy and the Case for Socialist Feminism* New York: Monthly Review Press

—— (1979b) 'Some Notes on the Relations of Capitalist Patriarchy' in idem (ed.) *Capitalist Patriarchy and the Case for Socialist Feminism* New York: Monthly Review Press

Elshtain, J.B. (1982) 'Feminist Discourse and its Discontents: Language, Power and Meaning' *Signs* 7, 3

197

Encel S., N. Mackenzie and M. Tebutt (1974) *Women and Society: An Australian Study* Melbourne: Cheshire

Fausto-Sterling, A.M. (1985) *Myths of Gender: Biological Theories about Women and Men* New York: Basic Books

Fawcett, M.G. (1873) 'Mr Fitzjames Stephen on the Position of Women' *Examiner*, reprinted as a pamphlet, London: NUWSS

—— (1881) 'The Women's Suffrage Movement in England' in T. Stanton (ed.) *The Woman Question in Europe* London: Sampson Low

—— (1885) 'Speech or Silence' *Contemporary Review* 48, September, pp.326–31

—— (1891) 'The Emancipation of Women' *Fortnightly Review* 50, n.s., pp.673–85

—— (1898) 'Home and Politics', address delivered at Toynbee Hall, London, published by the Central and East of England Society for Women's Suffrage

Fawcett, M.G. and E.M. Turner (1927) *Josephine Butler: Her Work and Principles and Their Meaning for the Twentieth Century* London: Association for Moral and Social Hygiene

Fee, E. (1974) 'The Sexual Politics of Victorian Anthropology' in M. Hartman and L. Banner (eds) *Clio's Consciousness Raised* New York: Harper & Row

Finnane, M. (1981) 'The Popular Defence of Chidley' *Labour History* 41, pp.57–73

Firestone, S. (1971) *The Dialectic of Sex* New York: Bantam

Foucault, Michel (1972) 'The Discourse on Language' *The Archaeology of Knowledge* New York: Harper Colophon

—— (1977) *Discipline and Punish* London: Allen Lane

—— (1978) *The History of Sexuality* New York: Pantheon

—— (1980) *Herculine Barbin* New York: Random House

Fox Keller, E. (1982) 'Feminism and Science' *Signs* 7, 3

—— (1983) *A Feeling for the Organism: The Life and Work of Barbara McClintock* New York: W.H. Freeman

—— (1985) *Reflections on Gender and Science* New Haven: Yale University Press

Freud, S. (1978) 'A Special Type of Object-Choice Made by Men' in *Standard Edition of Complete Psychological Works of Freud* (ed. J. Strachey) vol. XI

Furman, N. (1980) 'Textual Feminism' in S. McConnell-Ginet, R. Borker and N. Furman (eds) *Women and Language in Literature and Society* New York: Praeger

Gailey, C.W. (1980) 'Putting down Sisters and Wives: Tongan Women and Colonization' in M. Etienne and E. Leacock (eds) *Women and Colonization* New York: Praeger

Gallagher, P. (1985) Work in Progress on Poverty in Australia, 1981–82, paper presented at NSWCOSS Seminar, Sydney 25 June

Gatens, M. (1983) 'A Critique of the Sex/Gender Distinction' in J. Allen and P. Patton (eds) *Beyond Marxism? Interventions After Marx* Sydney: Intervention Publications

—— (1986) 'Feminism, Philosophy and Riddles Without Answers' in C. Pateman and E. Gross (eds) *Feminist Challenges: Social and Political Theory* Sydney: Allen & Unwin

Geering, R. (1978) 'What is Normal? Two Recent Novels by Christina Stead' *Southerly* 4, pp.462–73

George, V. and R. Lawson (eds) (1980) *Poverty and Inequality in Common Market Countries* London: Routledge & Kegan Paul

Geschwind, N. and P. Behan (1982) 'Left-Handedness: Association with Immune Disease, Migraine, and Developmental Learning Disorder' *Proceedings of the National Academy of Science U.S.A.* 79, p.5097

Geschwind, N. and A.M. Galaburda (1985) 'Cerebral Lateralisation: Biological Mechanisms; Associations, and Pathology' *Archives of Neurology* 42, pp.428–653

Geschwind, N. and W. Levitsky (1968) 'Human Brain: Left Right Asymmetries in Temporal Speech Region' *Science* 161, pp.186–87

Gilbert, S. and S. Gubar (1979) *The Madwoman in the Attic* New Haven: Yale University Press

Golder, H. and J. Allen (1980) 'Restructuring an Industry: Prostitution in New South Wales 1870–1932' *Refractory Girl* 18–19, pp.17–23

Gordon, L. (1982) 'Why Nineteenth Century Feminists did not Support "Birth Control" and Why Twentieth Century Feminists Do' in B. Thorne and M. Yalom (eds) *Rethinking the Family* New York: Longman

Gordon, L. and E. Du Bois (1983) 'Seeking Ecstasy on the Battlefield: Danger and Pleasure in the Nineteenth Century Feminist Sexual Thought' *Feminist Studies* 9, 1, pp.7–25

Gorham, D. (1978) ' "The Maiden Tribute to Modern Babylon" Re-examined: Child Prostitution and the Idea of Childhood in late Victorian England' *Victorian Studies* 21, 3, pp.353–79

Gould, S.J. (1981) *The Mismeasure of Man* New York/London: Norton

Green, D. (1974) '*The Man Who Loved Children*: Storm in a Teacup' in W.S. Ramson (ed.) *The Australian Experience* Canberra: ANU Press

Gross, E. (1986) 'Philosophy, Subjectivity and the Body: Kristeva and Irigaray' in C. Pateman and E. Gross (eds) *Feminist Challenges, Social and Political Theory* Sydney: Allen & Unwin

Gross, M. and M.B. Averill 'Evolution and Patriarchal Myths of Scarcity and Competition' in Harding and Hintikka (eds) *Discovering Reality*

Gunson, N. (1964) 'Great Women and Friendship Contract Rites in Pre-Christian Tahiti' *Journal of the Polynesian Society* 73, pp.52–69

—— (1985) 'Sacred Women Chiefs and Female "Headmen" in Polynesian History' in C. Ralston and N. Thomas (eds) *Sanctity, Power and Colonialism: Gender in Pacific History* (working title), forthcoming

Halladay, A. (1975) 'The Significance of Poverty Definitions to Australians' *Australian Journal of Social Issues* 10, 1

Hamburg Staatsarchiv, PP V676 'Zentralverband der Handlungsgehilfen und—Gehilfinnen Deutschlands—Hauptvorstand und Bezirk' Hamburg, 3 vols

Handlungsgehilfen-Zeitung 1908–1914

Handy, E.S. Craighill (1923) *The Native Culture in the Marquesas*, B.P. Bishop Museum Bulletin No.9, Honolulu: Bishop Museum Press
—— (1927) *Polynesian Religion*, B.P. Bishop Museum Bulletin No.34, Honolulu: Bishop Museum Press
Hanna, G. (1984) Gender and Mathematics Achievement: an Examination of the Canada (Ontario) Data from the Second International Mathematics Study, paper presented at the Fifth International Congress on Mathematical Education, Adelaide
Hanson, F.A. (1982) 'Female Pollution in Polynesia?' *Journal of the Polynesian Society* 91, pp.335–81
Hanson, F.A. and L. Hanson (1983) *Counterpoint in Maori Culture* London: Routledge & Kegan Paul
Harding, A. and P. Whiteford (1985) *Equity, Tax Reform and Redistribution* Canberra: Department of Social Security
Harding, J., Women and Science: Filtered Out or Opting In?, public lecture given at the University of Sydney, 30 April 1986
Harding, S. 'Why has the Sex/Gender System become Visible Only Now?' in Harding and Hintikka (eds) *Discovering Reality*
Harding, S. and M.B. Hintikka (1983) (eds) *Discovering Reality* Dordrecht/Boston/London: Reidel Publishing Co.
Harnard, S., R.W. Doty, L. Goldstein, J. Jaynes and G. Krauthamer (eds) (1977) *Lateralisation in the Nervous System* New York: Academic Press
Harrison, F. (1891) 'The Emancipation of Women' *Fortnightly Review* 50, n.s. October, pp.437–52
Hartmann, H. (1976) 'The Historical Roots of Occupational Segregation: Capitalism, Patriarchy, and Job Segregation by Sex' *Signs* 7, pp.137–70
—— (1976) 'Capitalism, Patriarchy and Job Segregation by Sex', in M. Blaxall and B. Reagan (eds) *Women and the Workplace* Chicago: University of Chicago Press
—— (1979) 'Capitalism, Patriarchy and Job Segregation by Sex' in Z.R. Eisenstein (ed.) *Capitalist Patriarchy and the Case for Socialist Feminism* New York/London: Monthly Review Press
Henning, C.M. (1974) 'Canon Law and the Battle of the Sexes' in R.R. Ruether (ed.) *Religion and Sexism: Images of Women in the Jewish and Christian Traditions* New York: Simon & Schuster
Herda, P. (1985) 'Gender, Rank and Power in eighteenth century Tonga: the case of Tupoumoheofo' in C. Ralston and N. Thomas (eds) *Sanctity, Power and Colonialism: Gender in Pacific History* (working title), forthcoming
Herron, J. (ed.) (1980) *Neuropsychology of Left-Handedness* New York: Academic Press
Hiddleston, P. (1984), Sex Differences and SIMS Data from Scotland, paper presented at the Fifth International Congress on Mathematical Education, Adelaide
Honeycutt, Karen (1979) 'Socialism and Feminism in Imperial Germany' *Signs* 5, pp.30–41
Howe, K.R. (1984) *Where the Waves Fall. A New South Sea Islands History from First Settlement to Colonial Rule* Sydney: Allen & Unwin

Hubbard, R. 'Have Only Men Evolved?' in Hubbard, Henifin and Fried (eds) *Women Look at Biology Looking at Women*

Hubbard, R., M.L. Henifin and B. Fried (1982) (eds) *Biological Woman— The Convenient Myth* Cambridge, Mass.: Schenkman

—— (1979) *Women Look at Biology Looking at Women* Cambridge, Mass.: Schenkman Publishing Co.

Humphries, J. (1977) 'The Working Class Family, Women's Liberation and Class Struggle: the Case of Nineteenth Century, British History' *Review of Radical Political Economics* 9, 3, Autumn, pp.25–41

Hunter, D.E. and P. Whitten (eds) (1975) *Encyclopedia of Anthropology* New York: Harper & Row

Ihrer, E. (1896) 'Wie sollen sich die Arbeiterinnen organisieren?' *Gleichheit*, reprinted in Gisela Losseff-Tillmans (ed.) *Frau und Gewerkschaft* series Die Frau in der Gesellschaft: Fruehe Texte, Gisela Brinker-Gabler, ed., Frankfurt a.m.: Fischer Taschenbuch Verlag, 1979

—— (1905) 'Die proletarische Frau und die Berufstaetigkeit' *Sozialistische Monatshefte*, reprinted in Brinker-Gabler (ed.) *Frauenarbeit und Beruf*, series Die Frau in der Gesellschaft: Fruehe Texts, idem, ed., Frankfurt a.M.: Fischer Taschenbuch Verlag, 1979

Irigaray, L. (1977) 'Women's Exile' *Ideology and Consciousness* 1

—— (1980) 'For Centuries We've Lived in the Mother–son Relation . . .' *Hecate* 9, 1–2, 1983

—— (1984) *L'éthique de la différence sexuelle* Paris: Minuit

—— (1985a) *Speculum of the Other Woman* Cornell University Press

—— (1985b) *This Sex Which is Not One* Cornell University Press

—— (1985c) 'Is the Subject of Science Sexed?' *Cultural Critique* 1, pp.73–89

Iseman, K. (1981) 'Our Father's Daughters: the problem of Filiation for Women Writers of Fiction' in N. Grieve and P. Grimshaw (eds) *Australian Women: Feminist Perspectives* Melbourne: Oxford University Press

Jackson, M. (1984) 'Sexology and the Universalization of Male Sexuality' in L. Coveney et al. (eds) *The Sexuality Papers* London: Hutchinson

—— (1982) 'Sexology and the Construction of Male Sexuality' in L. Coveney et al. (1984) *The Sexuality Papers* London: Hutchinson

Jacob, F. (1982) *The Possible and the Actual* New York: Pantheon Books

Jacobus, Mary (1986a) *Reading Woman. Essays in Feminist Criticism* New York: Columbia University Press

—— (1986b) 'Interview with Beate Josephi' *Australian Feminist Studies* 2, pp.45–54

Jannsen-Jurreit, M. (1982) *Sexism: The Male Monopoly on History and Thought*, trans. Verne Moberg, New York: Farrar, Straus, Giroux

Jay, N. (1981) 'Gender and Dichotomy' *Feminist Studies* 7, 1, pp.38–56

Jeffreys, S. (1982) ' "Free from all Uninvited Touch of Man": Women's Campaigns around Sexuality 1880–1914' *Women's Studies International Forum* 5, 6, pp.629–45

—— (1983) 'Sex Reform and Anti-feminism in the 1920's' in London Feminist History Group (eds) *The Sexual Dynamics of History* London: Pluto

—— (1985) *The Spinster and her Enemies. Feminism and Sexuality, 1880–1930* London: Pandora Press

Jones, F.L. (1984) 'Income Inequality' in D. Broom (ed.) *Unfinished Business* Sydney: Allen & Unwin

Kamakau, S.M. (1961) *Ruling Chiefs of Hawaii* Honolulu: The Kamehameha Schools Press

Kamerman, S. (1984) 'Women, Children and Poverty: Public Policies and Female-Headed Families in Industrialized Countries' *Signs* Winter, 10 p.2

Kaplan, G.T. and L.J. Rogers (1986) 'Definition of Male and Female: Biological Reductionism and the Sanctions of Normality' in *Feminist Knowledge as Critique and Construct* Section 3, Deakin University Press

Kardiner, Abram (1939) *The Individual and his Society. The Psychodynamics of Primitive Social Organization* New York: Columbia University Press

Keeves, J.P. (1973) 'Differences between the Sexes in Mathematics and Science Courses' *International Review of Education* 19, pp.47–62

Kinsbourne, M. (1980a) 'Brain-Based Limitations on Mind' in R.W. Rieber (ed.) *Body and Mind* New York: Academic Press

—— (1980b) 'If Sex Differences in the Brain Exist, They have Yet to be Discovered' *Behavioural and Brain Sciences* 3, pp.241–42

Kirby, V., The Politics of Representation: The Body as a Problematic, thesis submitted for MA Preliminary, Department of Anthropology, University of Sydney, 1986

Koblitz, A.H. (1983) *A Convergence of Lives. Sofia Kovalevskaia: Scientist, Writer, Revolutionary* Boston: Birkhauser

Kudilezak, S., T. Alaimo and L. Powell (1979) 'Survival Mathematics' in S. Ferguson (ed.) *Mathematics for the 80's* Melbourne: Mathematical Association of Victoria

Kuendiger, E. (1984), A Conceptual Framework for Analysing Sex Differences on an International Basis, paper presented at the Fifth International Congress on Mathematical Education, Adelaide

—— (1982) *An International Review on Gender and Mathematics* ERIC Clearinghouse for Science Mathematics and Environmental Education, Columbus, Ohio

Kuhn, T.S. (1970) *The Structure of Scientific Revolutions* 2nd edn, Chicago University Press

Lambert, H.A. (1978) 'Biology and Equality: a Perspective on Sex Differences *Signs* 4, pp.97–118

Lange, H. and B. Gertrud (eds) (1901) *Handbuch der Frauenbewegung* Berlin: W. Moeser Buchhandlung

Lantz, A. (1985) 'Strategies to Increase Mathematics Enrolments' in S.F. Chipman, L.R. Brush and D.M. Wilson (eds) *Women and Mathematics* Hillsdale, New Jersey: Lawrence Erlbaum & Associates

Larmour, C. (1985) *Labor Judge: The Life and Times of Judge A.W. Foster* Sydney: Hale & Iremonger

Leacock, E.B. (1981) *Myths of Male Dominance* New York/London: Monthly Review Press

Leder, G.C. (1981) 'Learned Helplessness in the Classroom?' *Research in Mathematics Education in Australia* 2, pp.192–203

—— (1984), Sex Differences in Participation and Performance in Mathematics in Australia, paper presented at the Fifth International Congress on Mathematical Education, Adelaide

Levy, J. (1977) 'The Mammalian Brain and the Adaptive Advantage of Cerebral Asymmetry' *Annals of the New York Academy of Science* 229, pp.265–72

Levy, R. (1973) *Tahitians: Mind and Experience in the Society Islands* Chicago: University of Chicago Press

Lewontin, R.C., S. Rose and L.J. Kamin (1984) *Not in Our Genes* New York: Pantheon Books

Liddington, J. and J. Norris (1978) *One Hand Tied Behind Us: The Rise of the Women's Suffrage Movement* London: Virago

Lidoff, J. (1979) 'Domestic Gothic: the Imagery of Anger, Christina Stead's *The Man Who Loved Children' Studies in the Novel* 11, 2, pp.201–215

Linton, R. (1939) 'Marquesan Culture' in Abram Kardiner *The Individual and his Society* New York: Columbia University Press

Le Doeuff, M. (1977) 'Women and Philosophy' *Radical Philosophy* 17, Summer, pp.2–11

—— (1980) *Recherches sur L'imaginaire philosophique* Paris: Payot

Lloyd, G. (1984) *The Man of Reason* London: Methuen

Losseff-Tillmanns, G. (1975), Frauenemancipation und Gewerkschaften (1800–1975), PhD thesis, Bochum

—— (1982) 'Einleitung' in idem (ed.) *Frau und Gewerkschaft* series Die Frau in der Gesellschaft: Fruehe Texte, Gisela Brinker-Gabler, ed., Frankfurt a.M.: Fisher Taschenbuch Verlag

Lowie, R.H. (1930) 'Adoption: Primitive' in E.R.A. Seligman (ed.) *Encyclopaedia of the Social Sciences* vol. 1, New York: Macmillan

Lueders, E. (1905) 'Die Arbeiterin in der Gewerkschaftsbewegung' *Correspondenzblatt*, excerpted in G. Losseff-Tillmanns (ed.) *Frau und Gewerkschaft* series Die Frau in der Gesellschaft: Fruehe Texts, G. Brinker-Gabler, ed., Frankfurt a.M.: Fischer Taschenbuch Verlag, 1982, pp.143–46

Lyotard, J.F. (1978) 'One of the Things at Stake in Women's Struggles' *Substance* 20

McDonald, P. (1985) *The Economic Consequences of Marriage Breakdown in Australia, A Summary* Melbourne: Institute of Family Studies

McDonough, R. and R. Harrison (1978) 'Patriarchy and Relations of Production' in A. Kuhn and A. Wolpe (eds) *Feminism and Materialism: Women and Modes of Production* London: Routledge & Kegan Paul

McGregor, P. (1985) 'Scope '84' *Education Alert* Australian College of Education and Australian Council for Educational Administration, Melbourne

MacKenzie, N. (1960) 'Vida Goldstein, Australian Suffragette' *Australian Journal of Politics and History* 6, 2, pp.190–204

Mackinnon, C. (1979) *Sexual Harassment of Working Women* New Haven: Yale University Press

McLaughlin, E.C. (1974) 'Equality of Souls, Inequality of Sexes: Women in Medieval Theology' in R.R. Ruether (ed.) *Religion and Sexism: Images of Women in the Jewish and Christian Traditions* New York: Simon & Schuster

MacMillan, C. (1982) *Women, Reason and Nature* Blackwell's

Maccoby, E.E. and C.N. Jacklin (1974) *The Psychology of Sex Differences* Stanford, California: Stanford University Press

Malo, D. (1951) *Hawaiian Antiquities* Honolulu: Bishop Museum Press

Manning, I. (1985) *Incomes and Policy* Sydney: Allen & Unwin

Manton, J. (1966) *Elizabeth Garrett Anderson* London: Methuen

Marcus, J. (1984) 'Islam Women and Pollution in Turkey' *Journal of the Anthropological Society of Oxford* 15, 3, pp.204–218

Marks, E. and I. Courtivron (eds) (1980) *New French Feminisms* Sussex: The Harvester Press Ltd

Marshall, M. (ed.) (1983) *Siblingship in Oceania: Studies in the Meaning of Kin Relations* Lanham: University Press of America

Marx, K. (1859) 'Preface', *A Contribution to the Critique of Political Economy* in *Selected Works*, vol. 1, Moscow 1947

Merchant, C. (1983) *The Death of Nature* San Francisco: Harper & Row

Miller, N. (1986) 'Arachnologies: The Woman, The Text, and The Critic' in N. Miller (ed.) *The Poetics of Gender* New York: Columbia University Press

Mitchell, D. (1977) *Queen Christabel* London: Allen Lane

Mitchell, J. (1975) *Psychoanalysis and Feminism* New York: Vintage

Mitchell Library (1979) *Guide to the Papers of the Scott Family* Part I, Sydney: Library Council of New South Wales

Modjeska, D. (1981) *Exiles at Home: Australian Women Writers 1925–1945* Sydney: Sirius

Moers, E. (1977) *Literary Women* New York: Anchor-Doubleday

Moi, T. (1985) *Sexual/Textual Politics* London: Methuen

Money, J. and A.A. Ehrhardt (1972) *Man and Woman: Boy and Girl* Baltimore

Montague, M. and J. Stephens (1985) *Paying the Price for Sugar and Spice* Melbourne: Brotherhood of St Laurence, National Women's Advisory Council

Moore, C.L. (1982) 'Maternal Behaviour of Rats is Affected by Hormonal Condition of Pups' *Journal of Comparative and Physiological Psychology* 96, pp.123–29

—— (1985) 'Another Psychobiological View of Sexual Differentation' *Developmental Review* 5, pp.18–55

Moore, C. and G.A. Morelli (1979) 'Mother Rats Interact Differently with Male and Female Offspring' *Journal of Comparative and Physiological Psychology* 93, pp.677–84

Morgan, D. (1975) *Suffragists and Liberals: The Politics of Women's Suffrage in England* Oxford: Basil Blackwell

Morgan, L.H. (1871) *Systems of Consanguinity and Affinity*, Smithsonian Contributions to Knowledge, vol.17, Smithsonian Institution, Washington

—— (1908) *Ancient Society* Chicago: Charles H. Kerr & Co.
Moss, J.D. (1982) *Towards Equality: Progress by Girls in Mathematics in Australian Secondary Schools* Melbourne: Australian Council for Educational Research
Mozans, H.J. (1974) *Women in Science* Cambridge: MIT Press
Mura, R. (1984), Sex-related Differences in Attitudes Towards Mathematics among University Students, paper presented at the Fifth International Congress on Mathematical Education, Adelaide
Nelson, B. (1984) 'Women's Poverty and Women's Citizenship' *Signs* 10, 2
Nienhaus, U. (1982) *Berufsstand weiblich: Die ersten weiblichen Angestellten* Berlin: Transit Verlag
Oakley, A. (1983) 'Millicent Garrett Fawcett: Duty and Determination' in D. Spender (ed.) *Feminist Theorists. Three Centuries of Women's Intellectual Traditions* London: The Women's Press
Oliver, D. (1974) *Ancient Tahitian Society* 3 vols, Canberra: ANU Press
Ortner, S.B. (1981) 'Gender and Sexuality in Hierarchical Societies: The Case of Polynesia and Some Comparative Implications' in S.B. Ortner and H. Whitehead (eds) *Sexual Meanings: The Cultural Construction of Gender and Sexuality* Cambridge University Press
Otterbein, K.F. (1963) 'Marquesan Polyandry' *Marriage and Family Living* 25, pp.155–59
Owens, L. (1981), The Cooperative, Competitive and Individualized Learning Preferences of Primary and Secondary Teachers in Sydney, paper presented at the annual conference of the Australian Association for Research in Education, Adelaide
Palmer, A. (1964) *World Without Strangers* Melbourne
Paris, C., P. Williams and B. Stimson (1985) 'From Public Housing to Welfare Housing' *Australian Journal of Social Issues* 20, 2
Pateman, C. (1982), What's Wrong with Prostitution?, typescript, University of Sydney
—— (1983) 'Defending Prostitution: Charges against Ericsson' *Ethics* 93, pp.561–65
——, The Fraternal Social Contract, paper to the Annual American Political Science Assoc., Washington, D.C.
Pateman, C. and E. Gross (eds) (1986) *Feminist Challenges. Social and Political Theory* Sydney: Allen & Unwin
Pattison, P. and N. Grieve (1984) 'Do Spatial Skills Contribute to Sex Differences in Different Types of Mathematical Problems?' *Journal of Educational Psychology* 76, 4, pp.678–89
Pearce, B. and H. McAdoo (1981) *Women and Children Alone and in Poverty* Washington: National Advisory Council on Economic Opportunity
Petocz, P. (1985a) 'Honours Bachelor Degrees in Mathematics and Statistics Completed in Australia 1983' *Australian Mathematical Society Gazette* 12, 4, pp.94–96
—— (1985b), Higher degrees in Mathematics and Statistics completed in Australia 1983, University of New South Wales, Sydney
Poiner, G. (1983) 'Difference Amplified: the Education of Women for the

Workforce' in J.M. Bennett and G.C. Lowenthal (eds) *Manpower Planning and Industrial Development in Uncertain Times* Symposium, ANZAAS (NSW), pp.59–74

Popper, K. (1969) *Conjectures and Refutations* London: Routledge & Kegan Paul

Power, M. (1980) 'Women and Economic Crises' in E. Windschuttle (ed.) *Women, Class and History* Melbourne: Fontana

Pybus, R. (1982) '*Cotters' England*: In Appreciation' *Stand* 23, 4, pp.40–47

Quataert, Jean H. (1977) 'Feminist Tactics in German Social Democracy, 1890–1914: A Dilemma' *Internationale Wissenschaftliche Korrespondenz zur Geschichte der deutschen Arbeiterbewegung* 13, pp.48–65

—— (1979) *Reluctant Feminists in German Social Democracy* Princeton: Princeton University Press

Radcliff Richards, J. (1982) *The Sceptical Feminist* Harmondsworth: Penguin

Rainwater, L. (1979) 'Mothers' Contribution to the Family Money Economy in Europe and the United States' *Journal of Family History* Summer

Ralston, C. (1983) 'Changes in the Lives of Ordinary Women in Early Post-Contact Hawaii' in M. Jolly and M. Macintyre (eds) *Bless This House: Christianity, Colonialism and Gender in the South West Pacific* forthcoming

—— (1985) 'Book Review Forum: K.R. Howe, Where the Waves Fall' *Pacific Studies* 9, 1, pp.150–63

Read, A.H. (1951) *A Signpost to Mathematics* London: Watts & Co.

Reid, I. (1979) *Fiction and the Great Depression* Melbourne: Edward Arnold

Richards, E. (1983) 'Darwin and the Descent of Woman' in D. Oldroyd and I. Langham (eds) *The Wider Domain of Evolution and Thought* Boston/London: Reidel

Richardson, S. (1979) 'Income Distribution, Poverty and Redistributive Policies' in F. Gruen (ed.) *Surveys of Australian Economics* vol.2, Sydney: Allen & Unwin

Ritter, G.A. (1976) *Arbeiterbewegung, Parteien, und Parlamentarismus: Aufsaetze zur deutschen Sozial und Verfassungsgeschichte des 19. und 20. Jahrhunderts*, Kritische Studien zur Geschichtswissenschaft 23, Helmut Berding et al., eds, Goettingen: Vandenhoeck und Ruprecht

Roberti, P. (1979) 'Counting the Poor: A Review of the Situation Existing in Six Industrial Nations' in DHSS *The Definition and Measurement of Poverty* London: HMSO

Roe, J. (1975) 'Social Policy and the Permanent Poor' in E.L. Wheelwright and K. Buckley (eds) *Essays in the Political Economy of Australian Capitalism* Sydney: ANZ Book Co.

—— (1983) 'The End is Where We Start From: Women and Welfare Since 1901' in C.V. Baldock and B. Cass (eds) *Women, Social Welfare and the State* Sydney: Allen & Unwin

Rogers, G. (1977) ' "The Father's Sister is Black": A Consideration of

Female Rank and Powers in Tonga' *Journal of the Polynesian Society* 86, pp.157–82

Rogers, L.J. (1981) 'Biology, Gender Differentiation and Sexual Variation' in N. Greive and P. Grimshaw (eds) *Australian Women: Feminist Perspectives* Melbourne: Oxford University Press, pp.44–57

—— (1982) 'Light Experience and Asymmetry of Brain Function in Chickens' *Nature* 297, pp.223–25

—— (1985) 'Lateralisation of Learning in Chickens' *Advances in the Study of Behaviour* 16, pp.147–89

Rogers, L.J. and J.M. Anson (1978) 'Cycloheximide Produces Attentional Persistence, and Slowed Learning in Chickens' *Pharmacology, Biochemistry and Behaviour* 10, pp.679–86

Rogers, L.J. and J. Walsh (1982) 'Short-comings of Psychomedical Research into Sex Differences in Behaviour: Social and Political Implications' *Sex Roles* 8, pp.269–81

Rogers, L.J. and J.V. Zappia (1985) 'Testosterone and Eye-Brain Asymmetry for Copulation in Chickens' *Experientia*, in press

Rose, H. (1984) 'Women, Work and Welfare in the World Economy' in C. Baldock and D. Goodrick (eds) *Women's Participation in the Development Process* Perth: Proceedings of the Women's Studies Section of ANZAAS Congress, May

Rose, H. and S. Rose (eds) (1976) *The Radicalisation of Science* London: Macmillan

—— (1969) *Science and Society* Harmondsworth: Penguin

Rose, S. (1976) 'Scientific Racism and Ideology: the IQ Racket from Galton to Jenson' in S. Rose and H. Rose (eds) *The Political Economy of Science* London: Macmillan

—— (1984) 'Biological Reductionism: its Roots and Social Functions' in L. Birke and J. Silvertown (eds) *More Than the Parts: Biology and Politics* London: Pluto Press

Rose, S. and H. Rose (1976) 'The Politics of Neurobiology: Biologism in the Service of the State' in S. Rose and H. Rose (eds) *The Political Economy of Science* London: Macmillan Press

Rose, S., L.J. Kamin and R.C. Lewontin (1984) *Not in Our Genes* Harmondsworth: Penguin

Rosenberg, R. (1982) *Beyond Separate Spheres: Intellectual Roots of Modern Feminism* New Haven: Yale University Press

Ross, E. (1985) *Living in Poverty* NCOSS Issues paper, NSW Council of Social Services, 3 June

Ross, M.W., L.J. Rogers and H. McCulloch (1978) 'Stigma, Sex and Society: a New Look at Gender Differentiation and Sexual Variation' *Journal of Homosexuality* 4, pp.315–30

Rover, C. (1967) *Women's Suffrage and Party Politics in Britain, 1866–1914* London: Routledge & Kegan Paul

Rowbotham, S. (1977) *A New World for Women: Stella Browne, Feminist* London: Pluto

Rubery, J (1980) 'Structured Labour Markets, Worker Organisation and

Low Pay' in A. Amsden (ed.) *The Economics of Women and Work* Harmondsworth: Penguin

Ryan, E. and A. Conlon (1975) *Gentle Invaders: Australian Women at Work, 1788–1974* Melbourne: Nelson

Sacks, K. (1982) *Sisters and Wives* University of Illinois Press

Sahlins, M. (1981) *Historical Metaphors and Mythical Realities: Structure in the Early History of the Sandwich Islands Kingdom* Ann Arbor: University of Michigan Press

—— (1985) 'Supplement to the Voyage of Cook or *le calcul sauvage*' in *Islands of History* Chicago: University of Chicago Press

Said, E.W. (1978) *Orientalism* London: Routledge & Kegan Paul

Salzman, F. (1977) 'Are Sex Roles Biologically Determined?' *Science for the People* July/August, pp.27–43

Sayers, J. (1982) *Biological Politics* London: Tavistock

Sayre, A. (1975) *Rosalind Franklin and DNA* New York: Norton

Schoeffel, P. (1977) 'The Origin and Development of Women's Associations in Western Samoa, 1830–1977' *Journal of Pacific Studies* 3, pp.1–21

—— (1978) 'Gender, Status and Power in Samoa' *Canberra Anthropology* 1, p.69

—— (1985) 'Rank and Gender in Samoa: the Genealogy of Salamasina' in C. Ralston and N. Thomas (eds) *Sanctity, Power and Colonialism: Gender in Pacific History*, (working title), forthcoming

Schorske, C.E. (1955) *German Social Democracy, 1905–1917: The Development of the Great Schism* New York: John Wiley & Sons

Scott, H. (1984) *Working Your Way to the Bottom. The Feminisation of Poverty* London: Pandora

Scott, R. 'Marriage', unpublished notes, *Rose Scott Papers* ML.MSS. 38/22/2

——, Peace and Arbitration, unpublished speech, *Rose Scott Papers* ML.MSS. 38/54, pp.251–53

——, Revolt against the Organs, unpublished notebook entry, *Rose Scott Papers* ML.MSS. 38/22/4

—— *Rose Scott Correspondence* ML.MSS. A2270–2284

—— *Rose Scott Papers* ML.MSS. Vols/Boxes 20–76

——, untitled notes, unpublished, *Rose Scott Papers* ML.MSS. 38/22/14

——, Untitled Notes on Men, unpublished, *Rose Scott Papers* ML.MSS. 38/22/24

——, Untitled Speech, unpublished, *Rose Scott Papers* ML.MSS. 38/25, p.295

—— (1903), Why Women Need a Vote, unpublished speech, *Rose Scott Papers* ML.MSS. 38/41, pp.173–249

—— 'Women's Political and Educational League', *Rose Scott Correspondence* ML.MSS. A27

—— 'Women's Work and Women's Movements' *Rose Scott Correspondence* ML. MSS. A2274

Segal, L. (1983) 'Sexual Uncertainty or Why the Clitoris is Not Enough' in S. Cartledge and J. Ryan (eds) *Sex and Love* London: The Women's Press

Segalowitz, S.D. (1983) *Two Sides of the Brain* New Jersey: Prentice-Hall
Shaver, S. (1983) 'Sex and Money in the Welfare State' in C.V. Baldock
and B. Cass (eds) *Women, Social Welfare and the State* Sydney: Allen &
Unwin
Sheehan, P. and P. Stricker (1983) 'Welfare Benefits and the Labour
Market' in R. Blandy and O. Covick (eds) *Understanding Labour
Markets* Sydney: Allen & Unwin
Sheridan, S. (1985) 'The Man Who Loved Children and the Patriarchal
Family Drama' in C. Ferrier (ed.) *Gender, Politics and Fiction* Brisbane:
Queensland University Press
Shore, B. (1976) 'Incest Prohibitions and the Logic of Power in Samoa'
Journal of the Polynesian Society 85, pp.275–96
Showalter, E. (1977) *A Literature of Their Own* Princeton: Princeton
University Press
—— (1979) 'Towards a Feminist Poetics' in M. Jacobus (ed.) *Women
Writing and Writing about Women* London: Croom Helm
Smith, D. (1978) 'A Peculiar Eclipsing: Women's Exclusion from Men's
Culture' *Women's Studies International Quarterly* 1, 4, pp.281–96
Smith, G. (1984) 'The Paradox of Women's Poverty: Wage-Earning
Women and Economic Transformation' *Signs* 10, 2
Sodersten, P. (1984) 'Sexual Differentiation: Do Males Differ from Females
in Behavioural Sensitivity to Gonadal Hormones?' in G.D. De Vries,
J.P.C. De Bruin, H.B.M. Ulyings and M.A. Corner (eds) *Sex Differences
in the Brain. Progress in Brain Research* 61, pp.257–70
Spacks, P.M. (1976) *The Female Imagination* New York: Avon-Discus
Spelman, E. (1982) 'Woman as Body: Ancient and Contemporary Views'
Feminist Studies 8, 1
—— (1983) 'The Politicisation of the Soul' in Harding and Hintikka (eds)
Discovering Reality
Spencer, H. (1966 reprint of 1904 edition) *The Principles of Sociology. The
Works* vol. 6, Osnabruck: Otto Zeller
Spender, D. (1980) *Man Made Language* London: Routledge & Kegan Paul
Spinoza, B. (1955) *The Ethics* in *Works of Spinoza* ed. R.H.M. Elwes New
York: Dover Publications
Starr, S.L. (1979) 'The Politics of Left and Right' in Hubbard, Henifin and
Fried (eds) *Women Look at Biology Looking at Women*
Stead, C. (1940) *The Man Who Loved Children* New York: Simon &
Schuster
—— (1944) *For Love Alone* New York: Harcourt Brace (edn cited, Angus
& Robertson, Sydney, 1966)
—— (1946) *Letty Fox: Her Luck* New York: Harcourt Brace
—— (1967) *Cotters' England* London: Secker & Warburg (published as
Dark Places of the Heart [1966] New York: Hold, Rhinehart & Winston)
—— (1976) *Miss Herbert (The Suburban Wife)* New York: Random House
—— (1986) *I'm Dying Laughing* London: Virago
Stehelin, L. (1976) 'Sciences, Women and Ideology' in Rose and Rose *The
Radicalisation of Science*
Stehr, K. (1926) *Der Zentralverband der Angestellten: Sein Werdegang,*

seine Gestalt und sein Charakter Berlin: Hausdruckerei des Zentralverband

Suggs, R.C. (1966) *Marquesan Sexual Behavior* New York: Harcourt, Brace & World

—— (1971) 'Sex and Personality in the Marquesas: A Discussion of the Linton-Kardiner Report' in D.S. Marshall and R.C. Sugges (eds) *Human Sexual Behavior: Variations in the Ethnographic Spectrum* New York: Basic Books

Summers, A. (1975) *Damned Whores and God's Police* Harmondsworth: Penguin

Swaab, D.F. and M.A. Hofman (1984) 'Sexual Differentiation of the Human Brain: a Historical Perspective' in G.D. De Vries, J.P.C. De Bruin, H.B.M. Ulyings and M.A. Corner (eds) *Sex Differences in the Brain, Progress in Brain Research* 61, pp.361–74

SWPS (1981) *Report on Poverty Measurement* Canberra: AGPS

Temple, D. (1983) 'Dr Who? Women in Science and Medicine' in B. Cass et al. *Why So Few?* Sydney University Press

——, Women's Place in Science and Technology, paper given at the Women's Studies Conference, University of Sydney, September 1985

Thoennessen, W. (1973) *The Emancipation of Women: The Rise and Decline of the Women's Movement in German Social Democracy, 1863–1933* trans. by J.de Bres, Bristol: Pluto Press

Thomas, A. (1981) 'Sex Differences in School Certificate Reference Test Results' *Reflections* 6, 3, pp.12–14

Thomas, N. (1983) 'Domestic Structures and Polyandry in the Marquesas Islands' in M. Jolly and M. Macintyre (eds) *Bless this House: Christianity, Colonialism and Gender in the South West Pacific* forthcoming

—— (1984), The Contradictions of Hierarchy: Myths, Women and Power in Eastern Polynesia, conference paper, Australian National University, Canberra

—— (1985) 'Unstable Categories: Tapu and Gender in the Marquesas' in Ralston, C. and N. Thomas (eds) *Sanctity, Power and Colonialism: Gender in Pacific History* (working title), forthcoming

Townsend, P. (1979a) 'The Development of Research on Poverty' in Department of Health and Social Security' *The Definition and Measurement of Poverty* London: HMSO

—— (1979b) *Poverty in the United Kingdom* Harmondsworth: Penguin

Travers, P. (1983) *Unemployment and Life History*, SWRC R & P, No. 30, University of New South Wales

Trimberger, E.K. (1983) 'Feminism, Men and Modern Love: Greenwich Village 1900–1925' in A. Snitow et al. (eds) *Powers of Desire: The Politics of Sexuality* London: Virago

Trivers, R.L. (1978) 'Parental Investment and Sexual Selection' in T.H. Clutton-Brock and P.H. Harvey (eds) *Readings in Sociobiology* San Francisco: W.H. Freeman

Tulloch, P. (1979) *Poor Policies* London: Croom Helm

—— (1980) 'The Poverty Line: Problems in Theory and Application' in P.

Saunders (ed.) *The Poverty Line: Methodology and Measurement*, SWRC, No.2. October, University of New South Wales

United Associations of Women *Papers* Mitchell Library, esp. folders labelled 'Equal Pay'

Urban, O. (1949) 'Zentralverband der Angestellten' in E. Gierke (ed.) *Zur Geschichte der Angestellten-Gewerkschaften* Schriftenreihe der 'Freiheit' Heft 1, Berlin: A.G. der Angestellten-Gewerkschaften

Van den Berghe, P. (1981) *The Ethnic Phenomenon* New York: Elsevier

Vicinus, M. (1982) 'Sexuality and Power: Some Recent Writing on the History of Sexuality' *Feminist Studies* 8, 1, pp.133–156

Vipond, J. (1986) 'Poverty After Housing Costs' in A. Jamrozik (ed.) *Income Distribution, Tax and Social Security*, SWRC R & P No.55, January

Ward, E. (1984) *Father–Daughter Rape* London: Virago

Watson, J.D. (1968) *The Double Helix* London: Weidenfeld & Nicolson

Weeks, J. (1981) *Sex, Politics and Society: The Regulation of Sexuality since 1800* London: Longman

Wexler, A. (1984) *Emma Goldman: An Intimate Biography* London: Virago

Weyl, H. (1935) 'Emmy Noether' *Scripta Mathematica* 3, 3, pp.201–220

Whiteford, P. (1982) 'The Earned Incomes of the Unemployed' *Social Security Journal* December

Whitehead, A. (1974) 'Christina Stead: an interview' *Australian Literary Studies* 6, 3, pp.230–48

Wild, R. (1975) *Social Stratification in Australia* Sydney: Allen & Unwin

Wilson, B. (1987) 'Where Have all the Women Gone?' *CSWP Gazette* (Newsletter of the Committee on the Status of Women in Physics of the American Physical Society), n.d., reprinted in *Wisenet*, No.9

Wilson, E.O. (1978) *On Human Nature* Harvard University Press

—— (1975) *Sociobiology* Harvard University Press

Wily, H. (1984), Women in Mathematics; Some Gender Differences from the IEA Survey in New Zealand, paper presented at the Fifth International Congress on Mathematical Education, Adelaide

Women's Bureau (1983) *Facts on Women at Work in Australia 1982* Canberra: Department of Employment and Industrial Relations

Zentralverband der Handlungsgehilfen und Gehilfinnen Deutschlands (1904) *Protokoll der 4. Generalversammlung v. 22.–23.4.1904*, Hamburg

—— (1906) *Bericht des Vorstandes und Ausschusses ueber die 5te Geschaeftsperiode 1904–05 nebst Protokoll der 5te Generalversammlung, 4.–5.6.1906 in Chemnitz* Hamburg

—— (1908) *Bericht des Vorstandes und Ausschusses ueber die 6.Geschaeftsperiode 1906–07* Hamburg

—— (1910) *Bericht des Vorstandes und Ausschusses ueber die 7.Geschaeftsperiode 1908–09 nebst Protokoll der 7. Generalversammlung, 16.–17.5.1910*, Hamburg

—— (1912) *Geschaeftsbericht fuer das Jahr 1910–1911 nebst Protokoll der 8.Generalversammlung, 5.–7.Mai 1912* Berlin

Zetkin, C. (1889) *Die Arbeiterinnen- und Frauenfrage der Gegenwart*, excerpted in Gisela Brinker-Gabler (ed.) *Frauenarbeit und Beruf*, Series Die Frau in der Gesellschaft: Fruehe Texts, *idem.* ed., Frankfurt a.M.: Fischer Taschenbuch Verlag, 1979
—— (1897) 'Kritische Bemerkungen ze Genossin Brauns Vorschlag' *Gleichheit*, excerpted in G. Losseff-Tillmanns (ed.) *Frau und Gewerkschaft*, series Die Frau in der Gesellschaft: Fruehe Texte, G. Brinker-Gabler, ed., Frankfurt a.M.: Fischer Taschenbuch Verlag, 1982, pp.154–6
—— (1898/1901) 'Schwierigkeiten der gewerkschaftlichen Organisierung der Arbeiterinnen' *Gleichheit*, reprinted in G. Brinker-Gabler (ed.) *Fraunarbeit und Beruf*, series Die Frau in der Gesellschaft: Fruehe Texte, idem, ed., Frankfurt a.M.: Fischer Taschenbuch Verlag, 1979, pp.149–54
Zinn, D. and R. Sarri (1984) 'Turning Back the Clock on Public Welfare' *Signs* 10, 2